MW00479034

BILL —

THANK YOU FOR BEING THERE

DON

THE PRISON WITHIN

A MEMOIR OF BREAKING FREE

DON CUMMINS

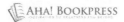 AHA! BOOKPRESS

AHA! BOOKPRESS
INSPIRATION TO GREATNESS AND BEYOND

www.ahabookpress.com

Library of Congress Control Number: 2020911233

Paperback ISBN: 978-1-7348926-0-4
Hardcover ISBN: 978-1-7348926-1-1
Ebook ISBN: 978-1-7348926-2-8
Audiobook ISBN: 978-1-7348926-3-5

This is a true story. The events and situations in this book really happened. The names of many, however, have been changed to protect their anonymity or privacy.

REVIEWS

A "gripping, heartbreaking and ultimately hopeful true story about the author's struggles with addiction, prisons both external and internal, and the long and painful road to recovery...a priceless resource, an offer of light for people fighting their way through what seems to be hopeless darkness."

— INDIE READER

The Prison Within is "masterfully written...the story of a true underdog."

— READERS FAVORITE

"As a recovery story, Cummins inspires. He strays from the standard 'a-ha' moment and narrates the work along with the many failures and relapses that come with a happy ending. Each story, in all its sadness, is a brick laid on his slowly paved path to recovery. His compelling story, paired with his witty and smart writing style, makes *The Prison Within* an easy and enjoyable read."

— INDEPENDENT BOOK REVIEW

For my boys Levi and Finn

CONTENTS

ACKNOWLEDGMENTS

"Our lives are not our own. We are bound to others, past and present, and by each crime and every kindness, we birth our future."
David Mitchell, Cloud Atlas

I am beyond grateful to all who have helped me on this journey. Some had a part in giving me this story to tell. And others helped me tell it, which was a journey in itself.

When Brianna met me, I was: a) forty-five, b) homeless, c) unemployed, d) on public assistance, e) declared by the courts to be insane, f) an ex-felon who'd served decades in prison, and g) I had an outstanding bank robbery charge. To this day I still have no idea what she was thinking. I love you Bri - 'till the wheels fall off.

Levi and Finley, my precious boys. For two years, somewhere between five and six in the morning, while the glow of my screen would fill the living room, I wrote and rewrote these chapters. It was then you'd wake up and crawl upon my lap on the couch. I'd close my laptop and spend the hour or two with you until mommy finally woke up. Those moments were truly the best of times. I miss them already. Thank you, both of you, for helping me be a better person.

My mother Susan is the glue that held our family together. No family is perfect, but her strength, loyalty and dedication made our family strong. She never expected a damn thing in return. I am forever grateful to her for creating a home that reminded me that love was real, even when I was in utter darkness and sick and unable to find my way. I love you Mom.

Liz, thank you for the texts when I was at my lowest. It helped more than you'll ever know. I love you little sis. And Jacqueline and Christine, big sisters, I love both of you so much.

Bob, my bro… Thank you for being you and for showing up. I love you forever.

I want to thank my Grandma Sally and my Grandpa Herman. I'll never forget you and the example you showed me and the faith you instilled in me. I hope you're proud of me, wherever you are.

Not a day passes that I don't think of my Dad, sensing both his absence and presence. I wish you could've seen the past four years, Dad, because they've been amazing. I love you forever. I hope we meet again.

A warm thanks to all the people who donated to my Kickstarter campaign. True, it did not get funded! But that's okay, because here we are and I wouldn't change a thing. I can't wait to put this book in your hands in appreciation for your support and belief in this story.

I couldn't do an acknowledgements page without thanking my editors. Michelle cut me to pieces when she critiqued my first draft, sending me back to the drawing board. Emma took me the next two rounds and helped me shape this book into the story it is today. She had deep insight into what I wanted to say, and her coaching helped me develop the skill to say it. And in the end, Brooks made sure I dotted those i's and crossed those t's, and then some. Thank you so much for helping me tell this story.

A special thanks to James. I owe you more than you can ever know. Without your guidance and support and example of the power of recovery, Part Three would never have been written.

FOREWORD

This memoir may seem like a story about Don Cummins. But actually, this isn't about Don at all — and he knows this. It's about the power of recovery to revolutionize lives.

It's also about the power of love and family and never giving up. It's one of infinite hope and inspiration for anyone who struggles with addiction or mental illness, or any disability really, and for their families and friends as well. Many professionals and providers, even judges, who dedicate their lives in service to the "hopeless cases" they see in the system every day, will be engaged and benefit by the inspiration and miracle of this story.

When I first met Don he was struggling greatly, but he truly wanted to stay clean. He continued to try, but the obsession and compulsion to use drugs would come over him and, despite his genuine desire to stay clean, he would sabotage himself and his progress once again. But with the support of those who continued to love him, Don kept trying. He finally reached a point of surrender, giving up and letting go of the ideas that had held him hostage for so long. Don poignantly and powerfully describes that moment in his story and the process leading up to it.

When Don speaks to groups, he talks about not giving up, no matter what your struggles are, and of discovering "the hero within" that exists in us all. Don's recovery has been a dramatic and profound transformation. In *The Prison Within*, he eloquently describes his journey through many, many years in the depths of hopelessness, desperation and self-destruction to the full, vibrant, productive, healthy and fulfilling life of love and service that he now lives. His message is one of infinite hope and promise!

It is not unusual for those who experience the transformation of recovery in their lives to feel and to say, "If I can do it, anyone can." In my 30 years of living a blessed life in recovery, never have I observed that to be a truer statement than in Don's journey.

It is said in the recovery community that being a sponsor is like having a ringside seat to the miracle of another's recovery. I have had the great privilege and blessing of having that seat to witness the amazing transformation and recovery of my friend and brother, Don. Through these pages, Don has provided that ringside seat for all to experience, and quite an experience it is!

James
June 6, 2020

PREFACE

I never dreamed I'd write a book - much less one about my own experiences.

But suddenly, it seemed, I found myself connected with others, in love with my beautiful wife, and completely taken by my wonderful boys. I owned a home, I had a solid career in software development, and I was thrilled to be alive.

It was around this time that I began to ask myself, "How in the hell did I wind up here?"

Of course, I knew the timeline and the events and the story. And clearly I had something to do with it — especially the parts about landing myself in prison and creating my own personal hell. Yet my role, I suspect, is only half of it. There are other forces at play as well. Ones that are mysterious, far greater than me and my own understanding. And so, to be perfectly honest, I don't quite know how to answer the question.

I probably never will. But I do know what I experienced, and what I thought and felt about it all. And as time passed and I gained more perspective, I realized I couldn't keep it in any longer. I had to tell my story.

I hoped it would entertain. But I hoped even more that it

would inspire. And even more than that, I was crazy enough to pray that it might not only help save someone's life, but that somehow it might help them create an entirely new one. One they absolutely love, like I do mine.

But if it does only the first thing, then bravo.

PART I

1

SOLITARY

M y heart is almost dead. But it must be beating for these words to exist, for these thoughts to even flow. I check my pulse, but I can't feel a thing – it's nowhere to be found. It's in some remote, lonely place, surrounded by a thick block of concrete and chains, encrusted with jagged barnacles. It's like someone put cement shoes on it and tossed it into the deepest of seas.

But my body and my brain, they don't know this. No, they say, we have a beating heart. We think something's wrong, that's all. We may not have any heart-feelings, but we have a heart.

Somewhere.

But what they do not know is that this heart is so diseased that it may as well be dead. It may as well be at the bottom of the goddamn sea, rotting away.

We. I chuckle under my breath and my laugh bounces off the cement walls, filling my cramped cell. Who was it that spoke using a *we* like that? Oh, yeah – Gollum. And how did I wind up thinking in the *we* like Gollum? Maybe it's just the vibe of this dungeon. It *is* kind of like a cave. That must be it, because I normally don't think in the *we*. No, I think in the *me*. Me, me, and *more* me.

But the point is, it's true. I can't feel my heart.

Maybe I don't have one. My pain threshold, if it exists, is like a skyscraper. No, like Mt. Everest itself. I can take one hell of a beating and stand there bloody and bruised and smirking, completely unfazed. And when I've got way too much time to think, like I do right now, I sometimes wonder if I'm just an experiment in some virtual lab. Maybe the researchers have engineered me for failure. They've designed me to spin out of control and crash and burn while they watch in horror and perverse delight. And when I say *engineered for failure*, I don't mean that I've had one or two train wrecks. No, I'm talking way more than you can count on fingers and toes. It's a crazy thought, I know, but it rings true to me: I may not have a heart. Because to withstand this kind of intensity and not come unglued, you can't have a whole lot of emotions getting in the way. No, I'm built for this shit.

Infinite numbness.

It's my third month in solitary confinement. There are no books allowed in here except for the Bible or the Quran. But not both. No talking to other inmates under the slit of this dirty cell door. No phone calls. I can have a pad of paper, some envelopes and stamps, and a bendable rubber pen that has quite the learning curve. It's supposed to make stabbings impossible, but you can blind someone with it if you want.

Me, I don't want. I'm not in solitary for murder or stabbing or anything like that. The truth is, I'm here for some real dumb shit. I'm under an administrative investigation for being part of an organized theft conspiracy. I was on the rec yard when I stumbled onto it.

"Hey bro, need any boxers?"

I looked up. It was Alex. Thick cursive writing wrapped around his neck, and tattooed teardrops spilled down his cheeks. His white T-shirt was starched and pressed, and his blue pants sported razor-sharp creases.

Alex worked in the laundry.

I only owned three pairs of boxers, and they were worn and grey, just like my T-shirts. My day to get new clothes was still forty-five days away.

"Fuck yeah," I said. "How much?"

"Two packs of Camels."

I got in line to buy the smokes, and an hour later the guards walked up to me, snatched my new undies, and slapped handcuffs on me.

"You're going to solitary," one of them growled.

So no, I'm not in solitary because I hurt anyone. I just wanted to stay fresh.

I have a routine to pass the time in here. I do a lot of pushups and sit-ups. I sing, too. Actually, I *love* to sing, and this cell has the best echo ever. Better than you can get in a recording studio. I wouldn't know because I've never been in one, but I'm pretty sure it does.

When I sing, I pretend I'm Al Green. Then I'm Marvin Gaye. Then Paul Rodgers. I make up words for the ones I forget, but that doesn't matter because the crowds love it anyway. They gaze up from below, their mouths gaping. They're screaming and absolutely freaking out. Sweat trickles off my body as I stand on stage and bleed out every last drop of my soul. My lean chest is bare, and my abs drive them insane. The men are envious, and the women on the verge of tears. They pull up their T-shirts and bare their breasts as an offering to me, a god.

It's at this moment that keys clang outside my cell door. I'm snapped out of my trance as the latch opens, and a plastic food tray appears.

"Chow time, Cummins!"

It's a middle school serving size of meatloaf, mixed veggies, and a cup of juice with artificial sweetener. The food is bland

and lukewarm, but I gobble it down. I even lick the sauce off the tray.

I leave nothing for the ants.

After lunch I write poetry and letters. I ponder. I have conversations with myself.

Out loud.

I'm on my fourteenth year in prison. I'm a convicted bank robber. I'm a dope fiend. I've been in a few mental hospitals, too.

I'm not normal and I know it. Normal people are uncomfortable around someone like me. I haven't been around too many normal people, but I'm sure it's true. And what am I supposed to do with that? Knowing that I'm...*deformed?* So much so that I've been banished to prison for the majority of my life?

I don't know what to do with it, or how to figure it out. I take a look in the rearview mirror of my life and I'm stumped. Some dots you can connect, and some you conveniently forget. And others, you stay the fuck away from.

I like to think I'm a genius. That I'm a manly man. That I'm a legend to the folks in my hometown, and that they still talk about me around campfires.

I like to think whatever it is that helps me feel okay about me.

I'm starting to recognize this, and it's not easy. I'm thinking that I might be a bit slow in some ways. Maybe even special. It's good that I'm finally starting to see some things, but it's coming at a slow drip. It's like a complex puzzle with a thousand tiny parts, all mixed up and spread out across the floor right in front of me. And so I sit, staring at them and scratching my head.

When I get sick of push-ups and writing and singing to sold-out arenas, I lie on my bunk and thumb through the Bible. When I do, I think of my grandmother. She would always tell me that one day my life will do a one-eighty. That I'd speak in front of crowds, telling them how Jesus saved me and turned my life around.

The last time she told me that was six years ago. She sat across from me in the visiting room in Raiford. Right after she said it, her gaze lost its focus, and her eyes became droopy. I reached for her hand and squeezed, but she didn't respond.

She was having a stroke, right in front of me.

Twenty minutes later, I waved and mouthed goodbye through the fences as they helped her into an ambulance in front of the prison. She couldn't possibly have seen me. But I did it anyway, just in case. That's the last time I ever saw her or talked to her.

She passed away a few months later.

I don't know what it's all about, or where we're all headed. It could be heaven with streets paved with gold just like the Bible says. But it could just as easily be more like aliens and space wars with winged galactic horses. Maybe it's all just a giant mud puddle of nothingness.

Fuck, I don't know.

But I *have* read a lot of books. My list includes the Bible. The Quran. The Bhagavad Gita. All kinds of history and philosophy. I've even read the entire dictionary. Plus, I've taken lots of college correspondence courses that my grandmother paid for. And if I've learned anything, it's this: no one knows. And if they say they do, they're full of shit.

Still, I want my grandmother to be right. I want this life to have a happy ending. A happy middle would be nice, too. And even though I might not have a heart, I want the same for everyone else. Because I just know there's got to be something to all of this – and that regardless of what you believe, with the tiniest bit of faith, almost anything is possible.

I was on a rural county road in Tennessee, my thumb sticking out as a car passed. The road had been cut in a sharp crevice between mountainous hills with wooded terrain that rose abruptly on either side. The sun had not yet risen, but the dark was slowly turning purple. The air was crisp, and breath poured from my mouth like a cold fog.

I loved hitchhiking and being eighteen. Not knowing what was going to happen next made my adrenaline kick in like a rocket. And when the thrill waned and I'd find myself in the middle of the desert or on some country road, I loved that, too. I'd take in the air deeply and exhale, and the negativity and confusion would leave my body. And afterward, the quiet of nature would whisper a truth: surrounding me was greatness. The sky and horizon and whatever lay underneath it all seemed to go on forever.

This trip hadn't been easy, though. I was coming all the way from Los Angeles, and it had taken me a week to get here. It had been two days since I'd eaten or slept. Some guy had picked me up in Texas, and he was generous enough to buy me lunch. I'm pretty sure that's how he drugged me. I woke up in a dingy motel room just off I-10, and he was on top of me. My body was paralyzed, and all I could do was scream at the top of my lungs. He jumped off me and rushed out of the room, leaving me sprawled on the bed. It took me an hour to regain movement. I gathered my belongings, stepped outside, and I just shook it off. I walked to the interstate and stuck my thumb out again. The next day, just outside of Houston, another hitchhiker stole my duffle bag as I walked to get us a couple beers from a gas station. And to top it off, after I finally reached Tennessee, my throat began to get raw. I was clammy, sweating bullets, and chills raced down my spine and limbs.

I stopped walking. I put my hands on my knees and panted. I steadied myself, and then I spoke.

"God, I'm tired and I'm hungry," I said aloud. "Please, help me."

I lifted myself up. There was no help coming. But fifteen miles down the road, there was a small town. If I made it there, I might find somewhere to crash.

But first, I had to take a piss.

I wondered what people might think if they drove by and saw a stranger whizzing on their country road at five in the morning. So I cut into the woods and as soon as I was out of sight, I unzipped my jeans. As I began to let it go, I noticed something big and bulky lying on the ground to my right. I turned my head, and my jaw dropped. It was brand spanking new. It was unopened. It was still in the thick plastic store wrapping.

It was a huge sleeping bag.

And that wasn't all. Lying right on top of it, placed neatly side by side, were two jumbo-sized candy bars. I looked more closely.

Snickers.

My legs went weak, and my heart began to pound.

"Hey!" I shouted. "Is anyone there?"

I waited.

I zipped up my jeans and turned around, squinting my eyes in all directions.

"Who's there?" I yelled again. "Anyone?"

My voice returned as a thin echo amidst the trees.

No one was there. It was just me and the sleeping bag and the Snickers bars.

And, apparently, God.

I unpacked the sleeping bag and spread it out on the forest floor. I crawled inside and began chomping on the first Snickers. It made no sense. It was as if someone had bought the sleeping bag and candy bars, driven all the way out here, walked into the woods, set them down, and then just turned around and left.

I finished the candy bar and saved the other one for later. It would be my breakfast.

I shifted around until I found a comfortable position. I wondered what my grandmother would say about all this. Whatever had just happened, one thing was clear. If God was real, he had one hell of a sense of humor.

Fucking Snickers bars.

A few moments later, I was fast asleep.

EVER SINCE THAT DAY, WHENEVER I SEE A SNICKERS bar, I think of God – and also how utterly unable I am to make sense of any of this. Somehow, though, I just know there's meaning. Because at the very moment I think I can't go on any longer, when I'm about to collapse on my face because of the beating I've taken, something picks me up and tells me to keep going. It might be a sleeping bag and candy bars. Or maybe just a word of encouragement. Whatever. The point is, there's got to be something to all of this.

Which doesn't make me some jailhouse preacher. No, I'm not even close. It's true that from time to time I have my moments. But there's a lot within me that balances out that God stuff rather nicely.

Like the fact that I'm not afraid to say it: I hate this shithole. And not only that, if the mystery meat I eat at dinner tonight miraculously turns into a Snickers bar from heaven, I won't be impressed. Not one fucking bit. Because to be honest, I just don't have it in me any longer. I don't think I can make it another year, no matter how filled with wonder it may be. I'm tired of doing time. It's eating at my insides and it's worn me out.

Like an old pair of boxers.

Prison's not like the movies, where in one scene you enter and a few scenes later, you exit the gates. No, you really have to do your time. Every frigging second of it. The past fourteen years have taken, well, fourteen years to go by. I don't think I can make it to fifteen – which is a good thing, because I don't have to.

In eight more months, it's over.

I have a life to look forward to. I'm finally going to have a chance to make up for all the years I've wasted. I have a family that will welcome me home.

I'm even going to have my own house.

I found out about that just a couple days before those officers put me in solitary. It was almost four months ago on a Saturday, right around noon. I'd just walked out of the chow hall when they called my name over the intercom.

I had a visit.

I walked to the admin building by the front gate and a correctional officer led me to a small holding cell. I stripped off my clothes, turned around and bent over and coughed while he checked my pockets. He tossed my clothes on the floor in front of me, and after I threw them on, he buzzed me through a thick metal door that led to the visiting room.

It was packed with chatty families and crying babies, and vending machines and correctional officers lined the walls. I scanned the tables until my eyes found my mom and dad. They sprung to their feet, smiles lighting up their faces. I hurried to them and we hugged and sat down and exchanged a flurry of questions and answers. My brother and sister and their families were doing good. My sisters in New York and their husbands, they were doing good. I was doing good.

Everyone was doing good.

My parents had visited every few months for the past decade and a half, but I'd never noticed they'd aged until that day. The lines and the greys had been there all along, I knew, but they had seemed to be just a whisper. Yes, I thought, they seemed older, yet on the other hand, nothing had changed. My mom was still beautiful and vibrant. My dad, he had a youthful energy and was always kidding around. They were doing good and very much alive – I could see it in their faces. But still, I asked.

"So, how are you guys doing?"

They looked at each other, then back at me.

"Donny, we have some news for you," my mom said.

My dad cleared his throat, then shifted in his chair.

"Well, it's not the best news," he began, "but it's going to be okay."

And then, he told me.

"I've been diagnosed with cancer."

I blinked.

"It sounds bad," my mom said, "but we're very optimistic. Your dad has a great doctor who's well-known at the Moffit Center. He says that of all the types of prostate cancer, this is the best kind to have. It's the least aggressive."

I'd never heard of a good kind of cancer.

"It's going to be all right, honey." She put her hand on my arm and looked me in the eye. "Really. It's going to be okay."

I looked at my dad. He reached out and took my hand, a slight smile forming on his lips.

"We're going to follow up and find out what steps to take next. And when we do, well, we'll take them," he said. "But you've got to trust that it's going to be all right."

He squeezed my hand.

My dad was a tough son of a bitch. From sea captain to master builder, from motorcycle racer to entrepreneur, he was tough. As nails, he was. Nothing could beat my dad.

Not even cancer.

I decided to believe them.

"All right then." I forced a smile. "It's going to be okay."

"Yes, it is," he said. "And now that we've gotten that out of the way, we have some good news as well."

He nodded at my mom.

"When you get out, we want to help you," she said. "We've got this small house we usually rent out, and we want you to stay there a year or two. As long as you like."

A second home? I had no idea. I looked at him, then her again.

"You'll be a mile from us," she added. "And your brother and sister, too."

My own place? I opened my mouth, but nothing came out. My dad spoke up.

"Y'know, all these years have passed, but you've never really had a break. We want to help you get on your feet and give you the best possible chance to succeed."

"We can't wait for you to come home," my mom chimed in.

When I left the visiting room that day, my head was spinning. It still is. Because when I left home at thirteen, we lived in a small Florida house and there were cockroaches galore. My parents shared a used car, and we didn't go out to eat or buy any extra stuff. My mom cleaned other people's houses to help make ends meet. Once I stole from her purse, and a ten-dollar bill was the only thing my hand found at the bottom of it. After she discovered what I'd done, she was furious.

"That was our last ten dollars!" she screamed. "Don't you understand? We're poor!"

And then, she began to sob.

But now everything's different. They've come a long way, and so have I. Good things are coming. It's like one moment I have no idea where I'll go or what my life will look like, and now, I do.

I'm getting out of solitary next week. When I do, I'm going to focus on reading everything I can about the modern world.

There's the internet now, and a lot of other stuff has changed since 1991 as well.

But the most important thing, I already have. And that's a family who loves me and wants to help me, and a place I can call my home. I'll help them, too. They're going to need me.

My *dad* is going to need me.

To hell with why I turned out like this. To hell with trying to connect these dots or to solve this puzzle. My time is almost over, and I'm not going to spend it on that. What matters is my future.

I'm finally going to return. To my family. To my hometown.

I'm going home to Safety Harbor.

2

I WILL BURY YOU

I'm in a holding cell, and I'm a mess. My breath is shallow and rapid, and my limbs are all twitchy. My foot's tapping like crazy on the concrete floor. I press my toes hard against the bottom of my jail-slippers to make it stop, and it does. Under my breath I chant. *I will not tap my foot. I will not tap my foot.*

And why should I not tap that foot? Because it would mean I'm anxious and jittery. And if I'm anxious and jittery, I won't be able to speak well. My voice will shake, and I might even forget the very words that could save my life. And if that happens, my life will be ruined – even worse than it already is.

I stretch my spine and throw my shoulders back, sitting tall as I can on this metal slab. I inhale deeply, till there's a sharp pain in the bottom of my lungs. I exhale and release those jitters to the Universe. To God. To whatever *is.* I visualize the anxiety leaving my body and dissipating into the air around me. And then, it's gone.

My body relaxes ever so slightly, and a deep warmth washes over me. A smile forms on my lips.

Ah, serenity.

I draw the next breath – and there it is again. My foot's

tapping. And now a school of tiny minnows has joined in. They're racing in circles within my belly as I'm stuck here, waiting.

Any moment, the bailiffs are going to walk me down the hall to a courtroom. They'll stand me in front of a judge, who will look down on me and bang that gavel and pronounce my sentence. Which means that today I might walk out of this place.

And then again, maybe not. It might wind up being a repeat of what happened a few weeks ago.

I was supposed to get released from DeSoto Correctional Institution. It was still dark when my eyes flew open and I sat up straight in my bunk. I threw on my clothes and stood at my cell door and stared out the thick plexiglass window for two hours. When the sun finally rose, an officer let me out of my cell and escorted me to the release desk by the front gates. The release officer opened a folder and pushed some paperwork across the desk to me.

"You got a hundred and eighty dollars coming." She pointed at a piece of paper. "Sign right there."

She fanned through a folder while I signed my name.

"Oh wait," she snapped. "My bad. You don't get any money."

"Why not?"

"You only get that if you are actually getting out." She gathered the documents into a file and closed it. "But you're not."

"What are you talking about?"

"The U.S. Marshals are picking you up," she said. "They'll be here about 10 a.m."

My bottom lip began to quiver.

Fuck. I knew it. I had a violation of federal parole from fifteen years before. Which would mean at least a few more weeks before I got out.

If I got out.

So now here I am, waiting to find out what my sentence will

be. I might walk free in just a couple hours. My public defender thinks so. She knows the judge and says he'll probably let me go because I've already served a humongous amount of time.

She's probably right, but you never know. My record is bad. As an adult, I have a slew of arrests. Four or five burglaries, a few grand thefts and grand theft autos, and a couple violations of probation. The rest are all bank robberies. Eight total if you count the two from Los Angeles. But in a way, my juvenile record is even worse because I was arrested twice as many times. Thirty-two, to be exact. I know for sure because a judge kept repeating it over and over right before he sentenced me. That was over twenty years ago, but for some reason it's always stuck with me.

"YOU TURNED SIXTEEN YEARS OLD JUST LAST MONTH. And you've been arrested thirty-two times?"

It was 1982. The judge looked up from his paperwork and stared down at me. I nodded my head and cracked my knuckles. He grunted, then turned his attention back to his paperwork. He thumbed through a few more pages, then he scowled at me again.

"Thirty-two times." He shook his head and sighed. "For Christ's sake, son. You've been arrested *thirty-two times*. And now you've busted out of the holding cell, right here in my courthouse."

It was true. A few months before, I'd pushed the metal holding cell door open with my feet. It was just thin enough to bend a few inches, and I was able to open it just wide enough to squeeze my skinny body through with only a few scrapes across my chest. When I got outside to the parking lot, I found a car with the keys in the ignition and whoosh, I was gone.

"Son, why do you keep running?" he asked. "You know why?"

I didn't. But he was right – I *was* a runner. The reason I'd been in that holding cell in the first place was because I'd been arrested the week before for escaping from the Okeechobee Boys School. And how does someone get charged with escaping from *school*? Great question. They just called it a school. But really, Okeechobee was a juvenile prison. A twelve-foot-tall barbed wire fence surrounded the place, and when kids managed to climb over it the staff chased them through the swamp with rifles and dogs.

And why did they send me to Okeechobee? A grand theft auto charge. The short version is that I ran away from a children's shelter in Tampa with a girl who *said* she had permission to use the car. But she had lied. And why was I at the shelter? I'd run away from the Teen Challenge drug program in Miami, then hitchhiked to Tampa, where the cops found me wandering around in the middle of the night. They scooped me up and put me in the shelter. And why was I sent to Teen Challenge? Actually, I wasn't – I went on my own. I'll never forget how proud my grandfather was about that. He beamed when I made the decision to go, and he drove me all the way down there himself. He hugged me tight before leaving me in good hands at the intake room.

And as for Teen Challenge, all of that happened three weeks after I got out of Okeechobee the *first* time. And the first time I went there, that was because I ran away from a youthful offender program in Jacksonville. I was in *that* program because a mental hospital I'd been committed to had advised the courts that the Jacksonville program was the perfect spot for me. I was in the mental hospital because I'd escaped from a youth ranch, and I was at the youth ranch because I'd run away from a youth home. I was sentenced to the youth home because I ran away for the tenth and final time from an in-patient drug program called Straight Incorporated.

I was thirteen when that entire leg of the journey began.

The judge cleared his throat.

"Son, what am I supposed to do with you?"

I shrugged my shoulders and told him I didn't know.

I had no idea what *I* would do with me.

He sighed and said it one last time.

"Thirty-two times."

Then he sentenced me to two years in adult prison.

SO YES, MY RECORD IS BEYOND HORRIBLE. BUT I THINK the judge might let me out today because I've just done one hell of a stretch. That's got to count for something. But there's another way you can look at it, too. You could argue with a straight face that the right thing to do with a guy like me is to keep me locked away as long as humanly possible.

Which would mean twenty more years.

I'm grappling with that thought when my cell door flies open. I rise to my feet, and a couple bailiffs grab me by the upper arms and spin me around and march me down a long corridor, through a couple turns and then a wide door. And there I am, standing before the judge's bench. It towers above me like an empty throne. The courtroom is wide, the ceilings are tall, and low murmurs fill the room as people in suits talk in hushed tones.

My public defender stands by a table with some other lawyers who are whispering and nodding their heads. She looks my way and smiles. She gives me a thumbs up.

A bailiff announces my case with a loud voice, and the room settles down as the judge walks in and is seated above me.

This shit is about to get real.

An attorney for the government clears his throat.

"Your honor, Mr. Cummins has been adjudicated by the State of Florida to be a habitual offender. A career criminal. He has multiple bank robberies and thefts going back decades. We think it's appropriate for the court to sentence him to an additional five years."

Five is a lot better than twenty. I sigh with relief, but then my body stiffens.

Five more years *sucks*.

"Your Honor, the defense objects to any more prison time at all," my public defender counters. "Mr. Cummins has just served a total of fifteen years in state custody for robbing banks. Notably, his federal probation was violated specifically because of the state conviction. In other words, his violation of probation is based upon the same behavior he just served fifteen years for. This court should not punish him a second time for it. Instead, the defense respectfully requests time served for this charge."

The judge looks over his glasses and stares at me.

My forehead gets hot. Then it gets moist. I want to wipe my brow. I think about raising my hand and volunteering to do a couple more years just to be safe. But before I can the judge speaks.

"Mr. Cummins, if I were to let you go today, what's your plan? What are you going to do?"

I have formal training in absolutely nothing. Well, there's the welding certificate I earned eight years ago. It was a three-month class and I hated it. But at least it's true – I *am* a welder. I can also say I already have welding work lined up starting the following Monday.

Which would be a lie.

I decide to tell the truth – the *whole* truth.

"Your Honor, I'm going back to Safety Harbor. And since I've been in, I've written a lot of songs. Six of them were recorded by a professional blues vocalist, and I even earned royalties on one."

His face is blank, but he leans forward slightly.

"Well, I want to keep doing that. I'm going to write songs and make a living doing it."

My attorney groans.

I turn my head and look behind me. My brother Bob is sitting in the first row. He's wearing a Pearl Jam T-shirt and jeans and he has long wavy hair and a goatee. He grins and shakes his head slightly.

"Mr. Cummins, there's a lot of drug use in the music industry," the judge says. "Do you have a plan for that as well?"

"I do. I'm going to stay clean."

I mean it. I really do. I want to stay the hell away from anything that might get even remotely out of hand.

"And how will you do that?" he asks. "Do you plan on attending meetings or support groups?"

I don't. I don't need meetings or support groups because my problem is simple: Cocaine. Which means the solution is also simple: Don't do cocaine. It's been fifteen years since I smoked crack, so I'm pretty sure I'm good. What I need to do is focus on the future. But if I have to attend some groups once in a while, I will.

"I'm ready to do whatever it takes," I answer. "If it means going to meetings, I'll do it."

"I hope you will, Mr. Cummins. You're thirty-nine, which is still young. You've got enough time left to do great things if you choose."

My heart starts thumping. He's about to let me go.

"However, I advise you to remember well what I'm about to tell you." His tone is stern, and he looks at me hard. "I've seen many bad records, and yours is one of the worst."

I nod my head.

"If you ever set foot in my courtroom again, I will have no choice," he says. "I will bury you."

I swallow.

"If that happens, I promise that if you don't die in prison, you'll be a very old man when you get out. Do you understand me?"

I nod again.

"All right then. I'm giving you time served. Which means that today, you will walk out of here a free man. Good luck, Mr. Cummins."

3

BOB

I'm standing in front of the jail's release desk, a few feet away from a metal door. On the other side of that door, a horn is honking. Then, someone's laughing. I know what's on the other side of that door.

It's freedom.

I shift my weight from one foot to the other, then back again. I've been standing here for thirty minutes and it's taking forever.

"Cummins," the officer behind the desk barks. "You ready?"

"Yes."

"Got any release clothes?"

"No, just my prison clothes."

"Can't wear those. Put these on."

He tosses me a blue, one-piece, paper biohazard suit. It's oversized and baggy, but I don't care. I throw it on and scrawl my signature on some paperwork, and the door opens.

And just like that, the jail is behind me. I'm standing in the sunshine, and warmth rests on my neck and shoulders. I look around and take it all in. Everything's moving and breathing, and noises are everywhere. They aren't raucous and echoey or bouncing off steel and concrete like they did in prison. No, not at all. A light breeze scrapes my ears gently. Cars whiz past on a nearby street. A bus hisses as it brakes to a stop. A plane buzzes in the distance, then another one soars alarmingly close. A shoe scuffles on a sidewalk. Someone shouts from across the street, then somebody else laughs and yells back.

It's a sonic, eclectic mashup, and it's happening all around me.

It seems to go on forever, this free world. So spacious it is, with no boundaries. I can go anywhere I want. To the left or to the right. For one mile or a hundred. I can even go down if I'm willing to start digging.

It's my choice – whatever I want to do.

My head is dizzy. This is way too much. I sit down on a wooden bench by some pay-phones. I grip the edge of the bench to steady myself. I'm going to stay put right here. Bob will probably pull up any second. There's a line of cars parked next to the sidewalk. They're all new and shiny, and I can't tell a Honda from a Chevy.

I don't see my brother anywhere, either.

There's a pigeon on the sidewalk. It's barely out of arm's reach, and I watch it as it paces back and forth. It can't make up its mind which way to go. It stops and stares at me. It cocks its head and looks at me with one eye. Then the other. Then it lifts off from the pavement and flies away. I wonder how it knows where to go, how it gets home.

I look up toward the street, and I see him. Bob is leaning against a car, his eyes fixed on the jail door I walked through just moments ago.

He's looking for me.

I watch him for a moment. I'm amazed he's here, and that he still treats me like a brother.

I'm damn lucky he *is* my brother.

IT WAS 1991 AND WE WERE GOING TO BE ROCK STARS. We practiced every night in Bob's bedroom, writing songs and making 4-track demos. We'd record his drums and then I'd lay down the bass and guitar tracks. Afterward, we'd stand in the driveway, smoking cigarettes and talking about the future. We were going to take over the local music scene, then go national. And always, before we went back inside, I'd walk to the end of the driveway and flick my cigarette into the street.

I couldn't take a step further because I didn't want to violate my house arrest. Because if that happened, it would trigger a federal parole violation. Which, in turn, would trigger a federal *probation* violation.

My legal issues made it hard to go out and mix up with musicians. So instead, they came to us. They'd come to be interviewed, vocalists and bass players from all over. Yet not a single one made the cut. That's because we required something none of them had: perfection. Well, not *we*. It was I who required it. Each note and every accent they played or sang had to exactly match the notes and phrasing I heard in my head.

Not only that, they had to *look* perfect, too. Because to make it big, we needed perfect hair and a perfect stage show, complete with perfect showmanship and perfect lighting and fog. We were going to blow everyone away with our concert debut, and after a few shows, we would land a massive record contract – the reward for absolute perfection.

But the truth was, I'd never been in a band before. Unless you counted Ill Repute. I was lead guitarist for that all-bank-robber, punk, death-metal band during my stint in federal prison. A lot of people *say* they're hard-core, but Ill Repute truly was. Especially the bass player, Brad. And a month after I got out, he showed up at our house right after Bob and I finished practicing.

I opened the door, and my jaw dropped.

"Dude," I managed. "What's up?"

"Hitman, what's happening?"

Brad never called anyone *dude* or *man* or *bro*. It was always *hitman*.

"I got in some serious fucking trouble in Vegas." He slapped me on the shoulder and laughed. "I made it here by the skin of my teeth."

I didn't even want to ask. When Brad went in, he pulled a bandana over his face, whipped out a huge handgun, and screamed for everyone to get on the floor.

A total maniac.

"So, um, what now?" I asked.

I hoped to God he didn't want to crash the night.

"Europe!" he gushed. "I'm headed to fucking *Europe*! Hitman, you've got to come with me!"

"Europe? Why Europe?"

"Well, we can't do music here because the pigs are on my trail," he explained.

I leaned my head out the door and looked down the street.

"But if we go to Europe," he continued, "we can get *asylum*. Hitman, we can go there and put a band together and get famous. Thrash metal bank robbers? They'll fucking love us. We'll make some connections, pull some strings and get pardons. Then we'll come back to the States. It'll be awesome!"

I didn't need a pardon. But if I hung out with Brad, that would probably change quick.

"Dude, I don't think so," I said. "I'm good."

"Well, okay." He looked to the left and right, then lowered his voice. "You know where I can at least score some coke?"

I didn't. And that was the last I heard from Brad.

So, to say my band experience was limited would be an understatement. But federal prison gave me a lot of time to think about it, and I was sure I had it all figured out. Bob and I would put in the hard work. And if we were relentless, we'd eventually find the right musicians. We'd have perfect chemistry, and people would be absolutely floored when we finally played our first gig. That would create the buzz locally and regionally, and it would be our path to success.

Not quite as dramatic as Brad's plan, but doable.

"Okay, we'll find the perfect people if that's what you want," Bob told me. "But really, bro, I'm just happy to play with you. Glad you're here."

I was, too. I was twenty-three, and it was the first time I'd lived at home since I was thirteen.

Six months later, I got off house arrest and within a few days I ran into some guys in a local band. They had gigs lined up already, and they asked me to join. When they did, I didn't hesitate.

"It's temporary," I told Bob. "I just want to make some connections. Then it will be easier to get our own gigs. Maybe I can even network with some talent scouts."

He was silent for a minute.

"Well, okay," he said. "Do what you need to do, man."

Two weeks later I was in a hotel room after a show, snorting cocaine like a real rock star. Two more weeks and I was shooting it in a dirty gas station bathroom – like a real dope fiend.

The ball was rolling, and I couldn't stop it. I'd go missing for days, lost on long binges. The paranoia set in quickly, and I began to lose my mind. I started hearing voices, and I thought the FBI was after me. I'd see them following me around, and I'd hear them taunting me and laughing at me.

When I finally landed in jail again, I'd been charged with six bank robberies. It was seven years before my brother finally visited me.

I didn't blame him. I was a horrible brother. I wouldn't have visited me, either.

I STAND TO MY FEET, MY EYES ON MY BROTHER AS HE looks toward the jail, watching for me. Those few months in 1991 were so long ago. I need to focus on the future instead. I hope he feels the same.

I take a few steps toward Bob, and he looks in my direction. His eyes light up, and we hug and slap each other's backs.

"Good to see you, Bob!"

"You too, bro!"

"Man, when you started talking about music in the court-room, I thought the judge wasn't going to let you go!"

"I know, right?" I laugh.

We jump into his car and pull out. We head to his place first because I need to ditch the paper suit and get some real clothes. He lights up a cigarette, and I roll my window down. The wind is blowing on my face. I want to hang my head out the window with my tongue out like a dog.

It's great to be free. To be with family. This time it's going to be different. I'm going to show them I've changed.

"Playing out anywhere?" I ask him.

"Yeah." He blows smoke out his window. "This weekend we are. And then got one lined up to open for that guy from Jefferson Airplane. Marty something."

"Oh, yeah? That's great."

I wait a minute before I speak.

"Maybe you and me can play again sometime."

I look out my window and pretend to watch the stores and parking lots on Tampa Road as they whiz by. Bob doesn't say anything. He just looks ahead at the road and takes another drag.

"Um, well sure, man," he finally says. "We can do that."

"Cool. I'm really looking forward to it."

"Me too, bro. Me too."

4

MOM

Today is the first day I wake up free. When I finally lay down last night, I crashed immediately. But now, my eyes pop open and I sit up straight like I've been struck by a lightning bolt. There's a digital clock by my bed, and the glowing red letters say it's 5 a.m. For a moment I wonder where I am, then I remember. I'm in the guest room at my parents' house.

I smell coffee, and I get out of bed and make my way to the kitchen. My dad's wearing a thin, flannel shirt and he's packing a cooler with bottled water and apples.

"Morning, D," he smiles. "Sleep good?"

"Good morning, Dad," I yawn. I pour myself a cup of coffee. "Best sleep in a decade and a half."

"I'll bet," he laughs. "Ready to catch some fish?"

He's got his 22-foot Pathfinder out front, hitched to the back of the Ford. It's already loaded with a cast net and a bunch of fishing poles.

"I am." I take a sip. It's the best coffee in a decade and a half, too.

When we pull up to the Safety Harbor Marina, the sky is beginning to turn orange. We launch, and he navigates the boat quietly through the shallow waters, out to the channel and then by the old wooden pier that juts out on the waters toward the East. He pulls his baseball hat low and tells me to hang on. We speed toward the northern edge of Old Tampa Bay. I hold on tight as I sit at the bow, and the saltwater sprays my arms and face as we skip across the water.

When we get there, we cast our nets to catch bait and we pull in plenty – all greenbacks and pinfish. We keep the greenbacks; they'll land us snook, or maybe some redfish. My dad doesn't want me to cut the bait because his knife is razor sharp and I haven't fished in years. So he does it himself, instead. When he does, he cuts his little finger deeply and swears loudly. He bandages his hand with a shirt and laughs hard at himself. I try not to, but I do, too.

We fish for a few hours and catch nothing. But we talk a lot and laugh a lot. By 10 a.m., my pale skin is burnt already because I've been in jail and out of the sun. We reel in our lines and head back to the marina.

It's going to be a big day. After lunch, my mom is going to take me shopping and get me set up at my new house. My dad will drop by afterward, too. Then tonight I'll be at my parents' again for dinner. My brother and sister will be there, too.

It will be all of us together again, just like it should be.

WHEN MY MOM TAKES ME SHOPPING, WE GET PLATES and cups and toilet paper. A coffee maker. Toothbrush and toothpaste and some shampoo. We get *lots* of food. I see a George Foreman grill, and I grab it off the shelf. I saw one in a magazine a few months back – I can cook five chicken breasts and two hamburgers in a half-hour. That's dinner for a whole week.

We load up the back of her car with the groceries. Actually, it's an SUV. Everyone's driving them now, it seems. They're nice, like a truck and a car rolled into one. I shut the hatch, and we get in and drive to my house a few blocks away and pull into the driveway.

The front yard is narrow, but it has thick grass and a small, wiry tree. Shrubs surround either side of the house, squeezed against wooden fences. It's an older block house, painted tan with brown trim. It's small, maybe even tiny to some. But to me, it's amazing.

My mom unlocks the front door and opens it wide for me. I step in and walk around. The place is completely furnished. I pass through a modest dining room, then into a tiny kitchen. I peek out the window above the kitchen sink. The back yard is overgrown, a couple feet high in a few places, and there's a small shed and a laundry room. I turn and find my way to the bathroom and living room. And then, the bedroom.

My bedroom.

I return to the living room and I plop down on the couch.

"Like it?" she asks.

"Oh, yeah," I nod. "I love it."

My place is the size of a one-bedroom apartment, but it's perfect for me.

We bring everything in from the car, and my mom starts a pot of coffee and helps me with the groceries. We finish filling the cupboards, and we sit at the dining room table.

"I can't believe I'm here." I shake my head. "This house, I just love it."

She takes off her glasses and wipes the lenses with a napkin.

"You know, Don, we let your brother stay here for a couple years. And then your sister, too."

"Really?"

I thought they rented it out to *other* people.

"Yep," she says, "they each had a couple years to get their shit together. And after a couple years, they were outta here."

She motions with her thumb like an umpire calling a batter out. We both laugh.

"I'll be out in less than two years," I tell her, "and I won't screw it up."

"I know you won't. We always knew you'd make it out one day."

She places her hand on mine.

"I'm so glad you're here, Don."

Her eyes are red, and they're welling up with tears.

My mom, she's strong. But the lines on her forehead say she's tired, too. It's probably my dad. Taking care of someone with cancer has got to be tough. But then again, having your kid get out of prison has got to be nerve-wracking, too. I've put them both through a lot, I know. I wasn't just bad. I was *extreme*.

Which, of course, called for extreme measures.

IT WAS ALMOST NOON ON A WEEKDAY. I DON'T remember what day it was, but I know I woke up on the couch. Our house was still, and for a moment I wondered if Jesus had returned and left without me. And then, there was a firm nudge on my shoulder.

"Get up and get ready," my mom said. "We found a new school for you."

I was in the eighth grade, and I'd been expelled from two schools in the past two months for possession of drugs.

"Really?" I stretched my arms and yawned. "What one?"

"Just get up," she snapped. "We need to be there in an hour."

I got dressed and wolfed down a sandwich, and we drove in silence. I'd been missing the past two days, but she didn't even bring it up. She knew I'd been out getting high.

Getting wasted was all I wanted to do. I didn't care if it was weed or alcohol or pills or mushrooms. Or even cough syrup. Nothing else mattered anymore except getting high – I'd even given up playing guitar and baseball and fishing. My hobby, my purpose, and my entire life was all about getting stoned.

I skipped school most days. I crawled out the window in the middle of the night to meet up with older kids to get high. I'd go missing for days. The police would canvass the neighborhood, knocking on my friends' doors. *Have you seen Donny Cummins?*

Just a few months before, when I was still twelve, I even got arrested for public intoxication. There I was, sprawled out in the back of a sheriff's car, the top half of my body hanging out the door. I was coughing on my own puke, which dripped down my cheeks and neck, making a small puddle on the concrete below. I felt someone staring at me and I looked up.

It was my dad.

He towered above me, and his brow furrowed. His eyes became narrow, burning a hole right through me. I couldn't tell if he was furious or just upset.

My eyes lowered to the ground and within, I cowered. He knelt down beside me, and a moment later, he spoke.

"Ready to come home, Donny?"

It was almost a whisper.

"Yeah, I am."

He reached out and helped me to my feet, holding me steady as he led me to his truck.

I *was* ready to come home. I was always ready when I was worn out and unable to keep going anymore. But after I'd slept it off and the sun came up, it would return to me. The gnawing. The jitters. The deep *knowingness* that I had to keep running – no matter how bad it hurt.

My mom and dad hired psychologists. The doctors were pleasant enough, and I think they did their best. They would talk to me and observe me while I did jigsaw puzzles. They'd play chess with me while they took notes. They'd give me tests with huge lists of true or false statements, like *At times I feel like swearing*. Or, *I am very rarely troubled by constipation*. Or, *I do not always tell the truth*.

The strangest thing, though, is that not a single one of them ever asked me straight-up why I liked to get high, or why I ran away from home. But that didn't matter anymore, anyway. My parents were done with psychologists. The priority was to find a new school, and on deck was school number three.

My mom parked the car.

"We're here," she announced.

It didn't look like a school. It was in an industrial section, and there were no school signs or school buses, no track or football field. It looked more like an old warehouse.

"You sure this is it?" I asked.

"Yes." She opened the driver's door. "C'mon, let's go."

We went in and a receptionist greeted us, then led us to an empty waiting room. She opened the door and motioned us inside.

"Someone will be with you shortly, Mrs. Cummins."

We went in, and the receptionist closed the door behind us.

The moment we took a seat, a couple boys burst through the door. They walked right up to me, less than a foot away, and stood in front of me with their hands on their hips and smirks on their faces. They were older, maybe sixteen or seventeen, and stout like football players.

"Hey Don, how's it going?" the taller one said, sticking out his hand.

I reached out to shake it, and that's when I noticed. Behind him, my mom was walking out the door. I rose to my feet, but they shoved me back into my chair.

"You're not going anywhere," the other boy laughed. "Welcome to Straight Incorporated."

I doubled over. It was like I'd been sucker-punched in the

gut. My heart raced and my stomach was in knots. I wanted to cry and beg my parents to give me another chance. But it was too late.

She was gone.

The two boys, they started talking rapidly, but my brain put them on mute. I rested my chin on my knees and drew myself into a ball and began to rock back and forth, staring at the floor. It was my fault. I had given my parents no other choice.

I was a rotten fucking kid.

I had to get out of there. I needed to get back home somehow. And then, I began to hear them. They were saying I could go home in a month or two if I worked hard. They were telling me that they had gone through the same thing themselves. Don't freak out, they assured me – I just needed to be honest and humble.

I needed to get straight.

Tears welled up in my eyes, ready to spill over. But there was no way I could let that happen.

They might never stop.

I took a deep breath, and the floor came into focus again. I exhaled.

Everything was going to be okay, I told myself. *I'll get straight. I'll turn my life around and earn my way home. I'll go back to school and get good grades. I'll play baseball and guitar again.*

But I had no way of knowing that this party was just getting started.

5

DAD

It was decades ago when my mom left me at Straight. When I remember it, even now my stomach still drops. But it was hard on her, too – and really, the hell I put her through must've been even worse. Still, I want to think that everything is okay now. Because today, I'm sitting with her at my kitchen table in my new house. I'm finally out, and I'm ready to do the right thing.

And that, I tell myself, makes it all good.

But I know better than that. Time cannot have healed all those wounds. And sitting here now, I think I see it. When I'm in prison she knows I'm safe, and she can breathe. But when I'm out, anything might happen – and she holds her breath.

I want to say I'm sorry, but over the years I've said it so many times. It will just sound hollow. But I don't care – I want to say it again. I hope that somehow, it will help.

There's a loud knock on the front porch door.

"Anyone home?"

It's my dad.

He walks in and takes a seat with us. He removes his hat and puts it on the table. His hair is thick and white, and it stands straight up, like he stuck his finger in a light socket.

"What do you think?" he asks. "You like it?"

"The hair?" I smile. "It's awesome."

He laughs, and runs his fingers through it, smoothing it down. I notice the band-aid on his pinky from this morning.

"I mean the house," he says.

"I was just telling Mom it's perfect. I absolutely love it."

My mom gets up and pours him a cup of coffee.

"I'm going to run some errands," she tells us. "I think you two have some things to do, right?"

"We do," he says. "First, a few things around here, then we're going to get our boy a phone."

He looks at me and smiles.

I'm getting a cell phone. Now *that's* high tech.

She gives us each a kiss on the cheek and leaves. My dad and I sit a moment, and then he speaks.

"So how are you doing, D? Must be a lot to take in at once."

"It is." I nod my head. "But I'm okay. I'm going to do good this time."

"I know you will. I believe in you."

I shift in my seat. My dad, he believes in me. That's a lot to take in, too.

"We just want to help. It's up to you to do the work, of course, but we're going to give you the head start you deserve."

His voice breaks. He takes a moment to clear his throat, then stands to his feet and smiles.

"So, let's give you the tour."

He takes me outside and shows me how to use the lawn-mower. It's been a long time since I used one, but they still work the same. *Check.* He shows me where the water meter is and how to turn the water on and off. *Check.* He takes me to the shed outside, and he shows me where to find all the tools. *Check.* We go back in the house and he shows where the breaker box is, and he points out each switch and tells me what part of the house it controls. *Check.*

"You see all the rooms yet?" he asks.

"Yep."

"Storage room, too?"

I haven't. He walks me through the kitchen to a door by the dining area and he opens it. It's a plain room, maybe nine by fourteen feet. In the corner, there's a rolled-up carpet and some cans of paint.

"Okay," I say. "It's a storage room."

"Yes, it is." He looks at me. "What do you think you want to do with it?"

He's quizzing me, I can tell. I'm not sure what to say. Maybe, "I'll store shit in it." But then it comes to me – a recording studio! It's a bit tight for a band, but I think I can make it work. I'll soundproof it and it will be my lab – my *sound* lab.

I turn to him.

"Music," I tell him. "I'll use it for music. I mean, unless you have something else in mind."

"Not at all." He grins. "Actually, that's kind of what I was thinking."

My dad's the one who taught me to play. I was six when he showed me my first twelve-bar blues riff. The guitar was too large for my small body, so he showed me how to lay it across my lap and make it work.

I eyeball the room again. I can split it into two sections. The main room and a closet-size room. That will be the control room, complete with thick glass so the sound engineer can see the musicians. Like a real recording studio.

"I'd probably want to do some building in there," I say.

"What you have in mind?"

"I'd probably want to put a wall in there. Add some sound-proofing. Do a few upgrades."

He strokes his chin and looks around.

"I can help you with some of that."

"Really? You want to build it with me?"

"Yep. Your old man will help you build it. And your brother, too. If you want, that is."

My dad, the master builder. He's built everything. Houses, cabinets. Wood crafts. When I was young, we built lots of stuff together. The Boy Scouts' Pinewood Derby car is the one that sticks out the most. He ground the front end to a narrow point after drilling a wide hole in it and packing it full of lead, which he concealed with green paint. The Green Hornet, that's what we called it. It was an illegal car, but it won me a trophy.

The point is, I know this studio is going to be over the top because my dad is an awesome craftsman.

The last thing he built with me in mind, though, I have to say I did not see *that* coming. It was an upgrade for my bedroom, and it was supposed to help save my life. And really, that's all he ever wanted to do.

I never doubted it for a moment.

STRAIGHT INCORPORATED WAS A SHITHOLE. I WAS thirteen and not allowed any contact with my family. No phone calls. I couldn't even write them a letter. They barely fed us, and our stomachs always ached. There was no air conditioning, and the Florida sun beat down on the metal warehouse roof, turning the place into an oven. Beads of sweat would trickle down my neck and my back and my balls fourteen hours a day. I drowned in a sea of three-hundred teenagers, tightly cramped together in metal folding chairs. The days started early in the morning with writing assignments and group talks and lectures that went on late into the night. The talks were led by staff members who swore and yelled at us. Sometimes, if they thought we were out of line, they would punch and kick us, too.

I started the program on First Phase, or as a *newcomer*. In the evenings, the program staff would send we newcomers home with the teenagers who had advanced to Second Phase. They were called *oldcomers*. The oldcomers were allowed to go home to their own families every night, and we newcomers had to stay at their homes. The oldcomers would march us around the warehouse and their homes like prisoners. They'd walk behind us, one hand gripping our shoulder and the other, the waist of our pants at the small of our backs. They would guide us and push us toward the bathroom. To the backseat of their parent's car. Into their homes. And then back into the front doors of the warehouse each morning.

We weren't allowed to walk anywhere by ourselves.

I wanted to make it to Second Phase, I really did. But I couldn't help myself; I ran away every chance I got. If I had to use my legs, I would. But if I could, I'd steal a bike because they were quicker than my legs. And if I had the chance, I'd steal cars because they're faster than bikes. I escaped nine times, and the ninth was the game-changer. When morning came, my oldcomer discovered I was missing. And when he poked his head out the front door, he realized his parents' car was, too.

The police found the car in the middle of a cow pasture out at Boot Ranch, dangling halfway over the canal waters. They charged me with grand theft auto, and the courts had no mercy. They sentenced me to what seemed the worst possible place ever.

They ordered me to complete Straight Incorporated.

Straight wasn't thrilled. I'd become a liability and they wanted me gone. But a court order is a court order, so they worked out a deal with my parents. Instead of going home with an oldcomer each night, Straight would let me go to my own home. But there were two conditions. First, an oldcomer had to come home with me and stay overnight. The second condition was for my dad. If he wanted his boy to come home, he had to secure my bedroom.

My parents agreed, and Straight assigned Mike to be my oldcomer. He was lanky, an entire foot taller than me, and he had his own car, too. As he pulled out of Straight and drove us to my house on the first night, he didn't say a word. He just hunched over the steering wheel as he drove, sulking.

Then finally he spoke.

"You think you're special, don't you?" he spat, glaring at the road ahead. "You run away every other week. Then you steal a car. You haven't even *earned* Second Phase. And now they're letting you go home?"

I smiled in the dark. Mike was a real hater, but I didn't care. I was finally going home.

We pulled up to my house, and he made me step out of the car backwards. His right hand found a place in the small of my back, and he gripped the waist of my jeans tightly. His left hand held my shoulder firm as he turned me around and guided me roughly toward the front door of my house.

When we got inside and the front door was locked behind us, he loosened his grip. He hovered over me as I hugged my mom and dad, then Bob. And then, four-year-old Liz.

My heart was lighter by a pound; I was home, and that was all that mattered. The living room was just like it was when I'd left the year before. I looked back at Mike, and then my family.

"This is Mike," I told them.

Bob and Liz stared at him.

"Where's your room?" Mike asked.

I pointed down the hallway. He tightened his grip on my jeans and guided me toward my room, and my dad followed. When I swung the door open, my body stiffened. Wooden two-by-twos were screwed tightly to the window frames, like bars in a jail cell. There was a small bed with wheels for Mike, which allowed him to roll it in front of the door each night before we slept. Then my eye caught something at the foot of my bed. A chain was secured to the bedpost. A thick sheath of plastic covered the last seven or eight inches of it, and there was a padlock on the end. I stared at it a moment, and then I understood.

The plastic sheath was so my ankle wouldn't get chafed while I slept. My dad had made it for me.

It was a loving chain.

When it was time to go to sleep, my dad helped me put it on. I sat at the foot of my bed while he knelt down and fastened it. He looked up at me and his eyes were moist, and his hands trembled slightly.

"I'm so sorry, Donny," he whispered. "I don't want to do this."

My heart was heavy. But it wasn't me I was sad for.

"It's okay Dad," I nodded. "I understand."

But later as I lay there in the dark, my fourteen-year-old brain felt like it was about to explode. This wasn't home anymore. There was a stranger in my house, my room was a jail cell, and I was chained to my goddamn bed.

I wanted to stick it out. I wanted to do good and prove myself so Mike would leave, the bars would come off, and the chain would be retired. But every night, I kept noticing it. Mike wore the key to that padlock around his neck. It hung there, dangling and teasing me. The chain on my foot was long enough for me to reach Mike while he slept. Which meant that I could take that key if I was desperate enough.

On day four, I was desperate enough.

Mike was fast asleep as I lifted the key from his neck and used a toenail clipper to cut it loose. As I did, I half-wished he'd wake up and try to stop me.

No such luck.

I opened the padlock and removed the chain from my ankle. I reached my hands through the wooden bars and eased the window up and removed the screen. My dad had misjudged how far apart the bars needed to be; it took a few moments, but I squeezed my head through. And once my head made it through, my body followed.

I landed on the grass below my window, and I shot across the lawn and over the fence. It was about six in the morning and it was still dark. The light went on in my parents' room. Probably coincidence, I thought. I felt sorry for my Dad. He'd put a lot of work into upgrading my room.

I wondered if there was any hope for me, or whether I would ever go home again. But I didn't have time to think about all of that. I needed to figure out where I was going.

The police would be looking for me soon.

6

LIZ

My thumbs are clumsy and slow. There's an instruction manual open on my lap, and I lean over and glance at it, then look back at the phone. I read what I've just typed.

For the third time.

"Hey, it's me, Donny. I got a cell phone today."

I press the send button with my right thumb, and I grunt.

I think it worked.

I stare at the screen and wait for Liz's response. In two-and-a-half minutes, it arrives.

"Cool! Omw."

Tonight we're all having dinner at my parents' house. We're getting together to celebrate that I've finally returned home. And when I say home, I don't mean my new place or my parents' place. To us, home is Safety Harbor. We all live here, within two miles of each other. It's been my brother's home since elementary school. It's been Liz's from birth, almost. Mine, since just before I started sixth grade at Safety Harbor Middle School. Before we moved here, we lived in eleven or twelve places, and Safety Harbor is where we finally settled. And now that I'm back, we'll all be here together again. We'll look out for each other and we'll be seeing a lot of each other, which is how it should be.

We're family.

Bob is already here. He's in the kitchen with my dad, piling slices of roast beef and cheese on crackers and shooting the shit. I can see them from the living room. My mom is sitting next to me on the couch. I show her the text and ask her what it means.

"On my way," she says.

I put my cell phone in my pocket.

"You look tired, Don. And you got a lot of sun, too."

I am. And I did. It's been a long day already. When I finally lie down later, I think I might go into a coma.

"A little," I yawn.

I glance toward the front door. Liz should be walking through at any moment.

"It's been a while since you've seen your sister," she says.

"Yeah. Almost six years."

I sigh. I love Liz. But when I think of her, my heart sinks like a brick.

"She's looking forward to seeing you, Don."

I hope so. Because I can feel her anger, even from afar.

She hates me.

I wince. No, she can't possibly hate me – she's my *little sister*. I may have been gone for decades, but we've shared a few good years. And when I think of them my heart doesn't sink. No, it soars.

Those times were good ones, and I smile as they come to mind. They remind me of how it really is. Because those years, they are the truth.

Yet there's another truth as well. It's one I've never quite grasped until now. The truth is that those years, they are the ones she will never remember.

BOB AND I SAT OPPOSITE EACH OTHER AT THE DINNER table. I was nine and he was six, and spaghetti hung low from our mouths, smearing on our bare chests with tomato sauce. It was a who-can-be-the-messiest contest.

"Boys, we have some great news for you," my dad announced, then he nodded at my mom.

"We're having a baby." She beamed. "A little girl."

Warmth flooded my chest. A *baby girl*.

"What's the matter, honey?" My mom reached out and took my hand.

I hadn't noticed the tears rolling down my face.

"I-I'm just happy," I managed. "We're going to have a sister!"

After Liz was born, I learned there's absolutely nothing better in the entire world than making a little sister smile. I showered her with silly faces and funny voices, and she laughed constantly. I cheered for her when she began to crawl and shouted with joy when she finally walked.

When she was taking her first steps, I was already beginning my nosedive into a cloud of substances. But I had moments of clarity, genuine presence, and happiness. During those, I would look into her wide eyes and tell her that her big brother loved her so much.

She was three when I turned thirteen. And a few months later, I was gone.

Ten years later and I was twenty-three, doing federal time out in the Arizona desert. I sat at a small wooden desk in a cramped cell. A wastebasket sat by my feet, full of crumpled notebook paper.

I was trying to write a letter.

It was like torture, but I wasn't going to give up. I *had* to write to her. She needed to know I was real. That when I got out, I would take her to the movies and to the mall. That I would make up for all the years I'd been away.

She needed to know her big brother was coming home.

When I finally finished it, I put it in an envelope and dropped it in the mailbox by the guard station before I could change my mind. A year later, with house arrest and federal probation and parole, I returned home.

When I got off house arrest, she was fourteen. I never did take her to the movies or to the mall. I didn't take her anywhere. It was six months after that when she burst into the guidance counselor's office at school, crying hysterically. Her big brother was just on the news, she sobbed. Arrested for a string of bank robberies.

Again.

Ten years later, I sat in yet another cramped cell. And next to me was another wastebasket full of crumpled pieces of note-book paper. I was trying to write another letter to my little sister.

I meant well. I really did.

I'M IN THE KITCHEN WITH MY BROTHER AND DAD when I hear the front door slam. I walk into the living room.

It's her.

"Donny!" Liz exclaims.

She rushes to me and we hug and laugh, and she pulls away and takes a look at me. She's so tall, and her smile, so wide.

I'd kept up with her by my parents' letters and the pictures they'd send me. I'd seen her playing volleyball in high school, then graduating. At her wedding. And then with her beautiful children.

And now, here she is, before me. My little sister is twenty-nine.

"Oh my god, it's so good to see you!" she cries. "I can't believe you're free!" She hugs me again.

"Me neither!" I take a step back. "You're looking great, Liz."

"Thanks, you too!"

"So, how's the family?"

"Oh, they're good. The kids can't wait to meet you." She smiles.

Liz has two, Raymond and Rachel. They're three and four. My mom says she's thinking about adding another.

"Me too. I'm looking forward to it, Liz."

I shift my feet. I love my family, and I know they love me. Which should be enough, I think. But right now, I feel out of place and awkward.

I wonder if I really belong here.

"I bet you're glad to get out, huh?"

I snap out of it.

"I am. It's, um, really nice out here."

We laugh. Of course it is. *Duh.*

"So anyway," I say, "when I get settled in, let's do lunch or something"

"That sounds great, Donny."

MY MOM AND DAD MAKE AWESOME SPAGHETTI. AND homemade bread, too. It's fresh-baked and the aroma fills the kitchen. We sit down at the table and join hands. We're about to pray, but not because we're religious. No, my mom cusses and sometimes even my dad will laugh and tell me to go fuck myself. But we used to go to church a lot. We started going after my mom and dad stopped getting high and found Jesus. That's when we began praying at dinner. And even though we quit going to church years ago, we still pray sometimes. Especially when it feels right, like tonight.

Praying isn't the only dinner tradition my family picked up.

After I left, they started another one. At holidays they would remember me. They'd set an empty plate on the table in front of a vacant chair, and they'd mention me when they said the prayer. I try not to think about it for too long because I get all twisted inside. I want to start bawling.

But tonight, my plate and my seat are not empty. My dad thanks God that Donny is finally home, and he asks God to help me stay here. We all say amen, and we begin to eat.

It really doesn't matter what rock I've crawled out from or how long I was there. That whole part of my life, well, it's just gone. It's like the past fifteen years, and then the entire decade or so before that, have been squeezed into the space of a few short hours that don't even matter anymore. It's like I was at school for the day, and I've just come home for dinner.

The spaghetti is good, and so is the bread. And the company, even better.

I'm so glad to finally be home.

7

MY HOUSE

It's 3 a.m., and I'm wide awake. I lie on my back, then my side. Then on my stomach. And then my back again. I stare at the ceiling. There are a bunch of stickers on it – the moon and planets with their smiling faces glow down upon me in the dark. They look faded and worn, like they were here long before this became my room.

My room. I'm lying on *my* bed in *my* room. I sit up again and look around again. Just yesterday morning I woke up on a hard, thin mattress in a concrete cell – just like I had for over 5,300 mornings in a row. But now I'm in a real bed in a real room. In a real house.

My house.

It's almost too perfect. Too quiet. Too damn comfortable.

My bedroom door is closed, but it's not locked. Which means that if I want, I can walk right out of it because now, I'm free. But on the flip side, someone can walk right in. Of course, they'd have to get through the front door of the house first, which is locked.

Or is it?

I get up to check it again to make sure.

It is.

I step into the living room and stand there a moment. I don't have to lie down again if I don't want to. I can even walk around the house naked if I want. So I do. I walk back and forth doing my naked walk. I feel weird, so I put my boxers back on and walk around some more.

It *seems* like a real house. Like someone actually lives here. Someone who has a life. There's a couch and a TV in the living room. There's dishes and groceries in the kitchen. There's a front door and a sidewalk out front.

I walk to the front door again and look outside. I can take a walk down the sidewalk if I want. Maybe getting some of this energy out will help me sleep. But it's late, and if a cop stops me and runs my name, they would know I just got out. I shake my head and decide that taking a walk at this hour is exactly what I will not be doing. I'll wait till sunrise and go for a jog.

Maybe another sandwich will help me sleep. I can if I want – it's entirely up to me. But if I do, it will be my third since 11 p.m.

I walk to the living room instead and sink down on the couch. It's like a huge, fluffy pillow. An acoustic guitar leans against the wall next to me. I smile as I remember the first time I saw it.

I was on my bunk when the officer slid the envelope under the door. It was a letter from my dad. I tore it open, and a picture dropped to the concrete floor. I scooped it up and held it in my palm. It was a guitar. A *Taylor*. It was beautiful – natural wood, the color of light honey. I unfolded the note. "Happy Birthday, Son. I can't wait to give it to you when you get out," it said.

I reach for the guitar. It's light and comfortable in my hands. I strum it softly, and the notes are crisp and beautiful in the stillness. Its tone resonates in my chest, and I hum a tune under my breath as I play.

I sigh. I look around the living room again. I can't sleep, but it's going to be okay. The newness will wear off in a couple of days, I tell myself, and I'll sleep just fine. I'll adjust and I'll find a job and make some friends. I'll build that recording studio with my dad, and I'll start making music.

Eventually I'll get a girlfriend, too. Maybe I'll meet a female vocalist and write songs for her. I'll be her manager and producer and at first our relationship will be entirely professional, but somewhere down the line she'll come to see the truth about me. I'm not just some ex-con. I'm a good guy.

Good enough to date and then marry and have kids with.

That's what I really want. A wife, two boys and a girl, and a house. And a dog, too. I want a chocolate-brown Labrador just like we had when I was seven. And I'll give him the same name, too: Bummer.

I know the family thing isn't for everyone. But it is for me. I want to be like my dad and my grandfather. They're perfect examples of what good men are like. They both worked hard, got and stayed married, spent time with their kids, and provided for their families.

They stayed out of prison, too.

So, it's settled. I'll work a regular job for the next year or two, then I'll shift to making a living doing music. Then I'll start a family. And along the way, I'll forget the past twenty-five years ever happened. By the time I get to that point, it won't matter, anyway.

There's only one thing I need to do to make all of this happen: stay away from cocaine. Which won't be a problem because I hate that crap.

I say it aloud, right here in my living room.

"I will *never* do that shit again!"

My voice startles me. It's powerful. Authentic. And it's true – I really *won't* ever do that shit again.

Why *did* I ever like it in the first place? I was young and crazy, that's why. A lot of people start out a bit wild, then they outgrow it as they get older and more mature. Which is exactly where I'm at right now. And I'm ready to focus on the life that's before me, not behind me.

Young and dumb, that's why. Case closed.

But what about the banks? The constant stealing and lying? What about going insane after long drug binges, thinking I was with the FBI, and shooting drugs with dirty needles?

Then there are the tellers I robbed. What about them? A few actually collapsed into tears as I left the place. I had always told myself I was never mean, and I'd even made a point to try to be polite about the whole thing.

But there's no polite way to rob anyone.

I don't like even going there because when I start thinking about this kind of stuff, I know that being young and dumb is no explanation for the craziness that is my life.

There's a more straight-forward answer with simplicity, elegant: I'm a fucking horrible person.

I stand to my feet again. Maybe it's true. Maybe there's something within me, lurking inside and waiting to pounce. And when it does, it will completely destroy me. I'll wind up dead or locked away for the rest of my life.

I will bury you.

That's what the judge said, and he meant it.

I shudder.

I pace the floor. I can't entertain these thoughts another second. I have an even more simple, more elegant explanation: I'm perfectly normal – I made some bad mistakes, that's all. I'm not going to get into the weeds with a bunch of negative, self-analytical bullshit. What I need to do is move forward. And going forward, there's no way I'm going to get high or steal or *any* of that crap.

I have a great start with great help from a great family who loves me, and that's all I need. I'm going to amaze everyone. I'm going to build the life I've always dreamed about.

But I have to admit, I have some challenges. I've never done anything like this before. I've never paid my own rent for more than a few weeks. I've never held a real job for more than a month or two. I've never had my own car and I don't know how to fix a flat or change the oil. I've never even been to high school and I don't know what it's like to have real friends.

I don't even know how to make small talk with people.

I go back to my room and lie down again.

My brain hurts. I can't think about this crap anymore. Somehow it will all work out. It just has to.

I close my eyes one more time. I think about the band room my dad and my brother and me are going to build. I can see it in my mind. There are guitars hanging from a rack by the control booth. I see sound equipment stacked against the walls. My dad, he's helping me tack some soundproofing up on the walls. The studio is finally starting to take shape.

It's going to be *great*.

A few moments pass and finally, it happens.

I'm dreaming.

PART II

8

SAFETY HARBOR

I t's 5 a.m. and I'm up. I'm *killing* it out here.

I have a routine. First, it's weights. Then ten laps in the pool, followed by a jog down Bayshore Drive just as the sun rises on Tampa Bay.

Jogging is the best part. In prison, I'd run five miles a day around a thin, clay track. On the third mile, I'd enter the zone. The fences and cellblocks would vanish, and nothing else existed except the sound, deep within my ears, of my pounding heart.

Out here in the free world, jogging is even better.

After I run, I go home and eat oatmeal, almond butter, and a banana. Then a shower, and it's off to work.

I've been out just over four weeks already. I still can't believe my dad got me a membership to the Safety Harbor Resort and Spa. It overlooks the Safety Harbor Marina and the pier and the waters of Tampa Bay. They give away vacations to this place on game shows and sweepstakes. Sometimes celebrities come here, too.

And here is where I get to start my day – every day.

I'm living the dream. A few weeks out, and I already have a

house, a job, and a reliable used car. Not to mention a high-end resort I exercise at every morning. There are guys in prison who would kill for a setup like this.

Literally.

I walk into the gym and warm up. I do a few pushups, then I alternate sets of shoulder presses and leg presses. In prison they call that a superset. Wait, I don't care *what* they call it in prison – I'm not there anymore. In fact, I'm going to remove the word *prison* from my vocabulary. I grin as I push the weight harder. No, I'm not a prisoner any longer. I'm free, I'm successful, and I'm looking good, too. When I jog and I pass women on their morning walks, they always flash me smiles and say good morning. I chuckle to myself. They don't have a clue.

Practically no one does.

I wonder if the spa management knows. I decide definitely not because if they did, they would've revoked my membership already. They'd *have* to. After all, members would surely get uncomfortable if they found out about the new guy who just got out for robbing banks. Management would need to be proactive about that kind of thing and politely ask me to leave – and to never come back again.

I finish my set and look up to see a guy standing there, waiting. I wonder if he's the owner and he's about to kick me out. I climb out of the leg press machine and stand up to see what he wants.

"Mind if I jump in?" he asks.

He's got a toothy grin, he's about my age, and he's balding already. I look him up and down. Compared to me, he's a little dumpy. I'm pretty sure I can beat his ass.

Geeze, what the hell is wrong with me? Why did I even *think* that? I sigh and shake my head. I'm terrible, that's why. Wait – *not* true. I'm just institutionalized, I tell myself. I'll grow out of it; I just need to give it some time.

What I really need to do is engage. I need to learn how to

talk to people – especially small talk. I need to learn to do it without being awkward. How will I ever sell my music if I can't chat it up a bit?

"Sure thing," I tell him, "it's all yours, boss."

As I start doing my shoulder presses, I remember what the speaker on a CD from the prison library said. To become a people person, he said, you have to consciously and intentionally engage in small talk. Ask people what *they* do, then go from there. And no matter how it goes, he said, don't be hard on yourself. Just keep doing it, and you'll get better.

I'm going to do it, I decide. I'm going to make small talk.

I finish my set as he finishes his. I move toward the leg press again and he's headed my way. What will I say? How about, *Hey, my name's Don – what's yours?* No, that's lame. What about, *Dude – those leg presses are looking good!*

No way in hell.

I know. I'll just introduce myself, plain and simple. We'll have a brief exchange and when it seems right, I'll pop the question. I'll ask him what he does. And when he's done telling me, I'll talk about what I do.

My palms are sweaty. I have jitters in my stomach. What the hell is wrong with me? It's not like I'm about to ask him to get married.

I decide that if I don't make small talk with this guy, I can't do any laps in the pool. And so, that settles it. I take a breath. I get ready. I'm about to open my mouth and speak.

And out of nowhere, he blurts out, "By the way, I'm Jim."

Damn it! If I want to get my laps in, I need to turn this around and go on the offensive. I thrust my hand out. It's an awkward shake, but I smile steady and look him in the eye as I do it.

"I'm Don," I say. "Pleased to meet you, Jim."

Jim. Jim. I need to remember *Jim*. What do I say next? I know, I'll ask him what he does.

"So, what do you do, Don?" he asks.

My jaw tightens, but I recover and force that smile back on my face.

"Um, I'm doing a temporary gig at the moment," I shrug. "I work at an electronics service company."

"Oh, that sounds interesting. What do you do there?"

I barely know. But I *do* know that it's hard. I'm learning about electronic parts and how to use a computer and spread-sheets. I'm always having to ask questions. One minute I'm stuck, staring blankly at a computer screen and not knowing what to do. Then the next moment I'm holding a tiny microchip with a pair of tweezers and looking at it cross-eyed, trying to figure out what type and model it is.

I've almost walked out three times already.

I'm grateful to have work. It's challenging for sure, but I can't help but think this job is meant to be. It's just straight-up weird the way some things come full circle, and my job is defi-nitely one of those things.

It was Rick who got me the job. I met him in 1993 in a prison dormitory. There were fifty bunk beds packed in there, no air conditioning, and it was the middle of summer. He walked in holding a thin, rolled-up mattress on his shoulder. In his other arm he clutched a bundled-up blanket which hung low, dragging the floor and leaving a trail of stuff behind him. A tube of toothpaste, then a pen and a worn pocket Bible. He dumped his mattress and belongings on an empty bunk a few down from mine, and then traced his steps back. He reached down to pick up his toothbrush at the foot of my bed. His glasses were thick, his pale skin had not a single tattoo, and his hair, well, he was clearly a ginger.

"Hey, man," he said. "I'm Rick."

"I'm Don." I closed the book I was reading. "Where you from?"

"St. Pete."

"Oh, yeah?" I answered. "I'm not far. Safety Harbor."

"Cool. I like Safety Harbor." He looked around the dorm, then back at me. "You know where the chapel is? I don't know where anything is yet."

"Yeah, man, I'll show you."

Rick started hanging out with me a lot. We'd talk about the mysteries of life. Like God and women and how to succeed when we finally got out. Rick didn't have to wait long because he only had an eighteen-month sentence. The day he left, he told me he'd write me once in a while.

I was surprised a few months later when a guard handed me a letter with his name on the return address. After that, I'd hear from him about once a year. Sometimes he'd even send a few bucks.

He wound up getting married and buying a house, and then he had a son.

The last time he wrote, I had only six months left.

"I really appreciate you being a friend when I was in there," he wrote. "Man, it's hard believing you've been in that place all this time. This year, I became president of my company. When you get out, call me if you need a job and I'll help you out."

I never did figure out why I'd made such an impression on him, or why he stayed in touch with me. He was the only person I'd ever met in prison who actually wrote when he got out. But whatever it was, I decided I'd take him up on that offer – I would need that job. At least until my music took off.

I SNAP OUT OF IT. I TELL JIM I WORK IN THE receiving department at my company. I open boxes and take out electronic chips and inspect them, then match the package to the right job in our system. I create labels and send the box on its way to the production floor. But it's temporary, I tell him. I'm actually a songwriter. I've got tons of songs and one day he's going to hear them on the radio.

I exhale under my breath. That wasn't too bad. I got through it at least. Now it's my turn.

"So, what do *you* do?" I inquire.

"I'm an attorney," he says. "I do patents, mainly."

I almost gasp aloud. Patents include stuff like copyrights. I want to jump up and down. This dude is going to help me publish my songs. Goose bumps spread across my body as I take it all in. He probably knows record label executives. I've got to make friends with this guy. But I need to stay calm. I need to be nonchalant.

"That's interesting." I pick up some dumbbells. "So, what do you focus on?"

"Technology, for the most part. Lately, a lot of robotics."

Robotics?

"Oh. Does that ever include stuff like copyrights?"

"Well, once in a while. Mostly for scientific papers. Writings about technology patents and things like that."

"Oh, that's cool." I set the dumbbells back in the rack.

"Yeah, it *is* pretty cool," he chuckles. "But not as cool as some other things, like publishing songs. Too bad I don't cover those kinds of copyrights."

Too bad is right.

I tell him to have a nice day. I go to the pool and do my laps. I don't need that guy, anyway. When my dad and my brother and I build my home studio, it will be state of the art. I'll make plenty of friends just by having the damn thing. Like, what kind of dude has a recording studio in their own home?

Um, me. That's who.

I'm not going to build a network by chatting with random dudes at the gym.

The sun is rising as I begin jogging by the water. There are a few women walking my way, and as I run past they smile and wish me a good morning. I smile back.

I really *am* killing it out here.

9

UN-SOCIAL LIFE

I t's 10 p.m., and I'm on my way to the grocery store. I have a car and I have a place to live. I'm just doing what normal people with cars and places to live do. I'm going shopping for food.

I like grocery shopping because I like practicing being normal.

I pull into the parking lot and find a space. I shut my car off and sit a moment before I go inside. I think about what I'm going to do. When I go in, I'm going to try to talk to at least one person without being weird about it. That's my goal, and in a way it's more important than the food.

I get out and walk in.

I grab a cart and move toward the aisles, making a quick list in my head. I'm definitely going to need milk and cereal. I turn toward the dairy section. On second thought, if I get the milk first, it will probably get warm by the time I get home, so I go to the cereal aisle instead.

There is a woman shopping in that aisle. We make eye contact, and my eyes dart away. I pretend I'm interested in some oatmeal. Why can't I just hold her gaze and smile, and *then* look at the damn oatmeal?

That's what a normal person would do.

It's because I'm a fake, that's why. I'm acting like I'm a normal person but I'm not. I'm something else and I'm not quite sure what. But whatever it is, it must be obvious. She's got to know I don't fit in. No, I tell myself, that's not true. What I need to do is take a deep breath and calm the fuck down. She couldn't know I don't fit in unless she's a psychic. And besides, I *do* fit in.

I turn around and wheel my cart out of that aisle. I'll get the cereal later. Now I'm in the aisle with the bread and peanut butter and jelly. There are ten different kinds of peanut butter, and I still don't know what my favorite kind is. I have no idea what they had in prison because I never saw the labels. I'd only seen lumps of it on my tray. I hope I don't wind up choosing that kind, whatever it was.

I notice an elderly man coming down the aisle, headed my way. He has a slight limp and walks with a cane. I wonder what happened to his leg. Probably a World War II veteran, like my grandfather was. They called them the Greatest Generation.

I decide to look him in the eye and hold a steady gaze while I smile. I'm going to practice being friendly to a member of the Greatest Generation. In prison I did not act friendly. I always looked away, like I was cold and cared about nothing. That was the safe thing to do. But out here, it's safe to be nice. So I do it. I smile like he's my grandfather. I look him directly in the eye with respect. His eyes meet mine for just a sliver of a second, then he looks away. He doesn't even notice I'm smiling at him.

I know what I am. I'm a real doof. I have no idea how to do this social stuff. To hell with this. I'm here to buy food, not to make friends.

Fuck that old guy.

I get the rest of my groceries and make my way to the

checkout line. An older lady is haggling over a coupon, and it's taking forever. A woman steps in line behind me, and I glance at her. She's looking at her phone. She's about my age, and she's cute. I want to say something nice and funny like an outgoing person would. But then I look down at my groceries on the conveyor belt. I've got a box of Peanut Butter Captain Crunch.

In plain view.

I want to cover it up with some healthy food so she won't see it and judge me. The only reason I got it in the first place was because when I saw it, it reminded me of being seven and watching cartoons with my brother. Maybe I should invite her to come eat cereal with me. In my head, I ask her, and she laughs and tells me how funny I am. It continues to play out like a scene from a romantic comedy. Our cereal date turns to serious dates. We laugh, we love, and we just live.

But I don't ask. Instead, I turn my attention to the line in front of me. There's a guy just a few years younger than me, maybe thirty-five or so. He's here with his little boy. He's holding the boy and they're pointing at the tabloids and magazines, laughing at the pictures. I want to talk to that guy because clearly, he's successful. He's clean-cut and he probably has a good woman at home. He probably has a lot of friends and doesn't get high.

I need friends like that. I've been out four months and I don't have any friends at all.

The lady at checkout out finally gets her coupon issue resolved. She finishes paying, and the guy in front of me steps up with his boy. He buys his orange juice, and the father and son leave.

It's my turn now. The checkout girl smiles and looks me in the eye.

"Did you find everything okay?" she asks.

At once, I feel real. On some level, I know I just made a connection. It's not some huge romantic thing. It's just a normal, everyday *real* thing. I'm an average guy in the checkout line like anyone else, just doing what your average person does. I'm part of a community.

The shopping community.

"Yes, I did," I say, and I return the smile. "Thank you."

I pay for my groceries, and she hands me the receipt and tells me to have a good night.

It *is* a good night.

I walk to my car and put my groceries in the backseat, and I get behind the wheel and start the car. And for just a moment, I feel like I belong.

I'M CREATING A PROFILE ON A DATING SITE. I validate my email, then it tells me I need to upload a picture. So I do. It prompts me to write about myself. But first, I need a headline. Something catchy, it tells me. I think about that for a moment. How about, *From the Big House to Your House?* God, I crack myself up. Or how about, *I'm Clyde – Want to be My Bonnie?* Too cliché. I need something simple and light, but serious, too. I settle on *Looking for Serious Relationship – Let's Talk!*

The next thing I need to do is list my hobbies. I like to play guitar and sing. What else? I press my lips together and mull it over. I try to think of all the things I *would* be doing by now if I hadn't been away the past fifteen years. I like to hang out with friends. I like to play on a men's softball team. I like romance and walking on the beach at sunset. I like nice restaurants and a glass of wine over a candlelit dinner.

It's not a complete lie, I think, because I really *do* like to do all those things. I just haven't done them yet, that's all – but I will! It's complicated, I know. I'm just, well, kind of giving myself credit for what my hobbies most definitely are going to be.

I finish my profile and click submit, and I'm ready to browse. I search within twenty-five miles for women of every weight and color with no kids but who want to get married and have kids. The page loads quickly, and there are thousands of matches. Some are actually online right now, it says, at this very moment!

The first one lives within five miles of me. I click the thumbnail to see her profile. She's Latina and she's cute. She's all about family and wants to get married. She's hard-working and has no time for BS, it says. Neither do I. She's a tad thick, which is fine by me. I can see us – we're cuddling on the couch. She's making us tacos. She wants to make a home with me.

She just might be the one. I inbox her, and I keep it simple. I say I like her profile and invite her to talk.

Less than a minute later, I get a notification. It says she viewed my profile! She's probably looking at it right now! I stand up and pace back and forth. I can't believe this is happening. She could message me back any minute. Which means I might be going on a date.

Internet dating is *amazing*.

I sit back down and watch the screen and wait. Another notification pops up. She messaged me! I open it. She says I'm interesting and she wants me to tell her more about myself.

I shoot up out of my chair, clench my fist, and kneel like I just scored a touchdown.

I scramble back to my chair. I take a deep breath and exhale slowly. I need to calm down. I need to stay even-minded and be realistic about how this might go.

I fast-forward a few dates. We're at a candlelit table at an upscale restaurant. We're enjoying light conversation over a glass of wine when I tell her I need to share something with her. It's something about me, I tell her, and it might be a concern for her.

I have her full attention.

I pause, then I let it all out. I tell her I used to be a drug addict. That I was a bank robber and I just got out a few months ago after doing fifteen years. But wait, I say, I've really changed. I explain that with maturity, I've gained wisdom.

I tell her I'm done with the thug life.

What I don't understand is that there's no explaining this. Her eyes become like fire, and her jaw tightens. She rises from her seat and begins shouting at me in Spanish.

I don't know what the hell she's saying, but I know it won't end well. She tosses her wine in my face and stomps out of the place. I'm soaked and red-faced, and the room has gone completely silent.

I snap back to the present. There is no frigging way I'll go through anything even remotely like that. Honesty really *is* the best policy. In fact, I'm going to come clean right now.

I write her a message and I tell her the truth. I tell her I just got out of prison for bank robbery. That I'm doing the right thing now and I really do want to start a family, and I really do want to do all the things my bio says. But if she doesn't want to talk to me anymore, I tell her, I get it.

I reread my message, then hit send.

As soon as I do, I realize I might have another problem. What if she says she's *okay* with my past? What kind of woman would say *that*?

A woman who's bat-shit crazy, that's who.

There's no way I can have a woman like that raising *my* kids. What I really need to do is meet a woman who would never date a man like me – but then somehow does it anyway.

I have another notification. She's already replied. I open it, and it's polite and brief. She thanks me for being honest. But it's a bit too heavy for her right now, she says. She asks me to not message her again. I close the message and I sigh.

I am so screwed.

I'M TWO WEEKS INTO MY NEW TECH SUPPORT JOB. I'M hunched over in my cubicle, blinking my eyes at the screen. I don't know squat about databases, but I'm trying. I have three more days to learn the system, then I have to take incoming calls from clients. My job is to be patient and show our clients that the problem is somewhere between their chair and their computer screen. But if it's a real issue, I create a support ticket so our programmers can take a look.

I groan. My head hurts.

Bill keeps telling me to push through it. He sits me down and gives it to me straight – for the third time. It was rough on him when he first started here, he says. He left Texas a year before, where he was strung out bad on meth. But now, he's doing great. He didn't know much about computers and software at first, but he struggled and pushed through it. And if he did it, he tells me, so can I.

I appreciate the encouragement. But if I were him, I would've left the meth out of it. I made that mistake at my last job. One night I had a few drinks with a guy after work and I wound up spilling my guts. Then the next day at work some *other* guy walks up to me.

"Dude!" he said loudly. "I would've never guessed. Bank robbery! That's so fucking cool!"

My face turned hot and I looked around to see if anyone heard him. Then I stepped close to him and threatened him under my breath to keep his damn mouth shut. I quit a month later when I got the offer to work here. When I did, I went to Rick's office and shut the door.

"Hey, Donny," he asked, "what's up?"

I shifted in my chair.

"Well, I found another job."

His face turned a shade red.

"Oh. Why are you leaving? You need more money?"

"Not really," I said. "I got an offer in tech support. It might turn into a real great opportunity."

He was silent.

"Rick, I really appreciate all the help you've given me."

"Yeah, well no problem – I hope it works out for you," he said. "If not, we'll have a spot for you here."

I felt bad for quitting, especially because Rick gave me my first chance. But the whole company probably knew about me after that blabbermouth started talking. I won't make the same mistake at this new job.

There's an alert at the bottom of my screen. It's a message from Scott. He's asking me to go out with them to see a band this Friday. Them, meaning Scott, Karen, and Dawn. It's the third time they've asked since I've been here, and each time I've said no. I look over the top of my monitor. He's a few cubicles down and he's smiling and giving me a thumbs up. I know why he's giving me that grin – Scott says Karen says Dawn wants to get to know me better.

He returns to his computer, then another alert pops up on my screen.

"Dawn keeps asking if you're coming," he says.

I really should go. I don't have a life and I still haven't made any friends. Plus, I *never* go out.

Well, that's not entirely true. Almost every weekend I go to a club and it's always hopping, which is probably why it's called *New York New York*. But that doesn't really count as going out because I go there by myself. Plus, it always goes something like this...

I pay the cover and enter. I walk around and get a feel for the place. I'm on the prowl, and I circle the dance floor and then the bar with a thick swag. I take inventory of the ladies, and I make a short list of who I'll be dancing with later. But as I do, I don't look them in the eye or let them know I'm interested. Instead, I ignore them. I do it on purpose because it makes them want you more. Plus, it requires no communication skills whatsoever.

After I finish making my rounds and putting out the vibe, I order a drink. I turn around and lean my back against the bar and take a swig while I scan the room again. I plant myself there and chill. I'll make them come to *me*.

An hour later, not a single woman has come to me. That's when I see the one I like most of all. She's on the dance floor. I put my drink down and wipe my mouth. Damn, she's really nice. And she's not with anyone. She's just laughing and talking and dancing with her friends. I'm going to go for it. I'm going to walk right over there and ask her to dance with me.

I hesitate. What if she asks me a question like "Where are you from?" or "Where did you go to high school?" I'd wind up having to tell her a huge whopper about where I've been the past couple decades.

While I agonize over what to do, some guy walks up and starts dancing with her. I finish my drink and I leave.

And that is how New York New York always goes. So no, that's not legitimately going out. But I want to legitimately go out. I want to hang out with Scott and Karen and Dawn. I *need* to. It's not good for me to be alone all the time. Plus, if I keep refusing to go out with them, it could get awkward. They might start thinking I'm stuck up. Or weird. And then instead of trying to include me, they'll try to exclude me.

I feel like I'm still locked up, and I don't know how to get out. A support group, maybe? But I know how that would go. There I'd be, sitting in a circle with a bunch of ex-convicts and some facilitator. We'd meet twice a week and talk about coping with life in the free world. The other guys would be court ordered. They wouldn't want to be there in the first place. Which means they'd be up to no good – using hard drugs and committing crimes and pretending to be doing well when they really weren't.

No, thank you. That's exactly the kind of group I *don't* need to be around.

There's another alert on my screen. It's Scott again. He wants to know whether I'm going or not.

I want to, but I just can't. I slump in my seat.

I'm tired of smoking weed at home alone. And then I have a thought. What I really want to do, is maybe smoke some crack.

Maybe I can handle just one hit.

I sit back up and I shake it off. I'll never do that shit again. But, if I could just once, I know it would be amazing.

I message Scott and tell him I can't go. Maybe some other time, I say.

10

I FALL DOWN

There's no storage room at my house anymore. I'm good with that because it's a band room now. And not just some DIY, low-budget setup, either. My dad and brother and I finished it about eight months ago, putting up a wall to split the space into a large practice area and a control booth. The booth is the size of a walk-in closet, with racks of equipment and speakers piled high. From inside you can look through the glass and see the practice area with the drums, guitar amp, mic stands, and walls covered with sound-dampening baffling.

This room is made to record hits.

I can see it now. An audio engineer enters the control booth, shuts the door behind him, then hits record. The band starts playing and slowly finds their groove while the engineer watches through the glass, holding his headphones with one hand and adjusting knobs and moving faders with the other. He's nodding his head to the beat. He looks at me through the glass and gives me the thumbs up.

It's a good take.

"This, my friend," he tells me afterward, "is how the magic happens."

But the magic has not happened yet. I've been out a year and a few months now, and I still don't know a single audio engineer, much less other musicians.

But I don't give a shit. My studio is bad-*ass*. Sometimes I like to smoke weed and just stare at it. I'll get around to networking when I'm ready. Right now, there's just too much going on. Like work. Then there are chore days, which eat up so much time with groceries, the lawn, laundry, and other things.

Besides, I'm still trying to get my music right. Networking makes no sense if I don't have a product, so I'm trying to create one. I'm learning how to build a website to host the awesome songs I'm going to record. Plus, I have to actually practice and record them. And to do that I need to learn how to use all the recording software I've spent over a grand on. Now *that's* a chore. I try to follow the manual, and I read and re-read the instructions. But it's confusing. Sometimes I get so bent out of shape that I toss the quick start guides down on the floor and stomp off to the living room. Then I smoke weed and watch *South Park*.

But I *do* love this studio. And jamming to oldies here with my dad and my brother, too. The first time we played we were halfway through the first song when my dad raised his hand and brought us to a halt.

"Before we get too far here, we need to settle one damn thing."

My brother and I stared at him.

"You two got an idea for a name?"

I looked at Bob and shrugged. We drew a blank.

"Okay," my dad said, "then why don't we just call ourselves Big D and the Two Squirts?"

From then on, Bob and I were the two squirts.

We practice every Saturday. After I finish the lawn, I move my amp into the corner and plug my guitar cord in and set up the rest of the band room. Then I go to the kitchen and check the fridge to make sure there's beer and chips. Then I go back to the studio and check my mic. Testing one, two, three, I say. My voice is loud and crisp with the perfect touch of reverb. That's when my dad pulls up in his truck, and then my brother in his. We shoot the shit for a little while, and then Big D and the Two Squirts, we start jamming.

They're in it just for the fun. But me, I'm always uptight and I fuck my parts up. We take a break between songs and take sips of our drinks and joke around. After a while I loosen up. We don't have any gigs lined up and we aren't trying to. I remember this, and it's okay. I'm happy just being one of the squirts.

When we finish, they load up their trucks and go to their homes to eat dinner with their wives. I walk into the living room, plop down on the couch, and pull out a bong from a drawer under the table. I take a massive hit and hold it in. When I exhale, I sink deeper into the couch.

I'm so alone.

That's how it usually goes. Today is a Saturday, which is usually a practice day. But today's not a normal Saturday. My sisters are down from New York, and they're coming over with my mom and Liz to watch us play.

It's going to be Big D and the Two Squirts – *live!*

Jackie and Chris are my older sisters from my dad's previous marriage. They grew up in Syracuse, the area that we used to live in, too. But when we moved to Florida, they stayed up there with their mom. The last time I saw them, I was fourteen. I showed up on their doorstep in North Syracuse after hitchhiking all the way from Florida by myself. I was on the run, an escapee from a youth program in Tampa. A week later, the Syracuse police caught me and escorted me to the airport. They put me on a plane and when I stepped off it in Tampa, I was arrested on the spot.

But that was so long ago. I can't wait finally see them again and show them my new place.

My chores are done. The room is set up. I'm about to make sure there's enough drinks when the doorbell rings.

It's my mom. It's a bit early, and I let her in.

"How's it going, honey?"

She has a grocery bag in her arms, and I take it from her and kiss her on the cheek.

"I'm good. Just got the room set up for Dad and Bob. How are you?"

"I'm good." She pats the bag. "Brought you some lasagna."

"Awesome. Bread, too?"

"Yep."

"Thanks, Mom."

She sits down at the dining room table and I put the food in the fridge.

"The girls on their way?" I ask.

"Jackie and Chris are, and I just talked to Liz. She'll be here at five," she says. "Your dad was getting ready when I left."

I take a seat next to her. The tablecloth is a bit wrinkled, and she smooths it out and straightens her placemat.

"So," she says. "You meet any other musicians yet?"

"Nope. Haven't had time yet. But I will."

"Still trying to network?"

"Yeah, but it's a slow process. There's so much to do. But I'm getting there."

She nods her head. We don't say anything for a moment.

"How are you doing, Don? You okay?"

My palms get sweaty.

"Yeah. What's up?"

"Well, I'm worried about you. It seems like you're holed up here by yourself most of the time," she pauses. "This just doesn't seem like what you really wanted."

"Holed up?" I force a laugh. "No, it's really not like that. I get out a bit. And I hang out with the folks at work now and then."

"You do?"

"Yeah," I reply. "And maybe I'm not holed up here all by myself as much as you think I am."

"Oh," her eyes widen. "I didn't know."

"Yeah," I laugh. "I just haven't met anyone I can bring over to meet you guys yet, that's all."

"Well, all right," she sighs. "If you need to talk, we're here for you. I want you to know that, okay?"

The doorbell rings again, and I jump up. It's Jackie and Chris. We hug and tell each other how good it is to see each other. They're both looking great. I show them around the place and show them the band room and the back yard, and we chat and catch up. Then Liz shows up, then my dad, and then Bob. Suddenly, everyone's talking. My place is so busy all of a sudden. I'm trying to keep up with everyone but it's hard. I'm getting dizzy.

I think about walking out the front door and leaving. But I shouldn't feel this way. I wonder what's wrong with me. I swallow and take a few deep breaths, and it passes.

When we start to play, my mom and my sisters are in the band room, cramped in a line on the wall in fold-out chairs. We play some Eric Clapton and Jimi Hendrix. Then we play Tom Petty's "American Girl." My sisters like that song. So do I.

When we launch into it, the rhythm locks me in and connects me to something huge, something way bigger than myself. And as I sing the words, I live them in my mind. I see a younger version of myself and he's eighteen and hitchhiking out on that old Route 441. He can hear the waves as they crash on the beach, as he tries to find his way back to his American girl. But my older self knows what he does not – it really *is* too late, and he really *is* too far out of reach. My sisters are singing along and cheering, and as we finish the song a deep sadness overtakes me. I'm not sure I'll ever find my way home.

Afterward, we pack up our instruments. We do our hugs and say our goodbyes, and I watch them pull out of the driveway.

I go to the living room and reach under the table and pull out the bong.

A COUPLE DAYS LATER, I'M DRIVING MY CAR AROUND North Beach and Pier Sixty. The past couple months I come here in the evening before sunset sometimes. Groups of people walk down the sidewalk in a leisurely fashion, laughing and then disappearing into restaurants or surf shops. Couples stroll, holding hands and smiling. Packs of teenagers cruise around in cars or on skateboards. Others make their way across the street to the powder-white beach to watch the sunset.

I think about what it would be like to be down here with friends. When I was young, I'd come here at night. It would be me and Jimmy Check. Or Paul and Scott. We'd find a way out here and we'd find a spot and we'd start slamming beers and smoking weed. We'd talk to girls as they passed and try to impress them with how much we could drink.

I don't have anyone to come here with now, so I come alone. I park and people-watch and wish I had a life. After the sun sets, I start my car and head home.

On the way I always catch a red light at this one corner. It's like it knows I'm coming and turns red on purpose just as I draw near. As I sit waiting for it to change, my attention is sometimes drawn to a small convenience store. It has a sign that says they sell lotto tickets and cigarettes and wine, and people are always loitering out front.

They're selling dope.

I know because they're always rubbernecking and staring at the cars that pass by, trying to catch the drivers' attention. I see cars pull up to the store with their windows down. Someone walks fast to the car, looking to the left and right, then they lean over to the window and do a quick exchange.

At first when I'd stop at this intersection, I'd look away. My hands would grip the wheel and I'd glue my eyes straight forward, fixed on the light. I'd wait for it to change and I'd pass the time humming a tune and tapping my foot.

But not tonight. I turn my head and stare hard. I watch the deals going down and I wonder what kind of dope they're selling.

I'm almost positive it's crack. But there's only one way to be sure.

Smoking weed is exhausting me. It's monotonous. I do it before work and after work. Before watching TV. Before and while and after I watch porn.

I'm bored as hell and I'm tired. And I'm tired of being bored.

Maybe if I smoke crack just once, it will be good for me. Maybe something will come to me – like some inner realization. Or a catalyst for true change that will help me break out of this cycle.

Somewhere inside, I know those *maybes* are complete bullshit. I'm not playing with the idea of smoking crack to find enlightenment. But tonight, I'm willing to believe for just a moment that my thinking is right on the money.

My body starts to tremble. I can't stop thinking about getting high.

Me: Smoking crack would be so exciting.

Me: No way – when the light turns green, I'm going home.

Me: Nah, just pull into that store and get twenty. Or maybe forty.

Me: No fucking way – I could ruin my life.

Me: You've already ruined it.

My pulse is loud in my ears. And as the light turns green, everything seems to happen in slow motion. I turn the corner and pull up next to that little store. I roll down my window.

There are some guys standing next to the building, and one of them starts walking toward me.

Something screams inside my head.

Leave! Leave now!!

But it's weak and unconvincing. Besides, I tell myself, it's too late. I'm here, I'm parked, and this guy is already at my window.

"What you need?" he says.

I hear the voice once again, but this time it speaks out loud.

"I need forty."

I reach in my pocket for the money and he reaches for the crack. We do the exchange quickly and I pull away and head for my house.

I break out in a clammy sweat. My mouth is dry, and my heart is thumping in my chest. I haven't even had the first hit, but my body already knows what's coming.

The voice that tries to tell me to do the right thing is silent. It's nowhere to be found. It's retreated to some dark corner within, mourning quietly.

It's lost the battle tonight, and it might be a long time before it has a chance to win again.

11

I GO BOOM

At dawn, sunlight seeps around the edges of my curtains and pours lazily into my room. I turn and I toss. I stretch and I yawn. And then I remember. My eyes snap open and I sit up straight and look around.

I'm not in jail. I'm not dead. The world didn't end.

Last night there was forty dollars' worth of crack on my living room table. Then there was only twenty. And then, there was just one hit left.

And then, it was all gone.

And what did I do next? Did I jump in my car and try to score more? Nope. I did the right thing. I grabbed a bottle of cheap wine and smoked a little weed. And an hour and a half later, I was out like a light.

This is amazing. I actually smoked crack and woke up normal. What can this possibly mean? It means I've *grown*, that's what. It means I'm more mature than I used to be. I'm *forty* now, and when you're forty, you're no longer driven by every stupid whim like you are in your twenties. Last night is proof – when I ran out of dope, I just stopped, no big deal.

Like a normal person would.

My life is changed. No longer do I need to be afraid I'll go down a slippery slope if I cut loose for just one night. No, it's up to *me*. I don't have to throw my life away if I don't want to.

I get ready for work and then leave the house, humming a tune as I drive. Getting high was cathartic. It did me good. And to think that as I pulled away from that store last night, I actually thought my life was over.

How dramatic was *that*?

When I get to work, I stroll into the building and plow through my tasks. I'm on the ball. I work hard, solve a few problems, and don't even think about getting high.

I leave my cubicle for my lunch break and get in my car. I have no plans, but I'm thinking Joe's Pizza. I put it in reverse and start to back out, then I stop. I put it back in park. It occurs to me that if I want, I can take the rest of the day off and go get high. Just for an hour or two. Of course, I don't *have* to. It's entirely my choice. I can take it or leave it.

I decide to take it.

I call work a few minutes later. I tell them some family issues came up and I need to take care of them. They tell me it's fine. Do what I need to do. I hang up and head for the corner store.

A few hours and a couple hundred dollars' worth of crack later, I'm out of drugs. I'm sitting in my car in the corner of some parking lot and I don't know what the hell to do. I was supposed to go to my niece's birthday party after work, but there's no way I can go now. I call Bob. When he answers I take a deep breath and exhale.

I need to sound casual.

"Hey, Bob, what's up?"

My voice is trembling, but just slightly. I hope he doesn't notice.

"Not much, man, what's up with you?"

I clear my throat. I try to sound smooth and natural.

"Not much, Bob," I say. "Hey, some stuff came up at work

and I need to stay late. Can you tell everyone I'm sorry I can't make it?"

"Yeah, man, sure," he says. "Sorry you gotta work, bro!"

"Me too. See you soon."

I roll down the window. My heart is palpitating, and I wonder if I should call an ambulance. No, I'm fine, I tell myself – I just need to take some more breaths.

Tonight's the first family get-together I'll miss, and I wish I hadn't gotten high. Whenever I go over to my sister's place, Raymond and Rachel run up to me, laughing and yelling "Uncle Donny!" And the littlest one, Allison, is just barely a year. I pick her up, and she smiles and giggles. She reminds me of Liz when she was a baby.

My heart calms when I think of my family. It's true what my mom says. Nothing is as important as family. Then my heart sinks again. I can't be with my family tonight because I'm too fucked up.

I decide I can't dwell on that crap. I need to think positive. And the upside is that now, I'm free for the rest of the night – which means I can get high just a little more.

I promise myself I'll get to bed at a decent hour. And I swear that after tonight, I'll lay off this shit for a while. I'll make it up to my niece soon. Uncle Donny will get her something special and drop by to surprise her.

When I finally make it to bed, it's three in the morning – *Friday* morning. And on Friday mornings at six I meet my dad at the gym. We do a light workout and talk a bit, then he goes home to my mom and coffee, while I go home to get ready for work.

My dad needs those workouts. His energy level is up a bit since we started. He says he feels better, and he seems happier. If we keep doing it, he might beat his cancer.

There's no way I can skip our workout. If I just stay in bed until it's time to leave for the gym and don't smoke any more crack, I can at least show up and get through the workout. I can still be a good son.

Plus, I can always get high afterward.

When five-thirty comes I'm still smoking crack. There's no way I'm going to the gym. I call my dad.

"Hey Dad, I can't make it today."

I'm speaking through my nose to sound nasally, like I'm under the weather.

"I came down with something," I tell him. "I'm about to give them a call at work, too."

"Oh, I'm sorry to hear that," he says. "I hope you feel better."

"I will," I tell him. "I'll be there next time. Probably see you before then."

"Take care of yourself, son."

His voice sounds tired. Maybe a bit sad. I wonder if he knows something is up. But either way, my dad needs me – and I let him down.

That thought sinks in, and I dig my fingers into my thigh until it hurts. I'm a horrible son. That thought hurts even worse, so I switch gears and think about my bank account instead. I still have a few grand. I get up and drive to the corner store. When I pull up, a guy steps up to the driver's side window. I peel off a few twenties, and he puts the drugs in my hand.

This is the last time, I swear. When I run out, I'm finally going to sleep.

It's almost midnight, and my car creeps along a dim street. I peer over the steering wheel, scanning the sidewalk, left then right. I'm trying to spot anyone who will make eye contact with me and give me the nod. I have sixty dollars on top of the console ready to go. If I can score just one last time, I'll turn around and go home and stay there.

This time I mean it. I smoked crack for the first time in years on Wednesday night. I woke up the next day like I was king shit. Then I blew off work and skipped my niece's party Thursday. Thursday night, no sleep. This morning I let my dad down, blew off work again, and went on to burn through another nine hundred dollars on crack.

I have to stop at some point. And after tonight, I swear to God I will.

I drive past the corner store again, but no one's there. I cruise down MLK, then I take a left at Tangerine. Usually it's hopping, but tonight the sidewalks are empty. There's one dude up ahead, he's walking slowly my way but he's looking down at the sidewalk. I lean forward and stare, waiting for him to look up. When he finally does, he meets my gaze for a split second then looks back at the sidewalk.

He shakes his head no.

He's telling me there's no dope.

Or, maybe he's signaling that the police are out, and that everyone's lying low. But that doesn't make sense because I haven't seen a single cop.

Maybe I read him wrong.

I take a slow right on the next street. I decide I'll make one more pass and if I don't see anyone, I'll go home for the night. As I come out of my turn, the dimmed headlights of a car parked to my left catch my eye. My windows are down, and I hear the hum of its engine as it idles. I cut my eyes toward the driver as I pass, and his eyes lock with mine.

It's a cop.

I snap my head forward, breaking his gaze. Panic seizes my entire body.

I'm breathing hard. I need to get the hell out of here. I take the next right on La Salle, which heads back to MLK. If I can get back there without him following me, I'll be good. On MLK, there are at least three ways I can disappear before he gets near me.

I keep a steady pace. My knuckles are white and my legs tremble as I glance in the rearview mirror and pray to God he stays there. I look ahead at the stop sign at MLK.

I'm halfway there already.

I glance in my rearview mirror once more. Nothing. It's looking good. I'm twenty yards from the stop sign now. I look at the street before me, then my eyes dart back to that rearview mirror. His car is racing toward me. Before I come to a stop at the sign, he's behind me.

Right on my ass.

I flip my left turning signal on, then come to a rest at the intersection before making the turn. Maybe he will go right.

He makes a left.

I look at my speedometer. I'm doing twenty-five, right at the speed limit. Ahead there's a four-way stop. I'll make another left when I get there. I hope he'll make a right this time. If he does, I swear to God I'll go home and stay there.

I'll quit smoking crack, too.

As I approach the intersection, the police lights explode behind my car, filling the night with strobes of red and blue.

I ease to the curb and turn off the car. I roll down my window and put my hands on the steering wheel. I peek in my rearview. He's parked behind me, and then a second police car pulls in behind him.

He probably ran my license plate. If he did, he knows my record. I do a quick mental check. There's nothing in the car. No drugs, no paraphernalia. Nothing illegal. That's slightly comforting.

It's going to be okay.

Through the rearview mirror I see two officers approaching

toward my left. They're twice my size, and they rest their right hands on guns holstered to their waists.

"Put both of your hands outside the driver's window!" one of them shouts. "Now!"

I stretch my hands outside of my window. The moment I do, they grab me by the arms and yank me through the window. My body spills out of the car and onto the pavement. I'm face down and a knee presses hard into the small of my back, and hands dig through my pockets and feel me up roughly. They jerk me up and push my back against my car.

"What are you doing out here?"

He's so close that spittle sprays my face. He's got his right hand with a firm grip on my neck, his thumb heavy on my throat. The other cop moves in, his arms folded, and he glares at me.

"What are you doing out here? Answer me."

"I was, uh, I was looking for someone."

His pupils dart from my left eye to my right eye then back.

"Bullshit," he says. "You're looking for crack."

"No, I really was looking for someone."

"You're looking for crack," he interrupts. "Just admit it."

"I wasn't," I protest.

The other officer smirks and shakes his head. Then the first cop turns to me again.

"Okay, look, I'm going to ask you one more time," he says low and slow. "If you lie to me, your ass is going to jail. Understood?"

"Yes."

I know there's nothing in the car. And it shouldn't matter why I'm down here because I didn't do anything wrong. Not this time, at least.

"One last time – why did you come down here?"

"I came here to look for someone."

He nods to his partner, who walks me to the back of my car

and stops. We watch the first officer rummage through the driver's area of my car. In less than a minute, he stops searching, stands ups, and walks over to us.

"What's this white stuff I found on your floorboard?" He holds up a tiny Ziploc baggie.

It's empty except for a speck of something white in the corner. But I know it can't be mine; I've never bought crack in baggies.

"I have no idea," I tell him.

He sets the baggie on the hood of the police car and pulls out a test kit from his glove box. He does something with it, and I can't tell what. But after a couple minutes he turns to me.

"It's positive for coke." He's grinning. "You should've just been honest with me."

He slaps the cuffs on my wrists and puts me in the backseat of his car.

"You're being charged with possession," he says. "You got out less than two years ago, right?"

"Yeah."

"Which means that when you are found guilty, you'll get a mandatory ten."

That sounds about right, but I'm not going to respond. I'm remaining silent.

I look at the floorboard. All I know is that I finally had a chance to have a life, and I threw it away. It's sad, I know. And I should *feel* sad. My family sure will be.

But I don't feel sad at all. In fact, I don't feel a thing.

Something *is* wrong with me. Maybe I *should* be locked away and live in a cage.

Because maybe that's what I really am – an animal.

12

BILLY

I'm done with booking at 5 a.m., and a guard leads me to a pay phone on the wall. I have two minutes, he tells me. I call my parents. By 7 a.m., the officers escort me back to booking.

My dad posted bond.

I walk out the front doors and he's waiting for me on the sidewalk. He doesn't smile, but he doesn't frown, either. I tell him thanks, and he nods his head, and we walk to his truck in silence.

As we pull out and head to my place, my entire being is still numb. But sitting next to him as we drive, a small corner within my heart begins to thaw. My face becomes hot with shame and soon, I'm fighting back the tears. I glance over at him. I want to say something. I want to let him know how sorry I am. I fumble for words, but I find none. No one's had the chances I've had. Nobody's ever had the love and support I've had.

And what do I do with it? I treat it like it's nothing.

We pull into the driveway, and he turns the Ford off. We sit there forever, he and I, saying nothing. I look down at my knees, waiting for him to lecture me. I'm fragile, and I fear that with the slightest rebuke, I'll be shattered.

And then, he turns to me.

"Donny, what happened?" His voice is broken, almost pleading. "My God, what happened?"

It's like a punch to my gut. I wish he were angry with me instead. But he's not – he just loves me. I owe him some kind of explanation at least, I know, but I'm unable to come up with anything.

I only know I've been pretending. At our dinners and family get-togethers, I smile and hug everyone. I say I'm doing great, but I'm not. The truth is that I've been treading water all along. And now, the inevitable has begun.

I'm finally starting to sink.

"I don't know." I shake my head and look down at my lap. "I'm sorry, Dad."

Inside, I'm collapsing. My voice shakes and I no longer have the strength to hold it back. It's been a couple days since I've slept, and I'm weak and I'm dirty.

Inside and out.

I bury my face in my hands and my body begins to heave, and I'm sobbing.

"Donny, I believe in you," I hear him say. And then his hand rests on my shoulder. "You screwed up, but it's not over. You can turn it around."

I flinch. Turn it around? I already had a chance to have a life. To be somebody and prove who I truly am. Sadly, I think I did precisely that. If there was ever any doubt, it's now removed.

I'm bawling now, and snot is running down my lip. My whole body is shaking and really, I'd prefer a bullet to my head than all this. Because there is absolutely nothing I loathe more than experiencing the crush of this burden, of this heaviness, of the reality of these emotions.

I know what I need to do. There may be many things I can't

control, like who I am. But there are some things I can control absolutely.

Like how I feel.

IN THE EARLY 1970S, BILLY WAS LIKE AN UNCLE TO ME. He and his brother Kip would come to our small house at Indian Rocks Beach, a block away from the Gulf of Mexico. They'd drink beer and hang out with my mom and dad, cranking up vinyl records and laughing and talking. Billy would play with me and Bob, throwing a frisbee in the yard and telling us jokes.

My dad was the captain of a commercial fishing boat, and Billy and Kip would go with him, far out in the Gulf for a week at a time. They'd bring home tales of sharks and whales. Sometimes a week at sea wasn't enough, and family day at the beach could turn into quite the scene. My dad or Billy would run to our house to get our tiny canoe and a huge fishing pole. Then they'd paddle out a couple hundred yards offshore to fish.

For shark.

I was barely seven, and I'd stand at the water's edge looking on in awe. When they finally hooked one, my dad would paddle hard to shore while Billy fought the great fish. A crowd would gather to my left and right, and they'd murmur. Those guys are fucking crazy, someone would say. Then my dad and Billy would return to the shore and stand next to the shark as it thrashed and flipped around on the sand. The crowd, they'd move in closer and watch.

My dad and Billy and Kip were hard-core, like pirates. But the drinking and drugging eventually got out of hand, and my dad moved us back to Upstate New York. That's when he and my mom got clean and began taking us to church. Billy and Kip followed not long afterward. It was good to see them again, but I missed the beach. There was no fishing in Rochester.

Or so I thought.

One night, my dad told me they were going fishing at the river and that I was going, too. We all took off in my dad's truck, me and Kip and Billy, all of us crammed in the front seat. I sat shotgun with Billy, sitting on his lap.

My dad backed the truck to the river's edge, and we cast our lines from the tailgate. It was drizzling, but we didn't care. We huddled under a large tarp and watched our poles. It was perfect weather for bullhead. Not as exciting as shark, I thought, but it would still be fun. We fished for ten minutes, and then everything changed forever.

Billy committed suicide right in front of us.

Out of nowhere he bolted from the truck, pulling out a large lock-blade knife as he ran. When he reached the river's edge, he dove upon it, burying it to the hilt in his own chest as he splashed face down in the shallow water.

My dad and Kip ran to him and grabbed him by the arms, lifting his tall frame and turning him around, facing me. Crimson seeped from the center of his chest, spreading quickly across the front of his white T-shirt. Billy's long blond curls were wet and matted across his forehead and cheeks, and his blue eyes locked with mine. They pierced me for a split second, then they fell to the ground and glazed over.

When the ambulance arrived, I was sitting in the front seat of my dad's truck. I watched as the paramedics hovered over Billy. They pulled a cover over his face in the rain, while my dad held Kip upright. I trembled and I hugged myself around my waist. As I did, I glanced at my face in the rearview mirror. The tears that spilled over my cheeks were enormous, huge like the drops that splattered on the windshield.

I clenched my jaw and forced a smile on my face. It was a big grin, and fake like plastic. I sat up straight, and I summoned a laugh. It was bullshit, and even then, I knew it. But I looked myself in the eye and then I began to lecture myself.

"You will always smile, Donny," I said sternly. "No matter what happens, you will always smile."

My tears vanished. The grief and the sorrow disappeared, just like that. I searched my chest, my stomach, and even my brain, but they weren't there.

I had turned them off, all right, but I had no clue how to turn them back on.

When we got home, my dad told me to go to my room while he broke the news to the women. Through the walls I heard Billy's wife Diane begin to cry and wail. And then my mom joined her. My jaw tightened. I no longer felt anything, and their stupid crying, it irritated me.

It was just a couple months later when my dad moved us back down to Florida, leaving New York behind once and for all.

We moved to Safety Harbor.

IT WAS OVER THREE DECADES AGO THAT I SAT IN MY dad's Ford by that river as Billy died. And now, these tears in *this* Ford, they're a piece of cake. It's like flipping a switch. And just like that, I shut them off – and my emotions, they vanish.

I wipe the snot off my face with my shirtsleeve, and I clear my throat.

"I don't think this can be turned around, Dad. The cop says he found that shit. Right on the floorboard." I shake my head. "I'm fucked."

"No, you're not. We're going to get you an attorney. You're going to fight this and you're going to get through it." He looks at me, his grip tightening on my shoulder. "It's not too late."

I want to believe it's not too late, but I can't. I don't deserve any more help because now I know for sure. I'm rotten to the core.

"Dad, no," I protest. "It's okay, I'll figure it out somehow."

"I'll tell you what," he tells me. "You focus on not getting high anymore. Go to meetings. Do whatever you need to do. And if you promise to do that, I'll focus on helping you get out of this mess. That's the deal, okay?"

"I can't let you do that," I say. "This is my fault."

"It's not about whose fault it is, Donny. You're *worth* it. Yes, you've made some mistakes. But you're a good guy, Donny. You've got to believe that. And as long as you're really trying, your mother and I are going to help you."

A good guy, he says. I feel sorry for him. He's the good guy. Always believing. Hoping.

Hurting.

Yet I know when it comes right down to it, I'm not going to turn away help. Yeah, I'll take the paid attorney. But not because my dad's finally convinced me that I'm a good, or that I'm somehow worth it.

He hasn't.

It's pretty simple, actually. Because after all, even a piece of shit wants to live.

13

CHICKEN SOUP

"This is 911, what's your emergency?"

"I'm having a heart attack," I say.

My heart is flopping like a fish in my chest. I keep getting dizzy, and everything starts going black. But before it does, my vision returns. That's why I'm calling. For the most part, anyway. There's another reason, too, but it's complicated so I don't even try to explain it to her.

The short version is this: I'm about to be murdered.

I cut my eyes toward the motel window. He's still outside. It's dark out there, but I can see him clear enough. He's leaning against the balcony rail in front of the room next door. He's got a baseball hat pulled low on his head, and a fishing pole rests on his shoulder. He raises a hand to his cheek and touches the side of his face.

I know what he's doing. He's speaking in a low voice into a microphone. Probably to the FBI. They're about to make a move on me. They're going to bust my door down and shoot me right here on this bed. They don't care that I'm not armed. They just want me dead.

There's only one way out of this room, and it's through the

front door. But I can't walk out there, because I'll surely be killed. I need an escort to safety. Which is the other reason I'm on the phone right now.

"Okay, are you on any medications?" she asks.

"No."

"Any drugs, street drugs?"

"Not at the moment."

"Not at the moment? What were you taking, and how long ago?"

"Um, just a little crack."

"Okay, and when was the last time you used the crack?"

"I don't know, maybe ten minutes ago."

"All right. The paramedics are on the way. I suggest you take a minute and get situated so that you don't have any drugs when they get there." She pauses. "You understand me?"

"Yeah."

I hang up. I hope the paramedics get here before I'm dead.

I make one more call, to my parents. They're probably worried. They haven't heard from me in days. Plus, I was a no-show at another family get-together yesterday.

My mom picks up the phone.

"Donny? Where are you?"

I start to speak, but there's footsteps outside my door.

"Mom," I whisper, "they're going to kill me."

"Where are you?" Her voice is shaking. "Who is going to kill you?"

I begin pacing the room, my eyes darting around as I look for crack. I know there's some around here somewhere. I need just one more hit before they get here, then I'll flush the rest.

"Donny? Are you there?"

"Sorry. I'm at the Motel 8 by Sunset and 19. And I don't know who they are, but they're outside my door."

If I get shot right now while I'm talking with her, that will be absolutely horrible.

"I have to go, Mom. I just wanted to say I love you."

When I hang up the phone, someone starts banging on the door and yelling. It's the paramedics, they say. I'm not sure it is, so I just sit on the bed, staring at the door. Then the lock snaps and the door swings wide open, and they all pour in.

The room is full of people talking. There's a pen light in my eyes, and I'm being hooked up to a machine. I wonder where the guy outside the room went. Maybe he's the guy taking my blood pressure. Probably not. He wouldn't try to kill me right in front of everyone.

I laugh a little inside. What a way to make my escape. I am one clever dude.

Then my heart starts doing flips, this time worse than before. It even registers on the machine. I hear the beeps, and the paramedics look at each other.

They strap me to a gurney and wheel me down the stairs to the parking lot. The ambulance is waiting with the engine running and the back doors swung open. Faces stare at me to my left and right as they wheel me toward it.

I see my mom. Her eyes are wide as she steps near and puts her hand on my arm and then looks at one of the paramedics. They tell her I'm headed to the emergency room, and she says she'll follow.

When we get there, they give me drugs. It's to relax me, they say. My heart's a bit irregular, but then again, they tell me, that's normal when you've been doing blow for days with no sleep. They also say I'm experiencing drug-induced psychosis. They don't think anyone is trying to kill me. But I don't care about that anymore because I feel a lot better now. The drugs are starting to kick in, and I'm relaxed.

To hell with the FBI.

A short while later they release me to my mom, and I nod off on the drive to my parents' house. When we arrive, I somehow make it to the guest room. The bed linen is crisp, and my head sinks into a plush pillow.

I'm safe. And moments later, I'm asleep.

IN THE MORNING, I AWAKE TO THE SMELL OF COFFEE and English muffins. I stretch and pull the covers over my face. Another hour of sleep would be nice, but my stomach vetoes that idea. I sit up and plant my feet on the floor. There's a pair of pajama bottoms and a shirt neatly folded across the chair at the foot of the bed. I think I left them there a few weeks ago when I slept off the last binge. That time, I showed up at the front door hungry and scared, looking over my shoulder as I begged them to let me in.

I've lost count of how many times I've stayed here since my arrest last year. My life has been dangling by a skinny thread. My parents kicked me out of my house because I kept getting high. I've been fired from work three times. I've been to detox twice. I've pawned and lost my guitar twice. I've lived in my car, on spare couches, and in crack houses. Sometimes I go missing for days and at the end of it, I wind up crouched in the corner of some alleyway or behind an abandoned building in my car, scared and delusional.

I keep thinking the government is after me. Other times I think it's just my conscience, blown up and exaggerated by the drugs. That makes sense to me, because my conscience knows I'm guilty of treason – against myself.

When the money's gone and I have nothing left to sell, I finally start to come down. My body begins to feel again, and my stomach aches for food. Just a sliver of sanity returns, and it reminds me that there's somewhere I can always go.

It's then that I show up on my parents' doorstep, begging for help.

Those are the absolute worst of times. But they are the best of times, too.

I stay for a week, and my mom nurses me to back to health, feeding me chicken soup and sandwiches. My dad takes me with him to run errands in his truck. We talk about the good old days. About the fish we caught and the places we dove in the Keys when I was a boy. At night my dad and mom and I watch sitcoms on TV together. We eat ice cream and laugh our asses off.

My parents love me just the way I am. Whatever happened in the past, it doesn't matter. They just love me. I know this, and I trust them no matter what. Even if they decided to put me out of my misery and kill me in my sleep, I would be okay with it.

There's no place I'd rather be.

But I know I can't stay forever. So after a week I decide to take another stab at it. I'm going to try to stay clean, and I hope something changes. Before I drive off, I hug them and thank them for their help. They tell me they love me, and to take care of myself.

Within a week I'm shaking and sweating, peeking out some window, and someone is trying to kill me.

Once again, I've lost my mind.

"ALL RISE!" THE BAILIFF SHOUTS.

I rise. My attorney stands to my right. A judge's bench sits tall before us, and the judge emerges from a chamber behind it. She takes a seat and begins thumbing through some files and paperwork. The state attorney is seated at another table. I look behind me, and there's my brother on the third row. He smiles and gives me a thumbs up.

This is what déjà vu looks like.

The arrest for the cocaine was a year ago, and my trial is

finally over. It lasted almost two days, and I replay it in my head – especially the jury's reactions during the trial. They knew I'd been to prison a long time. They knew what for, too. They knew I'd had drug problems. And they knew that I maintained all along that I had no idea the cocaine was on the floorboard of my car.

I watched as they passed around the evidence among themselves – the same tiny Ziploc bag the officer held in front of my face that night. A few of the jurors held it up to the light and squinted, before shaking their heads and passing it on.

Even the judge said she was amazed that anyone might have noticed it in the first place, especially on a floorboard at midnight.

I'm with the judge.

But that's for the jury to sort out. And what they must decide is whether I knew, or should've known, that the crack was on the floorboard. That's what makes me guilty or not.

I'm biting my lip because I know there's no way the jury is going to believe me. If they could, I think, the jury would probably find me guilty – *as hell*.

"Has the jury reached a verdict?" the judge asks the bailiff.

"They have, your Honor," he answers.

"Please bring them in."

The jurors file in and take their seats.

"Will the lead juror rise?" the judge asks.

The lead juror stands, and the judge continues.

"The State has charged Donald Cummins, the defendant in this case, with one count of Possession of Cocaine, a second-degree felony in violation of Florida Statutes 893.13. As to this charge, I understand the jury has come to a verdict. Is that correct?"

"Yes, your Honor," she replies.

"And what does the jury find?"

I swallow hard.

The juror looks down at the index card she holds in her hand, and she begins to read.

"We, the jury, find the defendant, Donald Cummins, not guilty."

I collapse forward and catch myself, grabbing the table with both hands to steady myself.

My lawyer pats me on the back and congratulates me. I stand up straight and shake his hand. A buzz of conversation has erupted in the courtroom behind me, but I'm barely aware of it.

I'm in shock. I've *never* gone to trial before. I've always pleaded guilty, even for stuff I didn't do. But today, I won. I want to shout. I want to raise my hands and yell at the top of my lungs.

I've got another chance at this life.

I'm not going to waste it. Right now, I've got a week clean and I'm going to keep it that way. This whole thing has been hanging over my head for a year. If it wasn't for this court case, I think I would've been able to quit last year. But the stress, though. It's been way too much.

When I get home, it's time to celebrate. I sink into the couch and roll a fat joint. I light up and take a huge hit and hold it in as long as I can.

No more crack, I tell myself. That shit is horrible for you.

14

CRAZY TRAIN

I've been driving for hours on the Courtney Campbell Causeway, a ten-mile strip of land that cuts through the middle of Tampa Bay. It's about as narrow as a football field, and each side is lined with palm trees and mangrove bushes and a rocky shore.

I drive all the way to Tampa, and then I pull a U-turn and head toward Clearwater. When I get there, I pull another U-turn and head for Tampa. I repeat for hours, and everything begins to look the same.

The only thing that changes is the moon as it moves across the sky.

My arms become heavy. It's like they're turning into rubber, and the wheel is getting too tight to turn. My entire rear is sore, and I shift my weight from one ass cheek to the other. But I can't stop driving. As long as they keep following me and their police radios fill my ears, I don't have a choice. I've got to keep going.

I have no idea where they are, but they must be close. They might be following behind me at a distance. Or they might be above me, watching remotely from a helicopter somewhere.

Regardless of where they are, the result is the same. They're taunting me and trying to break my will. They're trying to manipulate me into doing something.

They, meaning the FBI. Or maybe it's the CIA.

They've been following me hard for a couple days now. They track my every move and put thoughts in my head – then they watch to see how I respond. At this very moment, they might be looking through my eyes and hearing through my ears. And if they really want, they can probably start driving me, too, like I'm a human drone.

Maybe it has something to do with the drugs. Which is not to say this isn't real. Maybe it's the drugs that are making all of this possible in the first place. Like, there might be something in the crack that opens my mind to all of this – it creates a chemical doorway, making my brain vulnerable to the government's remote *fuck-with-your-mind* technology.

But then again, I haven't smoked any in over twenty-four hours.

Maybe being overtired is the better explanation. After all, it's been four days since I've slept. I yawn, and I decide that being thoroughly exhausted wins: it explains perfectly why I'm bugging the fuck out.

I'll stop driving. I'll force myself to crash somehow. It'll be hard at first, I know, but eventually my body will overpower my mind and drag me to sleep, silencing this insanity.

I pull over on the shoulder on the northern side of the causeway, and I park the car. Dense mangrove bushes line the shore, and through a few gaps I can make out the shallow water and rocks below. A row of thick palms hides me and my car from anyone driving on the causeway to my left.

I'm safe.

I turn off the engine and roll down a window. I smell the saltwater and I hear the waves lapping against the rocks softly.

Then, there's movement to my right. I cut my eyes toward the mangroves and I see them. They're hiding behind the branches and the leaves, wearing dark suits and aviators. They vanish, then reappear to my left among the palm branches.

This is not an overtired mind; this is really happening.

The radios get louder, their static becoming abrasive. It's getting tricky to decipher what the agents are saying with all that noise, but somehow, I do.

A few miles away, they're telling me, there's a bank in Safety Harbor.

I know the one they're talking about. It's the one I tried to rob eighteen years ago – the one I didn't get any money from. They're saying I need to go back there.

It's time to take care of unfinished business.

IT WAS DECEMBER 1992, AND THE JAIL CELL STANK OF urine and shit. Though the light was dim, I could make out the brown smears on the wall. I stood close to the door, trying to suck in air from the hallway outside. I'd always been proud of my cast iron gut, but it was queasy and it began to lurch.

The food trap on the door flung open.

"Mr. Cummins?"

I bent over and looked out. A welcome blast of clean air hit me in the face. I focused, and a pair of eyes on the other side looked into mine.

"I'm John Pierson," he said. "Remember me?"

John was my public defender. I leaned in a bit closer.

"Yeah, I do," I said. "What's up?"

"You tell me." He studied me a moment. "I want to hear it one more time – you understand where you are?"

"Yeah, I'm at the courthouse."

"What's the date?"

"December." I said. "December sixth."

"No. The seventh," he corrected me. "What year is it?"

"1992."

"Okay. You know why you're here?"

"Yeah. They say I robbed some banks."

"And did you?"

That's where it got fuzzy. After a year in jail, I still didn't know for sure. I knew I walked into six banks and demanded money. Almost all the tellers handed it over. Except the bank in Safety Harbor – they refused.

I understood fairly well what had happened. But I wasn't sure about the *why* of it all.

"Well, like I told you last time, I'm not really sure. They said the tellers would be waiting on me. That after I got the money, I'd hand it over to them so they could get some code from it or something. Something hidden in the money."

"And who are *they*?" he asked.

"The government," I answered.

We'd been through this a few times already. I might have been foggy about some things, but the dilemma I faced was clear as a bell: either none of that government stuff was real, which meant that I was completely off my rocker, or it *was* real, which meant I'd been caught up in a bizarre government conspiracy.

My lawyer was leaning toward the first option. The psychologists were, too.

Not me. I was thinking the second one.

"Okay, sit tight," he said. "I'll be back in a moment."

A few minutes later, a bailiff escorted me to the judge's chambers and stood me next to John. It was there that the judge offered me the plea deal.

"I would at this point offer twenty years habitual violent with a ten-year minimum mandatory on everything," the judge said. "That will be a guideline sentence."

John spoke up.

"Judge, in light of his mental problems right now, would the court consider some probation with the condition that he go for mental health counseling? It appears that he has a long history of drug abuse. He's been in Boley Manor and Horizon Hospital several times. He's on medication - Stelazine, according to one of the doctor's reports. With counseling, maybe he can deal with some of those problems he has. There's at least one report that he may have been insane at the time of the offense."

"When he is out is he able to work? Is he on SSI or something?"

"I'm not sure but I can find that out."

"I will add five years of probation to follow the twenty, John, but I won't take any away from it. Based upon his history I think a long period of incarceration is appropriate."

"I won't request the probation – I don't want to get him in a worse situation than before we started."

John pulled me aside for a quick huddle. We could go to trial, he explained, but if I was found guilty I'd face an enormous amount of time. The judge could give me a hundred and twenty years.

My psych meds were heavy and I was a bit loopy, but I could still do math. Twenty years in prison would suck. But a hundred and twenty? That's a life sentence.

I took the deal. I agreed to go away for the next two decades of my life.

Now *that* was insane.

Now, as I sit in my car on the causeway, I'm thinking that if I would've gotten that money from the bank in Safety Harbor, the feds would've never let me rot in prison all those years. But now, eighteen years later, I have the chance to finally make it right.

I can finally complete that mission.

The agents in the bushes are saying I need to go back to that bank and ask the teller for the money. She'll be the one on the far left, they say, and she'll be waiting for me. She's going to give me some stacks of money – there will be a note tucked inside one of them. I'll have to find it and hand it over to one of the agents.

What agent do I hand it to?

The note will tell you, I hear them say. Just find it.

Okay, I say aloud. Got it.

The sun is about to rise. I decide I'll drive around some more and think it over, because this is huge. Not many people know the government does stuff like this, giving important missions to nobodies like me.

I think they do it because they want to see if you're going to be loyal. Kind of like a hazing, but more hard-core.

I want to make it right. But I want to get the government off my frigging back, too. Maybe if I do this, I'll finally be able to break this cycle of madness.

I start the car and pull out.

"DONNY, PLEASE, TURN YOURSELF IN."

It's 4 a.m. the next day, and my mom is pleading with me. Her hand reaches for mine as we stand at the side of the road next to my car. Her hair whips across her face as an eighteen-wheeler blows by us. My dad puts his hand on her shoulder and steadies her. He looks at me.

"Everything will work out somehow," he says. "Just come with us. Please, for God's sake, come with us."

My parents tell me the police are looking for me because I

robbed a bank in Safety Harbor yesterday. The detectives had visited my parents, telling them I need to turn myself in. If I didn't, someone might wind up getting hurt.

My head is swimming – just moments ago as I drove to Tampa, my dad's truck suddenly appeared on the road next to me. The passenger window was open, and my mom was pointing to the shoulder of the road and mouthing for me to pull over.

I thought I was hallucinating, but I pulled over anyway.

"How did you find me?" I ask them.

"We couldn't sleep," my dad explains. "We had no idea where you were, but we knew we had to try to find you. We got up, and five minutes later there you were – you drove right past us."

"Come with us," my mom says. "We don't want to lose you."

I've got a handful of crack in the console of my car, and I'm on my way back to my motel room across the bay. Turning myself in is not part of the plan.

I screwed that bank up – for the second time. The teller gave me a stack of money, but as I left the bank it exploded in a huge plume of red smoke. I fell, and money rained down on the grass around me. I grasped for handfuls of loose bills from the ground, searching.

There was no note.

I did the only thing I could do: I panicked and ran. Lucky for me, the crack dealer didn't give a damn about the dye splattered on those bills.

But right now I don't care about that bank or the police or what's going to happen next. I only know that I've been up a total of five days now. I'm wheezing, and it feels like a knife is stabbing me in the chest each time I take a breath. Fatigue spills over my body and my eyelids become heavy, and I'm beginning to sway.

I look at my parents. They're just a few feet away but they're getting blurry.

"Okay, but can I go to sleep first?" I try to focus my eyes. "At your house?"

They hold me by the arms and guide me to my dad's truck and help me get inside. We take off toward their house and when we arrive, I'm already asleep.

15

THE OAKS

" S o how are you feeling today, Don?"

I'm sitting on a tiny, overstuffed couch. The room is stuffy and cramped, its walls covered with framed inspirational quotes like *One Day at a Time* or *Hope and Love*. Another reads, *Greatness Calls You*. There's a distressed, teal bookshelf packed with titles that have similar sayings. The room is still, almost motionless, except for the soft, steady tick of an old clock that hangs on the wall.

Leah sits opposite me, her back arched, ready with her slim paper notebook and thick, paisley pen. She peers at me over the rim of her glasses.

"Pretty good," I reply.

I've been at The Oaks for almost six months now. Today is my progress evaluation.

"Pretty good? That's great, Don. Would you care to tell me a little more about that?"

"Sure. I'm feeling okay. I still like it here and I want to stay."

I'm feeling a lot better now than I did in the beginning. At first everything was a blur. Doctors were always examining me. Court-appointed attorneys tried to visit me and ask questions, and social workers and case workers came to see me every other day. My meds were heavy and frequent, and my mind was thick, like peanut butter. But when I was ordered to live at The Oaks, my body and brain began to adjust. Now, months later, I'm alert again and my feet follow each other without dragging.

"We're happy you're here too, Don," she smiles. "We're glad that you're an Oakie."

"Me too."

"Okay, so let's talk about your diagnosis." She looks down at her notes. "It's important you come to terms with it, because once you do, the faster you will recover. Make sense, Don?"

"Yeah, it does."

"Okay, good. Did you read the pamphlet I gave you?"

I did. I know I'm not living the most normal life. And being at a residential mental health program means I might have an issue or two. And yes, my thoughts about the banks and the FBI are a bit extreme.

But it doesn't mean I'm a schizophrenic.

I think the drugs have a lot to do with it – and that's not the same as being mentally ill. After all, I see a clear pattern: when I go a few days without drugs, the voices always go away.

But that's not the only reason I'm not buying it. I think part of it is that I don't *want* to be a schizophrenic. I kind of hope the whole thing *is* real. Because if it is, it means I'm a little less sick than I already know I am.

"Yeah, I read the pamphlet. But I'm still not sure." I shrugged. "Just being honest."

"That's okay, Don," she said. "How about you give me some input on this: do you think that believing you're a part of a government conspiracy to stage a bank robbery is a rational belief?"

I look down at my shoes for a moment. I got them a couple weeks ago. A staff member had filled up the Oaks van with seven of us, unloaded us at a thrift store, and then gave us each a voucher for ten bucks. When I saw the shoes, I could tell they were nice, even though I don't know Allen Edmonds from Nike.

Now I'm wondering if there really *is* a crazy person walking around in them.

IT WAS 1981, AND I DIDN'T MIND BEING AT THE adolescent ward of Horizon Hospital one bit. The food was tasty, and I could even have seconds if I wanted. The staff scheduled activities for us like painting and pottery. A few times we went on field trips to the movies and to the beach.

There were girls in my ward, too.

I'd been in and out of the juvenile system and programs like Straight Incorporated for almost two years, and Horizon was way better than any of them – I would've never run away from there.

Horizon was also my last chance at juvenile rehabilitation. My parents had executed a campaign of letters and phone calls to anyone and everyone in the justice system, pleading for an intervention. They finally got one. When the judge committed me there, he told me that if I worked with the psychologists and made progress at the hospital, he would follow the hospital's recommendation and send me wherever I needed to go.

The staff at Horizon assured me that wherever that was, it would be even better than Horizon. It would be somewhere where I could do good and finally graduate and go home.

But after a few months, one of the counselors pulled me aside. I thought Dave and I were about to talk about the usual, like guitars or maybe Led Zeppelin or Jim Morrison. But he didn't want to talk about any of that. Instead, he said he had news for me.

I'd been diagnosed with schizoid personality disorder.

Dave went over parts of the report with me. The doctor had

written that I was *flat*. That I demonstrated a *lack of affect*. I showed little to no empathy for others. I was anti-social and evidenced an extreme level of emotional immaturity. On top of it, I was a budding criminal.

All of that, he said, made me a schizoid.

The solution, the doctor had written, was a long-term, in-patient therapy program. One that would help me learn how to express my emotions and have meaningful relationships. But the problem, Dave explained, was that there weren't any programs like that. Not for fourteen-year-olds. So instead, the hospital was recommending I go back to the juvenile justice system. He said in a week, a sheriff would transport me to a youth program in Jacksonville.

It was horrible news.

"Do you feel like you understand what's going on? Do you understand what it means to be a schizoid?" he asked.

I nodded my head yes.

"Do you have any questions?"

I shook my head no.

"Are you sure?" he asked. "If you do, you know where to find me, right?"

I nodded my head yes again.

I went to my room and shut the door. I found a spot in the corner on the floor and sat there and stared at the wall.

I didn't get it. The doctor hardly ever came to our floor. Once a week he'd meet with me for ten damn minutes. How could he even *know* whether I was cold and heartless? He thought I was a monster, but I didn't feel like one. I liked many of the kids on my unit, and I felt warm inside when I thought of them. And when they were discharged, I'd miss them and wonder how they were doing.

No, I couldn't possibly be a schizoid because I truly liked people. I really *did* care. I'd just never been that great at showing it, that's all. Okay, I was a bit stand-offish. Socially awkward. But I *wanted* to have friends.

When I'd lie on my bed in the hospital and look at the ceiling, I'd daydream. And in those daydreams, I had a girlfriend. She was cute, and she had brown hair and brown eyes. I was a pitcher on the school baseball team, and the other guys on the team and I gave each other high-fives, and we had each other's backs. I was a good guy and I only got in one fight ever, and that was to stop some jerk from bullying a little buddy of mine. Everyone in school and in my neighborhood, they knew my name, and I knew theirs, too. On weekends I would go to the mall and to the beach with my friends – my *close* friends. We had a great high school and I was proud to be there. Countryside High, home of the Cougars. That's where I was going to go to prom someday. That's where I'd graduate from. I was a part of something good. Something *wholesome*.

I was a happy, narrow slice of a huge apple pie.

No, the me in my daydreams was never alone. He was never cold. And he was never aloof or unkind.

That diagnosis is bullshit, I thought.

I felt it. I *knew* it.

But maybe the doctor knows me better than I do, I thought. What the hell did I know?

I didn't want to be a schizoid. I didn't want to be fourteen and in a mental hospital. I wondered if I'd ever be okay, and whether I'd ever be with my family again.

I wondered whether I'd ever have a life.

I sat there, rocking back and forth in that corner. My eyes burned, yet I held it all back and I just shook it off.

Being cold and emotionless was hard. I didn't wish it on anyone.

"SO, WHAT DO YOU THINK, DON?" LEAH ASKS ME again. "Is believing you're a part of a government plot rational?"

I sigh. I'm tired of thinking about this. Of reliving it over and over again.

"I know, it sounds crazy." I look down at my shoes again. "Looking back, I just don't know for sure if it was the drugs or if it was real."

"So, you don't think you're a schizophrenic, or is it that you're ashamed to be a schizophrenic?"

"I don't know."

I was having a good day until now. I rest my elbows on my knees and my head in my hands. I run my fingers through my hair. I don't want to keep going in circles about it. I just want to forget it all.

"Okay, Don," she says. "Enough, then. You're here, you're an Oakie, and if you're not sure what exactly happened, it's okay. Let's focus on something else."

That's fine with me.

"Okay, let's see." She starts thumbing through some paperwork. "I see you're still going to meetings."

"Yeah."

She looks up from her notes.

"How's that coming along?"

It's okay for the most part. I go to two meetings a week. Every Saturday night they load me and the other Oakies in a van and drive us to Gulfport. As soon as the van door opens, I put my head down low and quickly hoof it to the opposite side of the parking lot. Then I turn around and walk up to the meeting, pretending I'm not coming from anywhere near that Oaks van. I'm just a lone dude going to a meeting all by himself.

I started doing that after the third meeting. On that night, I had just found my seat when I heard a female voice behind me.

"There's those people from the Oaks again."

"Oh my God," another replied. "They are *so* creepy."

"I know it sounds horrible, but I wish they weren't here. They make me *so* uncomfortable."

I turned to look. They were about ten feet behind me, standing at a fold-up table under the pavilion, sorting books and pamphlets into small stacks. Then one of them looked me in the eye and began walking toward me.

I winced. She's going to ask me to leave, I thought.

"Would you read this when we call on you?" She smiled and held out a sheet of laminated paper. "It will be right after the meeting starts."

At the top in bold it said, *How Recovery Works.*

She had no idea I was an Oakie.

"Um, sure." I took it from her hand. "Thanks."

"You're welcome." She spun on her heels and walked back to the table.

So, I do like those Gulfport meetings because they're outdoors by the water, and it's cool and breezy in the early evenings. There are always lots of women there, too. But I'm tired of pretending.

"Yeah, I like going to the meetings," I tell Leah. "But I like the Freedom House best."

The Freedom House, I walk there by myself. It's only a block away from the Oaks and I know everyone there. They know who I am and where I live – and they don't give a damn. Some people at the Gulfport meeting call the Freedom House meeting "the meeting in the hood." But at the Freedom House, they just call it the Freedom House. A lot of the guys there have been to prison just like me, and just about all of them have been hard-core crackheads, too.

"Yep," Leah looks at her notes. "That's what I have here. Johnny's your sponsor, right?"

"Yeah."

I meet with Johnny every week after the meeting. We talk about how to stay clean. About life and how I can build one again. He gives me no-pressure writing assignments on topics like self-honesty, addiction, or courage.

"And I see you're all signed up for college. You're starting in about six weeks, right?" She smiles. "How cool is that?"

"It's pretty cool." I sit up straight and grin. "I can't wait."

Maybe everything really does happen for a reason, I think. Going to school is a big deal for me. I'll be in an actual classroom with real students, and there's no telling what might happen. It's going to be a place where I can explore and learn and discover what I want to do. I'm ready to let go of the old ideas about what I'm supposed to do so I can turn these lemons into lemonade.

I'm signed up for two classes: Basic Computer Literacy and Introduction to Speech. I don't know what the big picture is yet, but I'll take those two and figure it out later. The important thing is to just start. And if I stay clean and work hard, there's no telling what can happen. Johnny tells me that all the time. Leah does, too.

"Well, good luck, Don," she says. "It sounds like you're doing great. I'll be back to meet with you in a few weeks."

"Okay, sounds good."

We leave the community room, and I go upstairs to my room and lie down. I'm suddenly feeling a bit drowsy.

My meds are probably starting to kick in.

16

ATM BLUES

The applause is loud, and it catches me off guard. I do a double take. My classmates are smiling and clapping. A few are cheering.

I did it. I gave a ten-minute speech, and they liked it. It flowed and it was natural. I know because I could just feel it. I think maybe *this* is what I want to do. To speak to people about things that are important and meaningful, to make a connection with them as I do it, and to know in my gut that they get it.

Kind of like music, in a way.

Tonight I did both, actually. Because in my speech I introduced them to the greatest guitarist of all time: Jimi Hendrix.

I talked about him and his life, but I didn't just talk. The professor had said to use body language and give vivid examples, so I did. I demonstrated how Jimi played his guitar behind his back and behind his neck. I showed them how he played with his teeth.

I even humped my air guitar.

I have to give another speech toward the end of the term. I don't know what it will be about yet. But after this, I know I can do it.

After class is dismissed, I walk down the hallway and sit on a bench next to the elevator. I pull out an envelope the assistant handed me on the way out the door. It has feedback from the other students, written on notecards. I rip it open and pull out the first note.

I don't know much about Jimi Hendrix, but I'm going to check him out tonight. Thanks for the hookup!

I take out another.

Don, you were really great. I liked it when you showed us how Jimi played – a really vivid picture!

And another.

I just wanted to say that you did really great. I could tell you really believed what you were telling us. It made me want to go buy all of Jimi's albums.

Then, there's this one:

Don, there are a few things you can make improvements on, but when it comes down to it you've got it. You could use speaking to help make the world a better place, and I hope you do. Regards - Joyce.

I can't put a face to Joyce, but what she said is nice. It's kind of like what my grandmother would've said. Joyce is probably religious like my grandmother was. Those two would've gotten along great.

I stand and throw my backpack over my shoulder, and I head for the elevator. When I step off in the lobby downstairs, I see the ATM and I stop. My school money should come in any day now. I'm supposed to get five grand, which will cover my books and classes – and then some. Maybe I'll get some wheels. My car is long gone, and it would be nice to get around. Maybe I can meet some non-Oakie friends.

Maybe I can even find a girlfriend.

I deserve some normalcy because I've been clean almost six months.

I walk up to the machine and put my card in. I select the option to just get a receipt. A moment later it spits one out.

The balance is a little over five thousand dollars.

My stomach drops. I break out in a sweat. I inhale deeply and close my eyes.

Me: I don't have to do this.

Me: Oh yes you do.

Me: No, I like where my life is right now. I like school. I like the Oaks.

Me: Fuck school. Fuck the Oaks. You need to get high.

Me: But I don't want to get high.

Me: Bullshit. Just do it. Just this one time.

Me: But I can't do it just one time.

Me: Yes, you can. It's all in your head. Just make up your mind to do only a little, and you'll be good.

Me: If I get high, they're going to kick me out of the Oaks.

Me: Aw c'mon you lil' Oakie – you know you've never been able to stop. And you never will.

I whimper. It's true – I'm going to get high. I don't want to, but I know I will. It's like the full moon is out, and my body has just twisted and contorted and become something altogether different.

I've turned into the wolfman, and there's nothing I can do about it. It's my nature.

It's just who I am.

Sadness fills my body, and heaviness overtakes me. One moment there was hope, and the next it's been yanked out from under me.

I see my dad's face. Then my mom's. They're pleading with me. Begging me to come back, and to go to the light. Maybe it's not too late, I think. But it's as though an invisible fist punches me in my gut, bowing me over. My emotions shut down and my brain goes numb as it shifts to autopilot and my body begins to crave. I watch myself take four hundred dollars from that ATM. I witness myself call a ride. And as I take a seat in the car, I hear myself speak.

"Take me to Thirty-Fourth and Fifth."

The driver lets me off in front of a cheap motel. I pay for one night and go upstairs to my room. I put a hundred dollars in my pocket, and I hide my debit card and the rest of the money under the mattress, in the center of the bed. I walk out to the balcony in front of my room and light up a cigarette. I look around. I tell myself that it will be ten minutes till someone tries to sell me dope.

After five, I feel eyes on me. I cock my head to the side, and I notice the curtains move in a room two doors down. The door cracks open, and a guy pokes his head out.

"What's up?" he asks.

"Nothing, just looking," I reply.

"What you lookin' for?"

We're on the second story balcony, right out in the open. Anyone within a block or two with a camera could be snapping pictures or recording us. I cover my mouth with my hand as I speak.

"Hard white."

"How much?"

"A hundred."

"Hold on."

He shuts the door, then comes out a moment later. We do the exchange right there on the balcony. I go back into my room and lock the door and fasten the deadbolt.

Fifteen minutes later, I'm on my hands and knees on the carpet behind the bed, peeking around the edge. My pulse is racing, and my eyes are glued to the door. Sweat drips from my brow. I wonder if I locked the door good enough. Feet shuffle outside my room, and I hear whispering.

And then, a police radio.

Me: This can't be real. It's the dope.

Me: How do you know what's real or not? There it goes again – hear it?

Me: Yeah, but so what? It only happens after I start getting high.

Me: They're out there, all right. Go out and look.

I don't go out and look. No way. Instead, I take another hit. And then another. I tremble as I watch the door for another half-hour. And the doorknob – I swear I see it turn slightly. Someone's trying to open the door.

I wait. I sweat. I hyperventilate. I watch. I take another hit.

I repeat.

And then, I'm out of drugs.

I stay on the floor, my eyes are glued to the doorknob for another forty-five minutes. Gradually, my heart slows and my breath stabilizes.

Damn, I think. I should've bought *two* hundred worth.

I gather my stuff and leave the room. I walk a block away, glancing over my shoulder as I duck into the parking lot of another cheap motel.

A half an hour later I have more crack. I'm hiding behind another bed in another hotel room. And again, government agents are just outside my door. They're about to kill me.

My body can't stand much more of this, I think. I'm about to collapse from sheer terror, yet I know there's also part of me that absolutely loves it.

Two days later and I'm squatting next to a dumpster in an alley. It's been raining and there are puddles all around me. I'm filthy and I stink. My head is throbbing. I haven't eaten a bite since before speech class. My body is trembling, and my hands are shaking. My college bank account is empty. I have a dollar and change in my pocket, and my phone is gone.

I traded it for crack.

It could be worse. In the past two days I've almost been hit by two cars. I've been robbed twice, once at gunpoint. I was stopped by the police last night, but I don't remember why. I only know that when they let me go, they laughed and told me to go take a fucking bath.

I walk out to the bus stop on Thirty-Fourth and take a seat.

Just a few feet away, cars and buses whiz past. They're doing fifty. If my timing is right, I can aim my body like a missile so my head lands right in front of the bus wheels. I wouldn't feel a thing. My parents would be heartbroken, but maybe less so than by watching me go through this over and over again.

Taking myself out, I think, might be the most loving thing I can do for myself and everyone else. Plus, it's an opportunity to go out with courage and honor.

Like a samurai warrior.

I'm going to do it. The medics will probably curse me under their breath as they scrape me off the pavement, but they'll get over it. And so will everyone else.

I inch forward in my seat and glance to my left at the northbound traffic. There's a bus coming, about a block away. I tuck both my legs under the seat as my toes find a deep crevice in the concrete. I'll use the toehold to launch my body into the street. My entire left leg twitches, like it knows what's coming.

My body tenses, and I choke back tears and whisper goodbye to my family. But as the bus nears, it slows down. It stops right in front of me. The door swings open and the bus driver looks down.

"Getting on?" he shouts.

He's not supposed to do that. He's only supposed to pull over if I stand and step up to the curb.

I shake my head no. The door closes, and the bus pulls away.

It's twenty minutes till the next bus.

I stand up and look around. There's a payphone a half a block away. I should at least call my parents one last time.

My mom answers.

"Donny, are you okay?"

"Yeah," I mumble. "I'm all right."

"Where are you?"

"A street corner in St. Pete."

She's whispering to my dad in the background. He's saying something about the Oaks.

"Have you talked to the Oaks?" she asks.

"No, I don't think they'll let me come back."

"They will," she says. "They've been looking for you. They told your father they want to give you another chance."

I hang up and walk back to the bench. Another bus is coming soon.

Sometimes I think I'm like a dog in a laboratory. I'm hungry, but my keepers warn me to stay away from the food that's in my dog bowl. It's shit-food, they tell me. Instead, I need to wait a few hours. If I do, they say, then I can eat a huge, juicy steak. I picture the medium-rare sirloin in my dog-mind, and my tongue hangs out, my slobber spilling onto the concrete floor in huge globs.

But I am such a bad dog. And I'm a stupid dog, too. I'm stupid because I can't make myself wait for the steak. I don't know how to not eat the shit-food long enough to get what I really want. I want to learn to not do it, but I can't.

Yes, I'm that dog.

But there's a pinhole of light in this blackness. I can see it, faintly. To me it's a ray of hope. It's not likely, but it's possible. It's like I'm in the last second of the last quarter of the game and there's still a whole football field to go.

I'm hoping for a Hail Mary.

I have no idea how it might play out but suddenly, I think it's possible. If I go back to the Oaks, my life could totally change somehow. It just might be that something entirely unforeseen and completely out of my control will trigger some event that will finally teach my dog-brain to learn. But if not, at least it will be nice to shower and sleep, then wake up after twelve hours and eat a healthy meal.

I look up. The bus is a block away, and it's barreling in my direction.

I check my pocket. My bus pass is still there. I take it out and I step to the curb. The bus slows down and comes to a stop. The doors swing open, and I climb aboard.

I'm going back to the Oaks, and my fingers are crossed.

I'm hoping for steak.

17

PIDGEON

"I'm Don and I'm an addict."

My voice booms in the tiny room. I look around the circle. There's twelve or fifteen of us, and they all know me. They also know I've been missing, which usually means one thing.

I look down at the floor and take a deep breath.

"I'm coming back after a relapse," I announce. "I've got two days clean today."

The applause is like thunder, and they welcome me back wholeheartedly.

Glad to see you, Don!

Welcome back, brother!

Thank God you survived, Don!

I am too. That last go-around was a close call.

I like these guys a lot. I haven't had many real friends, but I'll bet they're pretty close to what real friends would be like.

After the meeting they give me hugs and wish me well. The room thins out and soon, it's quiet. It's just me and Johnny.

"My man Don."

We grip hands and embrace.

"How you doing, brother?" he asks.

"Okay."

He stands leaning with most of his weight on one foot, his body bent slightly while he holds himself up with a wooden cane. He shakes his head and grins.

"Yeah? You doing okay, huh?"

"Shit, I don't know. I'm alive, so I guess I'm all right."

"You are, Don. And don't forget that you're blessed."

He motions with his right hand.

"Let's take a seat."

I grab a couple folding metal chairs from a stack against the wall. I open one for Johnny and set it on the floor. He eases himself down onto it. I take a seat opposite him.

He removes his glasses and starts wiping them with a cloth. He holds them up to the light and squints, then puts them on his face again.

"Now, let me get something straight. Y'know, my old ass forgets sometimes."

"Sure," I say.

"I recall you and me sitting right here, just like we are right now. And you made a commitment. You remember what it was?"

I shake my head no.

"We agreed that you can get high if you want. But you got to call me first. Remember that?"

"Yeah, I do."

"So why didn't you call?"

"Man, I should've." I look down. "I'm sorry."

"You don't owe me no apologies. You should be apologizing to yourself."

I swallow. This talk isn't going to be easy.

"To be honest, calling didn't even occur to me," I admit. "I just got high."

"You even try to put up a fight?"

"For a second or two, but then I just caved." I shake my head. "Y'know, sometimes I think I can't ask for help because they're fucking with my head."

"The government?"

"Yeah. Like they're screwing with me and pushing me to use. And when I finally do, they just laugh at me."

As soon as the words leave my lips, I realize how insane it sounds.

"Sorry," I say.

"Look man, I ain't going to second guess them professionals about you being crazy," he says. "But I'll tell you what I know for sure, and that's this: Right now, there's something more important than figuring out whether the government's messing with you or whether you're crazy or not."

"Like what?"

"The solution, that's what."

"And what's that? Remembering to call you before I use?"

"No, that ain't it. If you can, then great. But the solution requires you to do two things. The first is to forget about them doctors. And your parents, too. Hell, forget about *me*. In fact, to hell with anyone who tells you they know what your problem is and tries to get you to follow *their* solution. Anyone who does that, well, fuck 'em."

"Yeah? And what about the FBI? Fuck them, too?"

"Yeah, fuck them, too. Which leads me to the second part of the solution, which is to remember this truth: you have God in you. And the one that's in you, Don, is bigger than the FBI and bigger than your addiction. And brother, if you really *are* crazy, then God is bigger than your crazy, too. You got to trust that somehow, some way, some big-ass help is coming, and that it's going to arrive just when you need it the most."

Johnny knows I believe there's something to all of this. When we talk, sometimes I say God. Sometimes I say, *The*

Universe or even *higher power*. And I'm not doubting any of that. It's just that right now, I'm not so sure God is going to step in and save me. I'm just not convinced I'm that special. Besides, I've probably used up all of my chances, anyway.

"Do you believe that, Don? Do you believe that God's got your back and will see you through this?"

IT WAS 2001 AND I WAS LIVING IN THE WEST UNIT IN Raiford, Florida. I was halfway through my ninth year when I found out.

"Hep C?" I asked the doctor. "What's that?"

"It is a virus that causes liver disease," Dr. Nguyen answered. "There's a treatment available for some, and there has been success with it. But not much."

"And what if the treatment doesn't work?" I asked.

"It depends on how aggressive the virus strain is," he answered. "It's not pleasant to think about, but you must be aware that it often results in death."

I gulped.

"I will order more blood tests to see if you qualify for the treatment," he continued, "and I'll let you know the results."

I walked back to my dormitory and sat on my bunk, and I began to thumb through the pamphlets he had given me. He was right. There was no official cure, and it really did kill people.

I wondered how in the world I could have caught it. The needles I'd dug out of a dumpster behind the vet's office in Woodland Hills? Probably not. Hep C wasn't really a pet disease. Sex? Remotely possible, but not likely. And then I remembered one incident during my stay at the federal detention center in Los Angeles in 1989.

I'd spent a month there waiting to go to federal prison after serving a couple years in the California state prison system. One day, my bunkmate returned to our cell from a visit with a wicked grin smeared across his face. He closed the door behind him quickly.

"Brother, I got meth and a rig," he whispered.

The meth and rig were in a green balloon, he told me – stuffed deep in his ass.

I pressed my face against the cell door's plexiglass window, keeping lookout while he dug it out. I could barely keep still. It was like Christmas, and Santa himself had just dropped off the motherload.

We shared the needle, priding ourselves on how we shared it responsibly. Each time we used it, we cleaned it meticulously, pulling bleach into the rig and pushing it out. Two pulls and two pushes, we'd agreed.

On the last one, though, I forgot to pull bleach first. And the split second before I slammed the drugs into my vein, I noticed it. It was a teeny, thin red ribbon floating in the middle of the clear liquid. I watched as it stretched and expanded. And then, it was gone. The liquid had turned a faint pink.

That ribbon had been blood. *His* blood.

I'd been in the room with him a couple weeks. He seemed like a tough guy. He was covered in tattoos and had an enormous beard. He definitely didn't seem the type to get HIV. Plus, he didn't seem sick at all.

I shot the dope.

Looking back, that was the only explanation I could come up with for the Hep C. But it didn't matter anymore, really. What I needed to do was come up with a strategy. And my first priority, I decided, would be to stay healthy. I already exercised daily – I'd need to keep doing that.

Like, immediately.

I stood up from my bunk and walked through a few gates

and into the rec yard. Carlos was already on the pull-up bars. He was about ten years older than me, in his early forties I guessed. He had a bald head and wore a thick metal chain around his neck. A fat wooden cross swung from it, and he was always lifting it to his lips and kissing it. He kissed it before eating. Before doing a set of bench presses. Before squaring off to fight.

I joined him at the pull-up bar.

"Hey, what's up," I said.

"Hey, bro," he said. "What's happening?"

He jumped up and grabbed the bar and pulled himself up.

"Same old shit," I said. "Well, pretty much."

He finished his set. I counted eighteen.

I jumped up and did mine. When I got to thirteen, I let go and dropped to my feet. He jumped up and grabbed the bar again.

"Just got back from medical," I said. "They told me I got Hep C."

He stopped mid-way through a pull-up looked down at me.

"You for real?"

"Yeah. I found out about an hour ago."

He dropped and landed on his feet. Then, he faced me.

"Serious? You really got that shit?"

"Yeah."

Maybe he's afraid he'll catch it, I thought. Maybe he thinks it's airborne.

Maybe he was about to kiss that cross.

"Homie, that's what I got!" he exclaimed. "I got that shit too!"

"You're messing with me," I said. "You got it for real?"

If Carlos had it, maybe things weren't so bad after all. He was a tough dude, and he didn't look like he'd be dying any time soon.

"Fuck yeah, I got it," he said. "And not only you and me, but lots of motherfuckers around here got it."

He began to name them off. Old Henry had it. So did Sidewinder. He was only nineteen or twenty. Lep had it, too. At least ten dudes that I knew had it. And they all seemed to be doing okay. But Carlos didn't think so.

"I'm telling you, that shit ain't no joke, homie," he said. "One day everything's fine. You think you got it beat. Couple days later, your stomach swells up and you start feeling sick as fuck. Three weeks later, you're gone."

He kissed the cross.

I started to laugh out loud, but I held it back. Carlos *was* pretty dramatic sometimes. I didn't think he had anything to worry about. He had a tough attitude, and his body was powerful. He could out-lift and out-run just about anyone there. But what he said turned out to be right on point – Hep C really *was* no joke. Because just six weeks later, Carlos was dead.

Seven months later, I thought I was going to die, too. I'd started the treatment just a few weeks after Carlos died. Pills twice a day and shots three times a week. I'd lie on my bunk groaning for hours each day. I lost twenty-five pounds, until I was a bony 150. I'd awaken to find patches of my hair strewn out across my pillow. My bones ached, and my joints, even worse.

I ran a slight fever on and off throughout the week, but it went up on Mondays, Wednesdays, and Fridays. Those were the days that I got the shots. My bedsheets stayed damp with sweat, and blisters covered my lips. I tried not to talk because when I did, they'd crack and bleed. I couldn't jog anymore because most days I was too short of breath to walk more than thirty or forty yards without a break. I had continual diarrhea, it was the middle of summer in Florida and there was no air conditioning.

I'd been that way six months straight. And as my body grew frail, and my face became gaunt, I began to hear it around me. Words spoken openly and loudly and in my hearing. Words that probably would've been whispered had I not appeared to have been fading.

"Hey man, you see that motherfucker? If that ain't AIDS, the Pope ain't Catholic."

"Always knew that cracker was a dick-sucker."

"That's the Lord's retribution – he's probably here for molesting children."

I'd read that the side effects might include not only physical symptoms like mine, but mental ones as well. Like depression. Anxiety. Suicidal and homicidal thoughts. And as the months passed, my mind deteriorated. Going through chemo *and* being in the middle of a twenty-year sentence was no walk in the park. And as my mind joined my body in sickness, I began to suffer.

I told myself I deserved every bit of it. I will surely die in this place, I thought, likely by my own hand.

It was at my lowest point during those days when some officers woke me up at 4 a.m. They shackled and handcuffed me, then boarded me on a van that set out for the regional medical center for the Florida Department of Corrections. It was a routine appointment to see a specialist. There were a few other prisoners already on board. One had tubes in his nose. Another was elderly, hunched over with a cane, wheezing as he breathed. The van had made its rounds earlier that morning, first picking up those guys from nearby prisons, then picking me up last.

We drove the thirty minutes from my prison to the medical facility at Lake Butler, and after we got through the gates we disembarked. The officers led us to the doors of the chow hall, then left us.

The others went in to eat, but something about the horizon captured my attention. I stayed in the courtyard instead. The sky was still dark, but it was rapidly becoming purple with a hint of red and orange. In the distance beyond the razor wire, clouds were becoming visible. They were spread out paper thin, like wings, taking on wisps of pink and yellow. Behind them, stars still shone against the darkness.

I stood in awe, my breath caught in my throat.

God has made all of this. And I, I am a part of all of this. No, I am this. And there is nothing to fear, because all is well. It always has been, and it always will be.

They weren't really words. They were more like ideas, in a way, but not ones that I thought. They were like ones I felt.

No, that I *knew*.

A whisper of mercy arose within me. It was a promise. A *knowingness*.

I was going to be okay, I knew. And I decided to shake it off, stand upon that promise, and keep putting one foot in front of the other.

I would not die in prison.

Warmth flooded my body, and tears ran down my cheeks. I smiled, and a crack opened in my lip and blood trickled down the corner of my mouth and chin. I wiped it off with the back of my hand, and I thanked God for being so good to me.

The treatment was scheduled to continue for six more months. But instead, I quit. Six months was enough for me.

Besides, I had a promise.

Two years later, in the middle of my eleventh year in prison, I sat before another doctor at another correctional institution. The blood work had come back, he said. And for the third time in a row in two years, they were unable to find the virus in my blood. According to the research, he told me, I was cured.

I THINK ABOUT JOHNNY'S QUESTION. OF COURSE, I believe God has my back. Miracles have always given me hope and kept me going. They've even saved my life at times. But really, all of that is beside the point, because they've never kept me free.

I glance down at the scuffed tile. Lots of people have been in and out of these doors. The Freedom House. I chuckle under my breath. I've been out over four years now, but I'm still a prisoner.

"Don, I'm going to be real with you." Johnny's voice is quiet. "You're in a real messed-up spot. Because if you don't have some kind of breakthrough soon, they're probably going to find you dead somewhere. In some motel or an alleyway. That, or you'll wind up back in the chain-gang for the rest of your life."

I nod my head. He's preaching to the choir.

"What do you know about homing pigeons, Don?"

"They fly and carry messages?"

"They do. But did you know that even real smart folks haven't figured out how them birds get home from over a thousand miles away?"

"A thousand miles? Really?"

"Yeah," he said. "You can take them birds, put them in a cage in the back of a truck, and drive a thousand miles away. And when you let them go, where you think they wind up?"

"Home?"

"That's right," he said. "Now, scientists think pigeons are hardwired with some kind of a map and a compass inside. Which means that when it's time to go home, they don't even think about it. They just do it."

I wonder what that has to do with me, but before I can ask, he tells me.

"Don, we're a lot like those pigeons. There's a part inside of us that knows how to get where we need to be." He leans on his cane a bit closer. "That part of us is connected to God. We just need to make the decision to go. And we trust we're going to get there no matter what – that something greater than ourselves is going to guide our steps."

"Okay." I sit up. "I guess you're going to tell me about some method that will help me get in touch with my compass and map? And then I can use it to get where I need to be?"

He grins and shakes his head no.

"Don, you ain't hearing me. It don't work like that. Besides, even if you could learn some technique to control all that you'd just fuck it all up."

"So what do I do then? How do I get where I want to be?"

"Where do you want to be?"

I pause and think about it. I want to feel warmth. To have friends. I want to have a family of my own. I want to feel joy and peace. I want to know what it's like to be okay with whatever is going on, and to not need to run away.

"I want to go to the place I see in my mind," I say. "I want to go home."

"All right." He looks at me and nods. "Then you need to make a decision. You need to decide you're going home."

I raise my eyebrows.

"That's it? Just decide I'm going home?"

"Simple as that. Don, you've got to make that decision from deep within. And when you do, you'll get there. *God* will get you there."

"But what if I get high again? If I do, I might not make it back."

He shifts his cane to the other hand, then wipes his brow and sighs.

"Don, you might not." His voice is almost a whisper. "But look man, that's not what we're going to focus on, because I believe you *will* make it back. That when you fall down, you'll get up again and remember your commitment."

"My commitment? To what?"

"To hold fast to your truth – the one you've decided and chosen for yourself. It's to cling to the reality that you're going home, no matter what."

My mouth is dangling. I'm speechless. The best advice Johnny has for me is to throw my hands up and trust the damn cosmos.

I leave the Freedom House and go back to the Oaks. I walk up the stairs to my bedroom and I shut the door and sit at the foot of my bed.

Johnny's right about one thing. If I don't stop getting high, I'm going to wind up dead. And *that's* what I need to focus on. Not some abstract decision to go home. Johnny means well, he really does. But that's just not what I need right now.

What I need is a solid *plan*.

I could check myself into a secure place where I *can't* get high. Like a detox or a long-term stay at a psych unit. Or I could talk to my doctor about an even stronger dose of my psych meds. Wait, I've got an idea – how about another twenty years in prison? If I get out in my mid-sixties, maybe this madness will be out of my system by then.

There are no good options for me. There are no solutions. It's clear: there's something I just don't know yet. There's something I haven't learned, and I have no idea what it is. I have no control over this thing, this *whatever* it is that's gripping me.

Maybe Johnny's right after all. Maybe I really *do* need a miracle.

If so, I need a big one. I need one deep in my mind and my heart. One that will do more than just get me through a tough situation – and then afterward ghost on me.

I need one that will stick with me.

I get down on my knees at the foot of my bed. I close my eyes, and I say the only prayer I know for sure that has ever worked for me.

"God, I'm hungry and I'm tired," I plead. "Please help me."

Then I add one more thing.

"And please, help me go home."

When I get up, nothing happens. There's no vision from heaven. No tears of joy. Not a single shiver down my spine.

I have no idea how this will play out. I'll do my best to not get high, and I'll try like hell to remember to ask for help. But there's one thing I decide I'll do for sure. As long as I breathe, I'm going to trust I'm going home and that somehow everything is going to be okay. Going forward, that will be my truth. I'm finally going home.

Even if it turns out to be my eternal one.

18

THE ITCH

The sun is beginning to rise as I stumble onto the Oaks property. It's been a rough four days. My stomach aches and my hands and legs are trembling. I fumble with my keys and try to open the door.

They've changed the locks.

I return to the streets and find a corner in an alley and I sleep there a couple days. Then I upgrade to a spot behind a dumpster next to a fast food place. There's an oversized cardboard box there already, and it seems abandoned. The dumpster stinks, but I find burgers and fries inside it that fill my hungry stomach.

It takes a couple weeks but eventually it happens. I wake up and I can't stand it anymore. I want to lather up with soap in a warm shower. I want to sleep in a bed. I want to sit at a breakfast table where I can drink orange juice and eat oatmeal.

This behind the dumpster shit sucks.

I talk someone into letting me use their cellphone, and I call my caseworker.

"Yolanda speaking."

"Hey it's me. Don Cummins."

"Don, where you at? We've been worried about you!"

By we, she means the team at Suncoast Center. It's been a year since the courts declared me to be incompetent and put me on disability. That's when they appointed the Suncoast team to look after me. The team makes sure I have a safe place to stay. That I get to my court dates and that I make any appointments with my public defender. They help me with a bus pass and make sure that my disability check is managed and that my bills are paid.

"I've been on the streets," I tell her. "They kicked me out of the Oaks."

"We heard. You all right?"

"Um, sort of."

Thirty minutes later I'm in her car. She takes me through a drive-through and hands me a hamburger. I begin inhaling it before she even parks.

"Damn, Don, you could sure use a bath." She grins and waves her hand in front of her face.

"I know." I swallow a bite. "Sorry about that."

"It's all right," she laughs. "I'm just kidding with you. I know it ain't easy. But you need to remember that a lot of people care for you, Don. You've got to believe that and keep moving forward."

She used to be a probation officer, she told me once, but she didn't like it. She took this job instead so she could help people.

"So," she says, "you ready to take that bath?"

"Yeah," I laugh. "I can't wait."

"Good," she says, "because I have a group home lined up and they have hot water *and* an opening today. What do you think?"

I think I want to give it a shot.

The group home turns out to be a lot like the Oaks. I need to submit to drug tests and I have to take my meds. After thirty days I can go to meetings or the library on my own, and after another thirty days I can get a job or go to school. Then it's weekend furloughs, and if *that* goes well, I can graduate and get my own place.

A couple months pass, and I'm doing good. It's time to decide whether it will be school or work. I like school, but my stomach gets queasy now when I see ATMs. I think my chances are better with a small paycheck from work every two weeks.

I start looking for a job but it's rough. I can't even wash dishes. No one wants to hire someone with an outstanding bank robbery charge.

I know Rick will put me back to work if he can, though part of me thinks it would be like going backward. But for me, maybe going backward might actually be like going forward.

I call him, and we catch up a bit. He's divorced now. He sold the house and he's renting a condo and his mom lives with him. He's been drinking a bit and he goes to the casino now and then, he says, but everything's okay.

He's still the president of the company. And right now, that's all that really matters.

I decide to ask him.

"So, um, you don't have any openings over there, do you?"'

"Well, I might," he says. "You sure you're ready to work?"

"Yeah, I'm not getting high anymore at all."

I wait a few seconds, and he finally responds.

"Well, things have changed since you left," he warns. "We've slimmed down a bit. If you come on board, you're going to have to wear a lot of hats. Probably put in a lot of hours, too."

The longer the hours, the longer I'm away from the group home.

"I'm all in," I tell him.

I start the following Monday. The week goes by like a blur. The mornings are a flurry of opening boxes with razor knifes and putting computer chips on shelves to be processed. I do a day's work in four hours, then I race upstairs to my own small office and start emailing and calling customers, trying to drum up leads and sales.

I learn about securing escrows and how to get electronic parts tested in a lab. In the evenings I try to learn to code by searching online. I need to update our website so people can search for parts on our site, but I have no idea what I'm doing. So I just copy and paste code until I figure out what works. In the end, that's all that matters, anyway.

Rick leaves it all up to me. No one's telling me what to do or how to do it. I'm handling it all myself.

Like a boss.

I work seventy or sometimes even eighty hours a week, and I'm making better money than I ever have. With my overtime I'm making almost seventeen bucks an hour, and that's not even counting commissions. My third sale was for sixty thousand dollars. A couple more like that, and we can hire someone else to open boxes, Rick says. I am exactly what he needs to help this company stay afloat.

But there's a flip side. I'm starting to get exhausted. I'm coffeed out and I'm drinking energy drinks all day. I wake up in the middle of the night with work racing through my mind, and I can't get back to sleep. My stomach is sour, and my chest burns. I need a vacation, I think. I need to escape.

I need to smoke crack – just once.

I've been daydreaming about it. I try not to, but then the thoughts come even stronger. I've got this fantasy, and in it I'm living at the house I rented from my parents. But in my dream, it has a basement like a bank vault – it's made of thick metal and it's reinforced by concrete. There are no windows, and there's only one door that's three feet thick and made of steel. It has a huge lock that opens only from the inside, and when I go in it, I close the door behind me and secure it tight. No one can come in and get me in there, not even the feds.

Finally, I can get high in peace.

It's sick, I know.

Rick's antennae begin to shoot up, and he starts eyeballing my every move. When payday comes around, he's biting his nails.

I'm getting the itch, and he knows it.

I'm eligible for weekend furloughs from the group home now, and he's afraid I'll take my leave and disappear. He offers me his couch for my furloughs so he can help me not throw my life away.

I agree, and we come up with a plan. We'll do things that are fun *and* safe. Things that let me scratch that itch yet still allow me to wake up on Monday and go to work like a normal person. On the first night of my first furlough, we follow the plan.

We go to a strip club.

I learn quick that I'm not the only one who needs to get it out of his system. Rick's in full character. He's got a wide-brim hat, and his Rolex is blinging on his wrist. His fur coat hangs to his feet as he shouts and peels off twenty-dollar bills over a dancer whose body writhes under blue strobe lights. I'm at the bar, sipping my third Long Island iced tea, watching. Laughing.

The only thing he's missing is gold teeth.

A woman slides next to me and leans in close.

"Hey, baby, want a private dance?"

She smells like a sweet flower. And suddenly, I feel like a drunken bee. But I'm not stupid. She's going to pretend she likes me. Besides, even if she really did, I'm not about to spend a single dollar with her. In the back of my mind, I'm thinking I might need it later for crack.

"I'd love to, darling." I smile. "But I'm dead-ass broke."

"That's okay. Your friend said he'd pay."

I look across the room at Rick. He's waving at me. I turn back to her.

"Seriously, I'm okay with just chilling."

"Really?" She sits up straight. "You don't think I look good?"

"Oh, you do," I tell her. "I'm just not into the dancing thing."

"Okay." She relaxes a bit. "You have a girlfriend?"

I think about telling her I'm married with kids and I'm crazy about my family. But I don't.

"No."

"Why?"

"I don't know."

"Are you dating?"

"You mean, am I available?"

"Something like that."

"Then yeah, I guess I am."

"Well, we can go on a date sometime if you want."

"You and me? No money involved?"

"Yeah, a real date." She laughs and puts her hand on my shoulder. "You seem nice."

She gives me her number on a napkin. Terri, it says. I tell her I'll call, and she leaves me at the bar. I wonder if she would be good for me. She might be exactly what I need right now. But I decide against it, and fifteen minutes later I drop the napkin in the toilet as I'm taking a piss. I feel a twinge of sadness as I flush her away forever.

When the club closes, Rick and I leave for the casino. We play blackjack and get even more wasted. Somehow, we make it back to the condo alive, and I find my way to his couch. Before I fall asleep, I'm relieved. It's nice being able to lie down, knowing that tomorrow morning I won't be homeless, and I won't wake up in a gutter.

And for the next month, every weekend, that's how my furloughs go.

When I finally graduate from the group home, I move in at Rick's. That's on a Monday. On Friday, I go missing for three days. I run out of money and steal from the company; I write a check to myself for a grand, and I smoke every last bit of it. When it's gone, I sell my phone so I can smoke another few hits.

Rick doesn't call the police. Instead, he searches the streets high and low. When he finally finds me, he talks me into coming back to his place and getting some rest.

When I wake up, I'm ashamed. I apologize for screwing him over. He says it's all good. We can work it out and come up with a plan to repay him, he says. And then, it's back to the grind.

For the next two months, that's how the cycle goes. I do good for a couple weeks, I binge, I repeat.

I'm starting to get scared. I know I can't keep doing this and live. One of these days I'll take that first hit and my heart will explode, and my body will drop on some motel room floor.

I'm trying to keep my commitment. I really am. Every time I screw up, I get back on my feet. I summon everything within me to try and believe that no matter what, I'm going home. I cling to the hope that something within will finally wake up and take me there.

But I'm getting weary. It doesn't seem like I'm headed in even the general direction of home. Instead, I'm wandering further away. I keep winding up lost in some motel room or some alleyway, terrified and shaking.

And then Rick finds me.

He really cares. He's just at a complete loss about how to help me.

And maybe himself, too.

"So what do you think, Don? Is everything predetermined, or is it all our choices?"

It was 1993, and Rick and I were sitting on my bunk in the dorm, waiting for our cups of Ramen noodles to cool. My stomach was growling – the hamburger they fed us for dinner was the size of a small breakfast sausage patty.

"Well, does it have to be either-or?"

"How can it not be?" he asked. "If God knows everything, then he knows how it's all going to play out. Which means it must be predetermined."

"I don't know. Maybe there's some guardrails in place, like some things we have no choice about. But we still have a lot of wiggle room about other stuff."

"But if we have wiggle room, how can he be in control?"

I wasn't a big fan of making rules on how God is supposed to act. They always get broken, anyway.

"Why does it need to be all bout control? Maybe God knows all the ways things can play out and is okay with it going however it goes."

I crushed up a bag of Cheetos into a fine yellow powder and stirred half of it into my soup. I handed the rest to him.

"Just a guess," I added.

"Yeah." He nodded and began stirring his soup. "Ever been married?"

"Yep. Two years."

"Wow, that's short," he laughed. "I guess *that* wasn't predetermined."

"Nope, it sure wasn't. We got married in a courtroom. I was in jail in Los Angeles waiting to go to prison, and we found a judge that married us the day before they took me up the road."

"No kidding?"

"Yeah. It was pretty sad, actually. I was wearing my jail clothes and had handcuffs on. She was wearing a pretty white wedding dress, and her face was all lit up with a huge smile."

"Damn. She must've really loved you."

"I don't know." I shrugged. "She probably thought she did. I think she was more in love with the fact that I'd hitchhiked all the way out there with only my guitar. She said it was romantic, like something out of a movie. Anyway, we divorced a year before I got out.

"So, what about you?" I changed the topic. "Ever been married?"

"No way. I have relationship issues."

"At least you'll be out in a few months." I smiled. "And you'll have plenty of chances to work on them."

We both laugh.

"So, how many girlfriends did you have issues with?"

"I don't know," he said. "Three or four."

"In love with any of them?"

"Just the first one. How about you?"

"Same. Just the first one," I said. "I still have regrets."

"What happened?" he prodded.

"Well, we were thirteen. She wanted to wait till we were married before we had sex, but not me. She finally gave in, but first she made me swear I'd never leave her."

"Then what?"

"I gave her my word, and I really meant it. But a couple days later my parents sent me away to a drug program." I shook my head. "I heard she hated me after that."

He was quiet for a moment.

"That's kind of like what happened to me. But different."

"Tell me," I said.

"Aw, I don't know. It's messed up."

"C'mon, man, you can tell me."

He sat up and cleared his throat.

"Okay. We were sixteen, and we were going to wait till we got married, too. We went to the same church, and even went to elementary school together."

His voice trailed off to a whisper.

"What happened?"

"Well, we tried to wait but we couldn't." He set his soup on the floor and pushed his glasses up on his nose.

"We had sex, but, um, she felt really guilty about it. Like it was bad or something."

He paused. He was red-faced and his lips were pressed together tight, like he was holding his breath. He put his palms on his knees and inhaled deeply through his nostrils. Then he continued.

"So, later that night she, um, well, she hung herself."

I sat up straight.

"She committed suicide?"

"Yep."

He stared straight forward, his body trembling. His eyes were clenched, almost shut, holding back the flood.

"Damn, man. I'm so sorry to hear that."

"Yeah," he whispered. "It really sucks."

IN HIS OWN WAY, RICK IS JUST AS MESSED UP AS I AM. But whether it was back then in prison or now, I know he's just done the best he can with what he's working with. Like any of us have, really. I'm glad for the help he's given me and I sure hope I turn a corner soon – for both of our sakes.

Because the truth is, I haven't been a good friend to him. And I'm not about to be, either. In fact, I'm about to screw him over.

Again.

It's a Saturday morning, and the sun isn't even up yet. I just woke up and I'm lying on his couch. It's dead quiet in here, and I'm just dying to get high. If I decide to do it, it will be the third time this month.

I decide to do it.

I ease off the couch and find Rick's wallet and his keys on the kitchen table. I tiptoe by his room and listen.

He's snoring.

I slip out the front door and put the keys in the ignition. I've got five hundred dollars in cash and I'm going to score. I'll be back in a couple hours, I tell myself. I'll just say I had to go to the store.

Five hours later, and it's 11 a.m. and I'm driving through a thunderstorm, my eyes glued to the rearview mirror. He's probably already reported the car stolen. There are a few cars following me. The drivers have dark shades, and they're wearing suits.

I know who they are. They're government agents.

My stomach is twisted, and my hands are shaking. I want another hit and I don't give a damn if those agents are following or not. The streetlight ahead turns red, and I slow to a stop. I hold my foot down hard on the brake, and I bend over, pretending to get something out of the glovebox. I suck in smoke until my lungs can take no more. Then I sit straight up and as the rush hits me, my ears start to ring.

I take another hit as the light turns green. I lift my foot off the brakes and drive through the intersection. Then, an explosion. A deafening, metallic crunch. My body flies into the passenger seat as the car spins a one-eighty. I raise myself off the floorboard and look around. The windshield is shattered, and the radiator is spurting liquid into the air like a fountain. The passenger door is crunched inward an entire two feet.

I've been t-boned.

I start to lift myself up when I notice the crack pipe lying on the floorboard. Next to it are a few large pieces of crack, and my lighter.

I grab the pipe and start stuffing it with crack.

A few moments later, I stumble out of the car and look around. A group of people have gathered on the sidewalk, and some guy yells at me. He's asking if I'm okay. I nod yes. Then I can't hold it in any longer. I blow out a huge plume of smoke. As the rush hits me I put my hand on the car to steady myself. I almost crumple to the ground, but somehow, I don't. I look up at the crowd.

They're all staring at me.

Adrenaline surges through my body, and I break into a full sprint. I run like a madman down the road, and I take a quick right into a residential neighborhood. I dart between two houses and I lie flat on my back in the thick, wet grass.

At once, the rain stops and the sun bursts out from behind the clouds. The wetness on the grass seems to turn to steam, rising from the ground all around me. I close my eyes tight. I play dead, lying as still as I can. I have no idea what's about to happen, but I know I need to stay put till I figure it out.

A helicopter is circling above, and dogs are barking nearby. They're starting to look for me.

I wish I'd brought the crack pipe.

The dogs get louder, and voices are shouting nearby. Then, footsteps in the grass right behind my head. A police dog is probably about to pounce on me. Or maybe a few officers are going to jump on me and pin me down right there. I clench my eyes tight, and my body tenses.

A few long seconds pass. Nothing.

I sense something. Someone is looking at me. I open my eyelids ever so slightly, and she comes into focus. An elderly woman is bent over me, peering into my face through large, thick glasses.

"Are you okay, young man?"

She leans over a bit closer.

"Are you all right, son?"

I try to say yes, but it comes out an incoherent, hoarse whisper.

I nod yes.

"Why are you lying here?"

"I'm waiting for them to come get me," I manage.

"Who?" she asks. "Who's coming to get you?"

"I'm not sure." I answer. "I-I'm just waiting for them."

Her eyes are a dark amber brown, the same hue as my grand-mother's.

"Honey, you don't know who they are?" she asks.

I shake my head no. My grandmother called me honey just like that. And for a moment, it's 1977 again. It's a Saturday, and I'm sitting next to my grandfather on their couch, watching an old black-and-white John Wayne movie. My grandmother hums a tune in the kitchen as she makes sandwiches and brings us a couple. *Thanks, Grandma,* I say. She smiles. *You're welcome, honey.* I'm glad I'm spending the night at my grandparents'. I'm happy and I'm safe and I'm loved. There's no one chasing me and my life is before me, not behind me.

I groan. I turn my face to the left in the wet grass.

"Are you thirsty?" she asks. "Would you like a glass of water?"

"Yes, please," I mumble.

"Okay. I'll be right back."

She walks away.

She's probably calling the police, I think.

Then, footsteps again. It's her. She bends over and holds out a tall glass of ice water.

"Thanks," I say.

I prop myself up on an elbow and take the water from her hand, and I drink.

"You're welcome," she says. "You know, I have a son. And if he was ever in trouble, I would want someone to help him, too."

She leans a bit closer and whispers.

"I called an ambulance for you. They'll be here any minute."

When the paramedics arrive, they kneel next to me and began flashing pen lights into my eyes. They take my vitals and ask me questions.

Are you hurt? No. *Are you in pain?* No. *Have you taken any drugs?* Yes. *What drugs?* I was smoking crack. *How long ago?* About twenty minutes ago. *What are you doing here?* On Earth? *No, why are you lying between these houses?* Waiting for them to get me. *Who is coming to get you?* I'm not sure – maybe the FBI. *The FBI? Why?* I don't know, but they were following me around. *Okay, we're taking you to a hospital – do you understand?* Yes, I do.

They board me in the ambulance and take off. We slow down a block away as we pass the officers and the dogs, and I raise my head and look out the window. Rick's car is still in the intersection, and it's crunched up bad.

I'm admitted to the psychiatric ward at St. Anthony's. I spend the rest of the day in the psych ward, watching TV and flipping through magazines. After dinner they hand me a small paper cup with a couple pills. I don't know what they are. I haven't even seen a doctor yet. For all I know they've mixed me up with some other patient. But I don't ask any questions. I take them and I hope they're good. An hour later, I'm sleeping.

The next day I see a doctor and he orders my discharge. They see it all the time, he tells me. Drug-induced psychosis. He advises me to quit, and he gives me a printout with some hotline numbers in case I need help. They give me my wallet and phone back and offer to cover a cab ride to wherever I want. I check my wallet. I still have a hundred dollars left.

When the driver picks me up, I tell him to take me to the Thirty-Fourth and Fifth. It's the closest place I know I can find crack.

19

MOTEL ON THIRTY-FOURTH

I'm standing in the doorway of a cheap motel room, looking for Mick. He should be back any minute.

We're all waiting, itching to get high again. It's me, Steve, and Tammy waiting on him. We've all been staying here together for a few weeks, since the day the doctor discharged me from St. Anthony's. All of us hustle up money every day to pay for this room.

We get dope with the rest.

There are two unspoken rules: always share the drugs, and never screw each other over. And I have to say, since the day I hooked up with this bunch, no one has broken the rules.

Steve has a thick, blond-brown beard and long, scraggly hair. Every day he sits on a crate at an intersection, holding a worn, cardboard sign with dirty fingers. They're dirty because he rubs dirt on them before he goes out. His sign says he's homeless and needs help feeding his kids. Behind it, he hides a beer and he sneaks swigs from it when he can. Sometimes he makes a hundred bucks a day, not counting beer money.

Tammy is in her early twenties and scrawny. She's in and out of the room all day and always makes a few hundred bucks by late afternoon. Usually she is soft-spoken, talking with a whisper. You have to lean in close and listen hard to know what she's saying. But in the mid-afternoon she always brings back two large pizzas, and if we say we aren't hungry, she looks at us sideways and her voice gets sharp. If we don't eat, she says, we ain't getting high with a goddamn cent of her money. So we eat.

Mick, I have no idea how he gets his money. He's in his mid-twenties and wears glasses and Oxford shirts and pressed pants and takes his laptop with him everywhere. Sometimes I think he's one of those undercover reporters, secretly working on a story about homelessness or addiction or something like that. But he gets high right along with us, and he contributes, too. He leaves late morning and comes back in the afternoon with a single one-hundred-dollar bill, like clockwork.

Me, I don't do much at all. I still have a valid driver's license, which we need to rent the room in the first place. That's my main contribution. But I also steal stuff and pawn it when an opportunity stares me right in the face.

Compared to them, I'm old as dirt. I've got almost twenty years on each of them, and they don't know anything about rock and roll, either. But I don't care – it's nice having people close by. When we get high I still get paranoid, but not as bad because they help me. They look out the window for me and tell me there's really no one there. And when the crack's all gone, they don't try to get more. They try to get some sleep, and they share their pills with me that help us all crash.

I'm thinking that maybe they care about me a little. Maybe they think I'm like a crazy uncle or something. I don't know. It's better than being alone, though. It seems like being around people helps me be a bit saner.

I make a mental note of that one. I need to think about that some more.

My phone rings, and I pull it out.

It's my brother.

It's not that I don't want to talk to Bob. What it is, is this: we're not going to just shoot the shit or talk baseball. No, he'll ask questions about why I'm doing what I'm doing. He'll ask me why I don't just stop. Mom and Dad are worried about you, he'll say.

He'll say things that make me feel guilty.

Liz knows I won't take calls when I'm getting high. So she doesn't bother. Instead, she texts me photos of her children. School pics. Or in-the-yard-smiling pics. Or we-love-you-Uncle-Donny pics. She sends them with short texts:

They love you, Donny. We all do. We hope you're okay.

When I see the pics and read the texts, I'm crushed even more than I already am.

My brother just calls and leaves voicemails, and he's left three in the past two days.

I take the call.

"Hey, bro, how's it going?" I ask.

"Hey!" he almost shouts. "You all right?"

"Yeah, I'm doing good. Hanging in there."

"Where are you? Got a place to stay?"

"I'm at a motel in St. Pete," I tell him. "Everything's good. How about you?"

"All good. Let's go grab a bite – I'll come get you."

"I don't know, Bob. I kinda got some stuff going on."

"C'mon, bro," he says. "Let's hang out for a few. I'll be down there in fifteen."

I shift my feet, then look back at the room. If I say yes, Mick will probably get back the moment I leave. I can meet my brother later, instead.

Then I see myself. I'm sprawled out on the motel room floor between the two twin beds. A crack pipe lies on the floor by my hand, and paramedics surround me, trying to resuscitate me. But my eyes are glassed over and my face is gray. I'm already gone.

I don't know why that flashed through my brain, and I'm definitely not superstitious. But it's enough to change my mind.

"Okay," I tell Bob. "I'll see you in fifteen."

I poke my head into the room and tell them I'll be back in an hour.

I walk five blocks to a breakfast joint and sit on a bench outside. Ten minutes later, Bob and I are inside at a booth. We order eggs and bacon and start talking. We don't mention addiction or where I'm staying or whether I should go to detox. Instead, we keep it light. We talk about new albums. New bands. Who's playing out at local clubs. He shows me prank video clips on YouTube, and we laugh our asses off. It's the third time he's showed me a few of them but I don't care. An hour flies by like it's five minutes.

Bob picks up the tab, and we step out into the parking lot.

"Well, all right, dude." He looks at me. "I just wanted to see you for a bit. You going to be all right?"

"Yeah, I'm good."

Mick must be back by now. If they're not getting high already, they're about to. Yet part of me doesn't even care. I wouldn't mind talking about bands all night long with my brother.

And then, it begins.

"Man, why do you keep doing this?" he asks. "Just stop and come with me, bro."

"I can't. I want to, I really do. But I can't."

"You can. We'll figure it out."

"There's no figuring this out," I tell him. "I wish I could, but I can't."

"Please." He's almost begging now. "How can we help? What can we do? Cuz man, if you keep this up you might not make it."

My brother loves me, I know. My whole family does. Yet here I am, torturing them. By merely living, by continuing to exist,

I'm causing them to suffer. I should've jumped in front of that bus. But I'm selfish.

I'm a coward.

Guilt and shame barrage me – they slam into me like a truck. I burst into tears and there I am, doubled over with my hands on my knees, bawling in the parking lot.

"There's something wrong with me, Bob," I spit out. "And I don't know what it is."

I've completely lost it. In between sobs, I'm babbling about what a horrible brother I am. What a terrible son I've been. That I'm a human deformity and a total fucking loser. And then I hear myself say something strange.

I say that somehow, despite all of this, I'm going home. I don't know how, and I don't know when, I say, but I'm going home.

It's so odd to my ears that it makes me snap out of it. I straighten myself up and I wipe the snot from my face and clear my throat.

"Sorry," I say. "I, uh, I just had a moment."

His eyes are red, and his hand covers his mouth.

"I'll be in touch," he manages. "Pick up the phone when I call, okay?"

I nod my head.

"I'm going to try to help. I don't know how. But I'll be in touch."

He hugs me and tells me it's going to be okay. He reminds me to look for that call.

I turn around and begin the walk back to the room.

I've got three and a half years on Bob. But I think we both know the deal. Age, it's just a number.

Really, he's the older brother.

20

FRIENDS

I'm seated at a bus stop right in front of a hospital. I'm leaning forward slightly and I'm stretched as tall as I can, peering over the traffic.

No bus yet.

I'm a bit early – three more minutes and it will be here. I close my eyes. I take a moment and inhale pure positivity. I envision goodness filling my lungs and pumping through my veins. I smile. I'm finally on the right track. I've been meditating again. I've been doing push-ups. I've been eating good.

I've been clean for three and a half weeks.

Detox was exactly what I needed. I'm finally going to make it because I care about me. Others care about me. People are for me and not against me. And whoever or whatever isn't for me, I've officially disinvited them from my life. That includes stress, worry, and anything that doesn't serve me.

I'm going to practice all the things we talked about at detox. I'm going to remember that feelings are a part of reality, and I won't try to ignore them and numb them with drugs anymore. No, I'll *feel* my feelings. I'll sit through them instead of running away. I'm going to find regular meetings and make friends, too, because I'm going to need them.

It was the day before I went into detox that I got the call from my brother. The renters who moved in the house after me had finally moved out, Bob said. My mom and dad were giving me one more chance. I could move back if I promised to go to detox, stay clean and go to meetings.

I was at the YMCA when he called, rummaging through open lockers and looking for wallets and loose cash. When he gave me the news, the wallet in my hand dropped to the floor with a small thud. I left it there and headed straight for a bench out front. I took a seat and didn't budge. I didn't even think about going back to the motel room and telling anyone goodbye. When Bob pulled up moments later, he took me to the house and handed me the keys. He gave me a hug and wished me luck, and he was gone.

I had plenty of rope to hang myself, but I didn't. I arranged an intake appointment at the hospital for the following day, spent one night at the house, then checked myself in. When I did, the staff told me I could check myself out any time I wanted.

I stayed.

I'm glad I did because right now, there's nothing stopping me. I just need to do what my counselors and I agreed upon, which is simple. I'll take myself to some meetings and put myself out there and talk to people. It's going to be weird, but I'll push through it. I'm convinced that if I do, it will turn out *more* than okay.

I envision it in my mind. I walk up to a small crowd after a meeting. There's three or four of them – there's a couple girls and a guy, or the other way around. They turn to me as I approach, and their faces light up and they extend their hands to shake mine. "Dude," they exclaim, "we see you are clearly an amazing person – welcome to our circle of friends!"

That's my cue to introduce myself.

I tell them I'm Don and with that, I've done my part. A week passes and I've already joined their softball team, we watch bands together, and we laugh and live and stay clean together.

I finally have my own crew.

It's going to be great because at last I get it: my life depends on being connected with other people. It's like oxygen to my soul. That's how one of the counselors had put it.

Tonight, I'm going to do my part and make it happen. I know I default to the overly positive sometimes. Maybe borderline unrealistic. But positive is okay, the counselors told me, as long as I also accept that I may face a bit of rejection. But then again, maybe I won't. It might go *better* than what I'm imagining. But however it goes, I'm in it to win it.

I've got to have that oxygen, because I've been suffocating a long time.

IT'S MY FIRST NIGHT OUT OF DETOX, AND I STEP OFF the bus. After a two-block walk, I'm standing in front of the place. It's an old, framed house with a wide front porch. There are a few people sitting out front, drinking coffee and smoking cigarettes. There's a sign out there with big bold letters: *The Serenity Club.*

It reminds me of the Freedom House. I step inside and explore. There's a pool table and a bar that serves only coffee, water, and soft drinks. I walk through a hallway over creaky wooden floors, poking my head into the meeting spaces. I finally find the right one, and I go in and take a seat.

I'm early, but it fills up quickly. Ten minutes later and there must be fifty people in there. They're all yakking away like they've known each other for years. When the meeting starts, I don't even notice; I'm too busy people-watching.

Afterward, everyone spills out a side door. I follow them, then I lean against the side of the building with my hands stuffed in my pockets. People are in small groups, talking and laughing like they're having a blast.

I'm not. I'm stuck and I feel all alone.

I'm having second thoughts about making friends tonight. I can find another meeting tomorrow night. But I've got to hand it to myself – for my first night, I didn't do bad at all.

Kudos to me.

I'm about to walk away when this guy steps right up to me and sticks his hand out.

"Hey, how's it going?" He's got a huge grin and lots of teeth. "I'm James."

He's about my height, maybe ten years older. He's got a short goatee and he's wearing a tweed blazer.

He doesn't look like a dope fiend. I wonder if he's a cop.

"Um, how's it going?" I shake his hand. "I'm Don."

"New to meetings?" he asks.

"No way," I tell him. "I've been to lots."

"Cool. How long have you been clean?"

"A little over three weeks. Just got out of detox today."

"Congrats! Three weeks is a miracle. It really is."

If he only knew.

"How about you?" I ask. "How long have you been clean?"

"Well, last week I celebrated twenty years."

"Serious?"

"Yeah man, twenty years." He chuckles. "I know, it sounds crazy. But it's possible, and you can get there, too."

I'd be thrilled to get just one year. Shit, six months would be awesome.

A tall, lanky dude steps up next to James. He's in his mid-thirties and his hair hangs past his shoulders. His faded jeans have patches of white on them. Dried grout, it looks like. He does tile work.

My dad had a tile business once.

"Hey, Don, this is Michael," James says.

"What's up, bro." Michael sticks out his hand and we shake.

"Michael has almost four weeks clean," James says. "Like you."

"Oh, yeah?" I look back at Michael. "Cool, man."

"Yeah, it is," he says. "I've been working with James and so far, so good."

I nod. I can't see James getting high at all. But Michael? Definitely.

"Do you have a sponsor?" James asks.

"No, but I'm working on it."

"Good." He strokes his chin. "Y'know, I have room for one more if you're interested. We can work together, even if it's just temporary. For now, it's important you start meeting people and get to know your way around. Michael and I can help you with that."

I look at Michael.

"Yeah, man," he chimes in. "Sounds like a great move for you, bro."

I trust Michael. I look back at James. I think I trust him, too.

"Okay. I'm on board."

"Great," James says. "All three of us can hit a few meetings together every week. Hang out a bit. Sound good?"

It sounds fantastic. I nod my head yes.

"Now one thing. No pressure, but I'm going to be straight up with you. When someone agrees to work with me, I look at it like this: what they really want me to do is help save their life. It's important, so we need to dive right in and get to work."

"Um, okay. What kind of work?"

"For now, there's three things I want you to do every day," James says.

I nod.

"I want you to call me once a day. If you get my voicemail,

just leave a short message and check in with me. It's important you do this because you're going to build a habit that will save your ass. Can you do that?"

"Yeah, that's easy."

"Okay. And the second thing is I want you to go to one meeting a day. We'll go to a few each week together, but when we don't you've got to get to a meeting on your own. There's at least ten a day around here so that should be easy. Sound good?"

"Yeah, sure thing."

"Okay. And there's only one more thing."

"What's that?"

"At each meeting, I want you to raise your hand and share. When you do, I want you to say one thing and one thing only. Say, 'My name is Don, and today I have a choice. Thanks for letting me share.'"

"That's it? Nothing else?"

"Yep, that's it. If you do that, after thirty days everyone will know who you are. You're going to meet plenty of people. And not only that, it will start to finally sink in. You really *do* have a choice."

He said *finally sink in*. Like he knows that's exactly what I need. I wonder if he's some kind of guru. I look at Michael. Maybe he is, too.

"Okay, I'll do it."

When they drop me off at my house, I go to my room and lie down and gaze at the ceiling. The stars and the moon are still up there, glowing and smiling down upon me. I remember looking upon them that first night at this house, and the excitement and hope I felt then.

I feel it tonight, too. I'm on the verge of something. Somehow, things are about to finally turn around for me.

THERE ARE MEETINGS GALORE AROUND HERE.
Sunrise meetings. Noon meetings. After-work meetings. Night
meetings. And they're everywhere. In churches. Parks. Ware-
houses. There are even meetings at the beach – right on the
sand.

James and Michael pick me up on a Sunday morning to go to
a meeting on Indian Rocks Beach. We pull up and we make our
way through a winding trail through some sandy dunes. It's the
last week of September, and in between the cool gusts of wind
the sun is direct and warm and the sky is a solid blue. There's
not a cloud in sight.

We approach, and there's about twenty people in the circle
already. The meeting starts in five minutes, and we take our
seats on the sand. There's one spot left, and whoever sits there
will complete the circle.

That spot is right next to me.

I look down the beach to see if anyone else is coming.

A woman emerges from the trail. She has on a wide floppy
straw hat and large Hollywood sunglasses. She walks toward us
with her hand on the hat, keeping it steady in the breeze. She
approaches and sits down next to me. I look over at her.

"Hi." I smile at her.

"Hi." She smiles back. "I'm Bri."

"I'm Don."

I want to keep it going. I want to ask her something remark-
able. Something that shows my depth and experience. Like,
Wow, that hat – is it an Estée Lauder?

But I'm stuck, and before I'm able to pry my tongue from the
roof of my mouth the meeting starts. When it does, the chairperson kicks it off with a question. He asks whether there's
anyone who's new and wants to introduce themselves.

Bri's hand shoots up.

"Hi, I'm new." She looks around at everyone and flashes that smile again. "I just got out of detox yesterday, and I'm so glad to be here. I'm staying at a women's halfway house nearby and I really need to get to know other people in recovery."

After Bri speaks, there's another fifty minutes of people talking and sharing and making announcements. But I don't hear a word. All I can think about is her. That Bri, she's got some audacity. She put it all out there and flat-out asked for help. That's way more guts than I've ever had. Which is a good thing, but it's a scary thing, too. Now everyone knows, which makes her vulnerable.

I look around the group and narrow my eyes as I take in each member. I feel a deep scowl forming on my face. I'm looking for vultures.

They'd better leave her the hell alone.

I glance at her again. Had she used like a complete maniac like I did? I doubt it. She probably just went a little bit off the deep end in college.

I say a quick prayer for her. I hope she does okay. There's something about her and the way she speaks. I can't put my finger on it, but it's soothing. It's *familiar*.

Soulmate? I laugh at myself. I don't really believe in soulmates. But if there *were* a real thing, maybe this is what it would feel like.

When it's over, James and Michael and I make our way through the beach trail back to the car.

"Pretty good meeting, huh?" I ask.

"I love the beach meetings," Michael says. "Nice vibe out here."

"Yeah, sure was. See that lady who sat right next to me?"

"Um, yeah – what's her name?"

"Bri."

How could he not remember?

"Man, I know it sounds crazy, but I had this feeling like I knew her already or something. She seems really cool."

We walk the rest of the way to the car in silence. When we pile in, James puts the keys in the ignition, then he turns around and looks straight at me.

"Want some solid advice, Don?"

"Sure."

"A good rule of thumb is that before you think about getting into a relationship, make sure you know at least one person who's going to be in it."

Michael busts out laughing and slaps his knee.

"Good one, James!"

I laugh, too – after we're a couple miles down the road.

A FEW WEEKS LATER, I WALK INTO THE MEETING ROOM of the Serenity Club. It's almost full, and I spot Michael in the third row. I squeeze my way through the row of chairs and take the seat next to him.

"Hey, brother!" he says. "How's it going?"

"Great, man. You?"

"Life is good. Can't complain."

I can't either. I look around the room. It's the same room it was a few weeks ago, but different. Now I know people. I wave to them when they come in and take their seats, and they smile and wave back and say hi. I'm starting to feel like I belong.

I've made friends I hang out with, too. When they walk through the door and find their seats, we greet each other and chat it up a bit.

Don Dortch walks in. He's the only other Don I know. He's about ten years older than me and he always wears a baseball hat. Sometimes red and other times, blue. He's given me a ride home a few times, too. On the way we always stop by a breakfast place first. We talk over scrambled eggs and coffee. We're going to do that tonight. He makes his way down my row and takes a seat by Michael and me.

Kevin and Kim are here. He's six foot four with long, wavy blond hair. She's five-two, with dark brown skin and a huge smile and heart. We hug before they take their seats. Kevin and Kim used to roam the streets and get high together, but now they come here together. Kim works at a women's halfway house, the one Bri lives at. Kevin and Kim have been talking about starting their own sober living home and helping others.

Bri comes in next. She's with her friend Meg, and they sit down in the row in front of us. Bri turns around and looks deep into my eyes.

I squirm.

"Um, how's it going, Bri?"

I think my voice cracked.

"It's going well, Don," she smiles. "How have you been?"

Right now, I'm fabulous. Bri and I have this connection and it's fire. We've talked maybe three or four times, and afterward I'm always stranded, lost on some back street in la-la land.

James says that according to many experts, that familiar feeling I'm talking about is what people feel when they subconsciously seek out the same unhealthy partner type they've always had before.

As in, codependency.

Just food for thought, he says.

I think that's bullshit. I don't have any patterns I'm subconsciously trying to perpetuate. Not with women, anyway. I'm practically a virgin because I've been away so long – both in prison *and* in oblivion. Which means that when it comes to relationships, I'm a clean slate.

As in, baggage-free.

"I've been good," I manage. "How about you? Getting used to things?"

"Yeah, it's going well. I applied for school at St. Pete College, and things are looking up." She flashes me another smile. "Nice talking to you, Don."

"You, too."

She turns around and faces the front again.

I sigh. I'm so stupid. And crazy, too. She's just being friendly, and I'm just imagining things. Like a creeper.

I remind myself of the truth: it doesn't matter if she likes me or not. It doesn't matter because change is coming in my life. God really *does* have my back, and I can feel it approaching. Good things are right around the corner – in spite of my stupid.

In spite of my crazy.

Yeah, life is looking good, and I'm going to live it – with or without her.

But it would be really nice to live it with her.

When we talk about Bri, James makes a lot of good points. He's got a lot of jokes when he makes them, too. But he's right – I need to focus on me right now, so that's what I'm doing. I try to keep it moving with her. I try to not stare too long. I try to pay attention to the meeting. Which is difficult, because whenever she's around, the next thing I know the meeting's over and I haven't heard a word.

Michael knows. Which is why right now he's elbowing me in the ribs. I snap out of it and look around.

The meeting's almost over. It's time to do my thing.

I throw my hand in the air, and the chairperson calls my name.

"I'm Don and I'm an addict," I announce. Bri turns around in her seat. From the corner of my eye, I see it. Another gorgeous smile. But I don't make eye contact. No, I hold it together like a champ and I finish what I have to say.

"And today," I tell everyone, "I have a choice. Thanks for letting me share."

Everyone claps. Some people are laughing. They hear it every night from me. And that's okay because it's right for me. For one, I committed to James I'd do it. And two, sometimes after the meeting people tell me it helps them. It reminds them that they have a choice, too. It's a good feeling to know I'm actually helping someone.

I think it's helping me, too. Because this new voice, the one that speaks these words every night at the meetings, it's different than the ones that have been in my head. At first it sounded fake and weak to my ears, but not anymore. It's starting to sound real.

Today, I'm starting to think I really do have a choice. Because today, I've got almost two months clean. And that's without even being in a program or some group home. I did this with just me and some friends.

Actually, that's not all. I feel like there is something much bigger than me, too. Something that cares for me on some level I can't define. And I'm glad I don't have to.

Yes, today, I have a choice. And I also have hope – hope that I'm about to finally get my life back. Actually, that's not exactly right because in a way, I never really had one.

I believe something better is going to happen. I'm going to get an entirely new one.

21

GUNS

I've been clean for almost three months.

I've got friends. I like Bri a lot, and I'm pretty sure she likes me. I've been working for Rick again and I'm starting to make money. I haven't heard a single peep from the FBI. Yolanda says if I keep doing well, the courts will eventually dismiss the bank robbery charge.

Things are looking up. But there's this one thing…

Something's not right, and I can't quite put my finger on it. But whatever it is, it's growing. It's creeping.

Wait, I know what it is.

It's that itch again.

It's insane, I know. After all I've been through, I'm baffled at how it can still get a grip on my brain. It's beyond explanation. Maybe I haven't learned a damn thing.

Maybe I *can't* learn. Like, maybe I have some kind of learning disability.

I could blame it on the job. That would be easy because I *am* working my ass off again and I'm getting stressed out from the hustling and the deals. I've been so caught up with work this past month that everything else has become an afterthought.

But I know that's bullshit. It's not the job. What it is, I think, is that the newness has worn off. It's just not exciting anymore. I find myself asking the question: is this all there is – going to work, to meetings, and having breakfast at 10 p.m. with Don Dortch in random diners?

I think about talking to James about it, but I can't because I feel stupid. I shouldn't be going through this in the first place. I should be grateful. Gung-ho and motivated. But I'm none of those things.

I'm just bored.

Luckily, I have a solution. I know exactly how I can spice things up. Lightning bolts shoot down my spine and my heart quivers at the very thought of it.

Now *that's* excitement.

I'm thinking about taking two hundred dollars, buying some crack, and holing up in a dirty motel for just a few quick hours. And when I run out of dope, I'll simply stop. I'll pack it up and leave and go back to my house and pretend it never happened.

Just like that.

I know, it sounds like I'm bullshitting myself because I've never been able to stop before. I don't deny it. But now, something's different. Because today, I have something I never before.

Today, I have a choice.

So I do it. I get the money and the crack and the room. And when I spend all my money and I'm out of dope, my body and mind scream for more. I've been fooled once again, and I know that absolutely nothing has changed.

Now that I've begun, I know that today I no longer have a choice.

I shake and tremble and I want to cry. That first hit was like Russian Roulette – I had no idea where it would take me, and I still don't. I'm afraid. But right now, there's something way more important than being scared.

I need more crack.

I take a bus to work. It's night and the place is empty. I let myself in quietly with my key, and I rummage through Rick's desk. He's hidden the company checks from me, but I search until I find them and I write one to myself for fifteen hundred. I catch a cab to an Amscot and cash it, then I head to a motel. Two days later, when the money is gone, I write another check and find another motel room.

But this time I can't find dope. I walk the motel parking lot. I walk the few blocks around the motel. I wander the streets a quarter mile and back, looking for familiar faces.

There's no one.

I've been up for three days and I'm getting tired of dragging this body around. And that's when I see her. She's leaning against the side of the store, barefoot with red shorts and a soiled white T-shirt. I've never met her. I've never even seen her before in my life. Yet, I know who she is.

She's a crackhead just like me.

I ask her if she can get any. She says she can, but I have to share. No problem, I say. She walks behind the store and returns, and we walk back to my room.

The dope is good. So good that after one hit, I run to the bathroom in a panic and lock myself in. My ears are ringing, and I start to sweat. I'm certain the cops are about to break down the door. When I finally calm down, I come out of the bathroom.

She's gone.

And so is the rest of the money. And almost all the drugs.

I dig in my pocket. The pipe is there. A few hits of crack are left on the nightstand, and I stuff all of it in the pipe and hold a lighter to it. I fill my lungs till they can hold no more, then I blow the smoke out fast and take a second hit before the first rush hits me. When it does, my vision dims and my knees buckle. I did too much, I realize. I begin falling to the floor in slow motion, and on the way down, everything goes black.

I don't know how long I lie there. But when I come to and

open my eyes, I can't see. I wonder if someone came in the room and shut the lights off. Maybe they're in here now. If they are, I wouldn't know because I can't hear, either. I try to move, and my body won't budge.

I'm blind, deaf, and paralyzed.

Maybe I fell and broke my neck, I think. Or maybe I'm dead. Maybe this is how I'll spend eternity. Any moment, I'll see little devils with sharp pitchforks, like the kind on the hot sauce label. For the remainder of eternity, they'll stick me and poke me and howl at me for wasting this life.

My vision slowly returns. The lights in the room are still on. No, I'm not in hell – but I'm close. I'm sprawled out face down on the floor. A crumpled cigarette butt is on the carpet just a few inches from the tip of my nose. There's a dull ache in my jaw and the taste of copper fills my mouth. It's my blood; I feel it between my teeth and coating my tongue. When I suck in a breath of air, there's a low gurgle in my chest and sharp pain in my left ribs. The ringing in my ears fades to a low hum.

I lift myself to my hands and knees, and that's when someone starts to pound on the door.

"Hey, motherfucker, I know you're in there!"

It's not the cops.

"If I don't get my shit, I swear to God I'm gonna kill your ass!"

I have no idea who it is but clearly, they're pissed.

The woman. It's got something to do with her. She must have burned them, and now they think I have their money. Or their drugs.

Or both.

Footsteps scuff on the sidewalk as they walk away. Then they come back. There's a voice outside my door. Then there's two, maybe three. Then footsteps walking away again.

And then, silence.

I need to get out of here, I think. Like right now. I pull

myself up and go to the door. I turn the deadbolt and crack the door slightly and peek out. It's night, and I scan the parking lot.

It's empty.

I fling open the door and half-walk, half-run to Thirty-Fourth. I hear feet on the pavement behind me, so I break into a sprint and bolt into the street without looking. I land on the median. Cars are whizzing past at fifty miles an hour in both directions. I look back. A couple dudes are on the sidewalk, pointing at me and screaming. The traffic is too heavy – they can't get to me. I lose my balance and almost fall, but I'm able to steady myself. The median is wider than a balance beam, but not by much. I run north on it as fast as I can.

In the corner of my eyes I see them. They're running parallel to me on the sidewalk. I run faster, but I can't look forward or I'll be blinded by the headlights of oncoming traffic. The cars zoom toward me then whish past a couple feet to my left. I collapse and stumble, almost falling into an oncoming car. A horn beeps in my face as I dart to my feet and keep sprinting forward. To my left, I hear a gunshot. Then another. I don't bother looking – I can't. I need to keep moving forward. Death is at my heels and I can hear it panting as my body plunges forward in the dark.

Ahead, there's a four-way streetlight with a gas station on the south corner. I cut across the street through traffic and burst through the front door.

"There's someone out there with a gun!" I scream. "Call the cops!"

There's a woman behind the counter. Her eyes are wide and her mouth is gaping.

"Where's your restroom?" I yell.

She's frozen.

"Where's your goddamn restroom?"

She raises her arm and points toward the back.

I run inside the bathroom and bolt the door behind me. I

crouch between the toilet and the wall and hug my knees against my chest.

I'm going to die, I just know it. Bullets are going to start flying through that door or I'm going to have a heart attack. Whatever comes first.

I wait.

I hear police radios, instead. For a moment, I wonder if they're real. And then, there's loud pounding on the bathroom door.

"Police! Unlock the door, step back, and keep your hands in view!"

I decide it's real.

I unlock the door, and the second I do it bursts open. The next thing I know, two huge cops are on top of me, pushing my face into the grimy tile floor. A third stands behind them, his gun drawn. I'm spread eagle, and the officers pat me down and lift me to my feet. They spin me around, and one pushes my head back against the door and puts his face in mine. His eyes dart from my left eye to my right.

"When's the last time you smoked crack?"

"Um, fifteen minutes ago."

"Got any on you?"

"No."

He studies my eyes a moment, then he spins me around and slaps handcuffs on me and walks me out of the gas station.

"Stand here," he snaps.

I look around the parking lot and the street while the officers sit in the squad car. I don't see anyone with guns except the cops. But they could be on the side of the building. Or across the street. They could be anywhere.

I'm a sitting duck.

The officer gets out of the car and tells me to turn around. I do, and he removes the cuffs.

"Get out of here," he barks.

"Serious?" I stare at him. "You're not going to take me to jail?"

"Nope," he replies. "You didn't do anything wrong, and you don't have any drugs on you."

"Fuck, man, can't you give me a ride a few blocks north, at least?" I plead. "There's people after me."

"No one's after you," he laughs. "You're just freaking out. You're in psychosis."

"No, I'm for real!" I protest. "They were shooting at me!"

"Oh, yeah? See that guy over there?"

He points across the street to a bus stop. There's a scraggly guy sitting there with a blanket wrapped around him next to a shopping cart that's packed with cardboard boxes and scrap metal.

"He's been there over an hour and he hasn't heard a single shot." The officer smirks. "Neither has anyone else around here."

"Man, that can't be. You've got to help me."

"Look," he says. "This is *your* problem. You caused it, so you handle it."

I sway a bit, and everything goes out of focus.

I'm losing my balance.

The next thing I know I'm on the sidewalk, lying on my back. Rick is kneeling over me. He's talking to me, then to the cop. And then I'm in the backseat of a car.

Rick's car.

"Rick? That you?"

"Yeah. You okay?"

"I think so," I mumble. "I'm really sorry, man. I think I cashed a check or two."

"Don't worry about it right now. We're going to get you somewhere safe."

"Man, thanks. I really appreciate that."

"It's all good, bro. I know you'd do the same for me."

I don't quite know what to say to that.

I pass out again and when I wake up, someone's asking for my name and my age. Then, my social security number. I'm being admitted somewhere.

And that's the last thing that I remember.

PART III

22

DOMINOES

A scream pierces through my thick slumber. Someone's begging somebody, or something, to stop. I open my eyes slowly. I'm lying on my side, and there's a grey concrete wall a few inches from my nose. An icy draft is blowing directly on my bare toes. I look down. A worn, green blanket is wrapped around my body, and it stops at my ankles. I unravel myself from the blanket and prop up on an elbow.

My head's pounding. My tongue is thick and heavy, and my mouth tastes like cat shit.

I'm beyond groggy.

I force my eyes open as wide as I can, and I suck in air until my lungs can take no more.

The door is a few inches ajar, and outside of it there's a cluster of couches. A woman with a mop of gray hair is seated on one of them in front of a small TV. She clutches a green blanket like mine tightly around her body as she rocks back and forth, her eyes fixed on the television.

I lay my head back down on the thin pillow and sigh.

I've been here before – It's *PEHMS*, a mental health crisis unit.

When they call me to the nurses' station, they tell me why I'm here: acute psychosis. It's related to my primary diagnosis of schizophrenia, they say, which is a slam-dunk since it's my second time here for the same type of thing.

I disagree. I tell them I'm not delusional at all. I know for sure there's no one after me. In fact, I'm relaxed and calm. I'm serene, I tell them. I smile.

See?

Can I go now? *Please?*

Not a chance, they say. They need a few days of observation before we even talk about it.

A few days pass and I'm in no rush to go. They have daily support groups here, and I like them. I talk about how I want to stay clean and pick up where I left off with James and Michael and my friends, and with Bri. When you boil it down, it seems like everyone else here wants the same thing. I've met a few people I like, and we talk about our lives as we eat our meals in the cafeteria. And with every meal, they have chocolate milk – all you can drink.

Things could be *much* worse.

There's another reason I'm in no hurry. I no longer have a place to go when I get out. I found out when I called my parents yesterday.

"Don, you can't stay at the house," my dad had told me. "We need our lives back. You're going to have to figure it out for yourself this time."

I want them to have their lives back, too. They deserve it.

Plus, I've realized something. The house, that's all it ever was. Just a house. A physical structure in a geographical location. It was never really my *home*. Not compared to what I've experienced the past few months. I'm thinking that home is what happened when I was *not* in that house. Like finally having friends. Hanging out with them. Having a sense of purpose and feeling like I was going somewhere.

I think home is more like a good feeling deep inside. One that lets me know I'm right where I'm supposed to be. I'm thinking that maybe home is anywhere that I know for sure that today, I have a choice. Which means that I can be at home right here.

In a mental ward.

It's day three at the crisis unit when I come to this realization. The moment I do, a caseworker pulls me into his office and tells me they're discharging me the next day. He asks for my address. They need it for release paperwork, he explains.

I tell him I don't have one. He makes a call to a homeless shelter and gets me on the waiting list. Now I do, he says, and I need to call the shelter daily to keep my place on the list. A bed should open up within a week.

When I leave his office, I return to the ward and I call James. I haven't spoken with him in a week, and I bring him up to speed. I tell him everything. I tell him about getting high and what happened at the motel and the gas station. I tell him that I'm at a mental hospital.

I tell him I'm sorry.

I grip the phone and my body tenses as I wait for his response.

"Wow, sounds like you've been through a lot. Glad you survived."

I relax slightly.

"Yeah, me too."

"I'll be honest, Don. I'm glad you made it, but I'm disappointed because we've been clear. If you want me to help, you've got to let me in. You can't trust your thinking right now. You've got to tell someone you trust what's going on with you because it will save your life."

I'm nodding my head as he speaks. He's right and I know it.

"Y'know, back when I was just getting clean," he continues, "I called my sponsor one day and he asked me where I was. I said, 'In my living room.' Then he asked if I was alone. I told him I was. And then he started screaming at me at the top of his lungs. He said, 'James, get the hell out of there! Quick – right now!!' He said it like it was an emergency, and I figured he must know something I didn't. So I ran straight out the front door and onto the front lawn – in my boxers!"

I began to chuckle.

"Then, y'know what he told me?"

"What?"

"He said, 'James, do you realize that just now, you were all alone in a house with a fucking maniac?'"

I roar with laughter.

"Don, it's true," James says. "Right now, when you're all by yourself, you're with an insane person. But it's nothing to be ashamed of – you just can't manage it all by yourself. And that's why I'm here.

"The good news is that it will get better," he continues. "Your thinking will change as your own truth begins to take shape. And instead of taking you out, your truth will take you up – to places you never dreamed. It just takes some time, brother. And lots of work."

James is a good dude. I'm really lucky we met. I decide that going forward, I'm going to trust him.

"Okay, so there's a recovery workshop this Saturday," he says. "Michael and I are going – want me to pick you up?"

"Yeah, but I have no idea where I'll be."

"Don't sweat it. We'll find a couch you can crash on till you get to the shelter."

When I hang up the phone, I think I've caught a second wind. I'm ready to give it another shot.

I GET OUT OF THE HOSPITAL THE NEXT DAY AND I'M

all set up. I have a couch for a week, which is all I need. During the day when no one's at home I have to leave, so I spend my time at the public library flipping through self-help books. I check out *A Return to Love* and *Awakening the Giant Within*. I finish both in a few days. There's something about them that speaks to me. I sense that somehow fear has been my enemy, and that love is the answer. And I've always believed I really do have a giant within. The problem is, I think mine might be Godzilla.

But there's got to be a flip side to that, I think. Maybe my giant can make something strong and beautiful out of this wreckage.

Something *great*. Something based in love, and not fear.

I feel like the dots are starting to connect, and I think I'm getting closer. Whatever it is, I pray I find it – or that it finds me – before it's too late.

Every day I call the shelter. And every night I go with James and Michael to a meeting. I try to cling to my truth. *The* truth. That somehow, I'm going home.

THE DAY THE WORKSHOP ARRIVES, IT'S OVERCAST AND cold and windy. James and Michael pick me up, and it's drizzling all the way to St. Pete. We pull up outside an old, red-brick church with a huge cross by the front doors and we park out front.

"Is this a religious thing?" I ask.

"Nope. The people who put on the event rent space from the church, that's all." James smiles. "But if you listen really hard, you just might have an awakening."

We count to three, then we run and duck under the front foyer, out of the rain. A tall guy welcomes us and points us to a room in the back. There's a bunch of chairs in there, and about fifteen people are seated already. We take our seats, and a few minutes later, it's underway.

A pudgy guy with curly grey hair is speaking. His voice is nasally, and I'm annoyed already. It's going to be a long six hours. He says we'll have a short break about every hour, and halfway through, we'll have pizza for lunch.

Someone hands out pens and pads of paper, while he tells us to be ready to do some soul-searching.

I thought we'd jump right into talking about drugs. But we don't go there at all. Instead, the first part is about a mindset. He's talking about a particular mindset, one that often goes along with addiction. It goes with other things, too, but right now addiction is the context, he says. He's focusing on why some people keep going back to using dope, even when they know it's ruining their lives. He's asking why, when people get over the physical part of addiction and get out of detox or rehab or whatever, would they go back to the same shit over and over again? *Who does that?* he asks.

I almost raise my hand.

It's way beyond physical addiction, he continues. What those kinds of people usually share in common, he says, is that they're in the grip. But it's not drugs that's gripping them.

It's *self-centered fear*.

I cock my head slightly at that one. I'm all ears.

He keeps explaining. These types of people are like one-year-olds. They think everything that happens around them is *about* them. They might not be conscious of it, but on some level they believe that everyone else is focused on them. And while most one-year-olds grow out of this mindset, he says, these people have not. As a result, their growth has been stunted.

They wind up with a mental posture of fear and defensiveness. Insecure at their core, they need validation and constant reassurance that they are okay. They try to get it from others or from some fantasy, or from a substance or some experience that doesn't last. But regardless of how they get it, it's never enough. They're uncomfortable in their own skin, which makes connecting with others difficult, if not impossible. It's like they're in a war zone, and intimacy and trust are the land mines. So, what do they do? They build strong walls. They avoid connecting, and isolation becomes their comfort zone. Like a trench in the midst of a hellish war.

Me: This guy is a maniac. He made this entire presentation just to fuck with me.

Me: Wow – but my reaction. It's kind of proving his point...

Me: No, it's not. Because anyone who knows me knows I'm not afraid of a damn thing.

Me: Yeah, but he's not talking about being afraid of 'things.' He's talking about being afraid of human beings and connection.

I have no counter to that one. And in that moment, it happens.

The light bulb begins to turn on.

It's true. I've always been afraid. Focused on protecting myself from what I imagine people are thinking of me. From the possibility that I really don't fit in. That there is something wrong with me.

For some reason, I'm scared I'm unworthy and that I'm fucked up to the core.

I've always felt this way on some level. And because of this, I've known only isolation – and not just because I've been locked away physically. This goes way deeper than that. There's actually a prison within me. A cruel, steel fortress that surrounds my very heart and soul, more unforgiving than any correctional facility I've ever been in.

My mind is racing. How did I not see this before?

And *why* am I afraid?

The moment I ask the question, I begin to see the answer. My fears, they're lined up like dominoes. And the domino at the very beginning is the cause of all of my suffering. My problems aren't because of the drugs, or the prison time or because of a diagnosis. At the heart of it, I'm afraid I'm inadequate, that I'm not enough, and that I'm defective. It's all those rolled into one.

This is what's been driving the car all along, steering me into a ditch over and over again.

It's almost too much. My scalp, it becomes all prickly, and chills run down my spine. My mind is officially blown, and my brain is coming undone.

I look around at the faces in the room. They're fixed on the speaker, heads nodding as he talks. I think of the people at meetings I've been to. I think of the college professor in my speech class. Of the judge who gave me twenty years. The newsman on TV. In my mind, I see some of the inmates I left behind in prison, many of whom will surely never get out. I see co-workers and the bosses I've had.

I see my dad and my mom. My brother and sisters.

Are they all better than me? More adequate?

More *real*?

Immediately, I know the answer. It's a big, fat *no*. I'm just as good as they are, and I'm *more* than enough, and I'm definitely not a fake.

Yes, that's the correct answer. Yet deep within, there's a worm of doubt. It's burrowed in there, somewhere deeper than my brain. Is it in my heart? My soul? I don't know, but wherever it is, it's the part within that questions and second-guesses.

Why?

And in this moment, when I need it more than ever, I experience the miracle.

I see scenes from my life, and they play out in my mind's eye like a movie trailer. I'm four, and a neighbor is abusing me, terrifying me beyond description. I see my nine-year-old self, shocked and horrified as Billy commits suicide in front of me. I'm twelve and drunk and handcuffed in the back of a police car, covered in my own puke. Then I'm fourteen, in the corner of that mental hospital room, trying not to bawl my eyes out. I'm eighteen and exhausted on the road, distraught and confused and crying aloud for God to save me. I witness afresh the numerous times I've turned my back on goodness, and instead embraced self-abuse. I watch as previous versions of myself throw my precious life away, over and over again. I experience once more the crush of the suffering I've caused myself – and others as well.

It's all true. My life has been a tragedy. I would never, ever wish it upon anyone. Yet as I watch, I don't cringe. I don't recoil in horror. I'm not angry or disturbed at that, that...that *human being* I see. Nor do I feel the need to cover up what I'm seeing, or to hide it from my own self.

No, instead I embrace it. Because, well, it just is. And it's okay.

I'm okay.

I was just blind, that's all. And who in the world blames anyone for simply being unable to see? No, there's no blame to be had anymore. I've suffered enough.

As I see this truth, compassion floods my soul. It's warm and it's powerful, and I feel a newness that's strange and incomprehensible.

It's empathy – for me, the nine-year-old. The nineteen-year-old. And the thirty-nine-year-old as well.

I'm not the first one to feel this. I've crossed paths with others who loved me simply because they saw my true self. They believed in me. They'd known all along what I am just now beginning to see.

I *am* worthy of love. Just as much as anyone else. As much as those people who are good and beautiful and seem to have all the answers.

As I embrace this, it becomes my truth. And with it, the very foundation of my self-imposed failure, insanity, and self-abuse begins to topple.

Like dominoes.

When we leave the workshop, I'm quiet. I don't feel like saying a whole lot. I just need to process it.

We all get in the car, and as we pull away, James starts talking.

"Don, you get anything out of it?" He looks back at me and grins. "You have an awakening?"

"Yeah. It was definitely a Jesus moment. But I don't think I can explain it right now."

They both laugh, but they know I'm serious.

The only thing I know for sure is that my life has changed. One moment it was headed one way, and now it is headed somewhere entirely different.

It's about damn time.

23

HEP

After five days, a bed at the shelter opens. It's a couple weeks before Christmas, 2011, and on Christmas Eve my whole family will be getting together. They'll be at my parents' house – my brother and sister and their families. They'll all eat dinner together and exchange gifts. My sister's kids will be tracking Santa on some website, hopping up and down with excitement and waiting for the hour when Santa and his reindeer finally get to Tampa Bay. Except for Ashley – she's the newest addition and she just turned one. Yes, my family will be together, warm and cozy on Christmas Eve, drinking hot cocoa by the fireplace.

We don't really have hot cocoa by fireplaces in Tampa Bay. But that's how my mind sees it. And that's how my heart feels it. I want to spend Christmas with my family – not in a homeless shelter.

I think about passing on the shelter. I can always sign up again after Christmas, or maybe after the New Year. But the moment I consider it, I know I can't do that. Because if I manipulate it so that I stay with them for the holidays, that would be my old way – the easy way. But I can't afford the easy way any longer.

It's way too expensive.

The shelter's going to be hard, there's no doubt. But there's another way to look at it. The space they have for me isn't just some bed at a shelter. It's my doorway to success. Going through with this is going to show me what I can do. What I can accomplish, from the dirt up. And on the other side, I know something awaits.

Something great.

I call my parents and ask for help. But I don't ask to stay for Christmas. I don't try to avoid the shelter. I just need help getting there, and I ask them for a ride.

When we pull up, I climb down from my dad's truck and grab a gym bag from the floorboard. It's stuffed with some jeans and T-shirts, a jacket, soap, toothpaste, and my phone charger. I throw the bag over my shoulder and look up at my dad and mom. I want to tell them I've finally seen the light. That I'll never get high again. That everything is different now. But I've said all of that before. So instead, I just thank them and tell them I love them. I turn around and walk through the intake door of HEP – the Homeless Empowerment Program.

After we take care of the paperwork, a staff member walks me to a small, crowded dormitory with metal bunk beds. She shows me to my bunk. It's on the top.

"Your counselor will get in touch with you sometime today," she says. "She'll review your plan and whether HEP might be a long-term fit for you."

I climb up on the bunk and look around the room. There are about fifteen other guys in here. The guy across from me, he's lying there reading a Carl Hiaasen novel. The dude next to me is staring at the ceiling, mumbling. There are a couple scruffy old-timers from New York in the corner, arguing about which home-less shelters are best: New York or Florida.

I say Florida wins. This place is clean, and although I haven't eaten the food yet I hear it's good. The staff and the counselors are pleasant, and they seem to care. Then there's the location. The Serenity Club is in walking distance, and so is Michael's house. And there's a bus stop right in front of the place, too.

The only thing I don't like is the bunk beds; they remind me of prison.

A staff member sticks his head in the doorway.

"Donald Cummins?"

"That's me."

"You need to report to Gloria's office," he says. "She's in the admin building next door. Second floor."

I make my way to her office and take a seat. When I do, she gets right to it.

"How do you want to use your time here?" she asks. "I want to help, but you need to help me by letting me know what you really want to accomplish."

I tell her I want more than a place to crash. I want to stay clean, and I want to go back to school or work or both. I tell her I want to build a new life.

"You going to meetings?" she asks.

"Yeah, every day. I have a sponsor, too."

"Awesome, Don," she nods. "If you maintain your sobriety and become a part of this community, I'll help you with the other stuff. Sound good?"

"Sounds great."

"Okay. Now, during the day you need something to keep you busy, so I'll hook you up with some volunteer work." She raises her eyebrows. "You willing?"

"Sure. What will I do?"

"How about four hours a day at the thrift store?"

The shelter owns the thrift store next door. It helps fund the homeless outreach.

"Works for me," I say. "When do I start?"

"In the morning. I'm putting you on the list for a bus pass, too. That should take a few days." She looks at the computer screen. "You get benefits, right? And Yolanda is your caseworker?"

"Yes."

"Good, because when you leave the shelter, we can work with her and maybe help with assisted, long-term housing."

I nod my head. I'm not sure that's what I want. I want to get *off* assistance.

"It's an option, that's all," she adds. "It might be a good move to take it easy for a year. Focus on your recovery instead of making money."

James had told me the exact same thing. He said I didn't have to prove anything to anyone, and that if I can get by each month with my tiny check, then I should forget about work for a year. That if I take the opportunity to invest in my recovery and learning how to live, I'd pay society back ten times over.

I leave Gloria's office with a bounce in my step. I have a place to stay and food to eat, I'm clean, and I have a couple of friends I know I can count on.

That's a lot more than some people have.

I'm not afraid to work, either. In fact, I'm going to work my ass off.

On my recovery.

AFTER A FEW DAYS AT HEP, I GET IN LINE TO GET MY bus pass. When the staff member hands it to me, my body goes stiff. A brand-new bus pass is worth ten bucks on the street. Which means I can walk three blocks away and trade it for a hit of crack.

Maybe two.

My stomach churns, and my mouth goes dry. My guts feel like they've collapsed within me, and suddenly, I have to shit.

You know you're going to fail! Just go ahead and get it over with – just go get high!

Panic rushes in like a flood. I become heavy and lopsided, like a boat that's capsizing.

But then, there's another voice. It's not loud. It doesn't scream at me or accuse me. It's steady and strong, and it's familiar.

It belongs to James.

It's just a feeling, Don. And this feeling, it will pass.

And then,

If you feel like getting high, call me. If you can remember to do this, it will save your life.

I fumble for my phone and I dial. It rings once, then twice. I wait.

It goes to voicemail.

I put the phone back in my pocket and I stand at my full height.

Somehow, just making the call is enough. My stomach is no longer sick, and my heart is beating at its normal pace again. I'm going to make it.

I'm going to live.

I'm dumbfounded. It's the first time I've ever *not* obeyed that voice. And it's not because I'm strong or because I've finally worked up enough willpower to resist.

I just reached out for help.

I grin. I want to jump and shout. I want to sing at the top of my lungs.

I'm *free*.

Just for this moment, it's a victory. No longer do I have to bow down to that voice. I now know from experience, and not just theory. If I ask for help, the very act of doing so releases an incredible power.

One that will save my life.

I'VE BEEN AT HEP AN ENTIRE MONTH NOW, AND IT'S
not so bad. I climb onto my bunk and pull out a book. Then I lay
it face down on my chest and take a deep breath. I reflect on the
day, and over the past few weeks as well.

Every day I've been waking up at 5:30 a.m. Then I throw on
some shorts and my sneakers and creep out of the dorm quietly.
I jog the surrounding neighborhoods as the sun rises. I smile at
people and tell them good morning as I run by. I do push-ups
every two blocks. An hour later, I walk into the dining hall and
find a seat with some of the residents. We make small talk as we
eat our breakfast together.

Late mornings and early afternoons I hang out at the thrift
store, pulling clothes from donation bins. I sort them then fold
them, or I hang them on racks. When I do the women's clothes,
I hold the dresses up and I study them. I try to figure out which
ones Bri would probably like. I also help customers as they
browse through the shop. I step right up to them and ask if they
need any help. Some are nice, and others are crabby. I don't care.
What really matters is that I'm doing it.

I'm talking to them.

I take the bus to the library in the afternoons and I read and
check out books. Some days I walk the seven or eight blocks to
Michael's place. We smoke cigarettes and talk about life and we
listen to music. He has a guitar, too, and we play a little.

The afternoons end with me back at the shelter. It's dinner, a
shower, then afterward, I'm off to a meeting.

When I finally lie down at night, I'm out like a light.

This routine is working for me. It's enough to keep me busy,
but not so much that I'm stressed out. I lift my book off my
chest and start thumbing through the pages again. As I do, a guy

walks in and sits down on the empty bunk below me. He's got a large plastic bag of clothing and a rolled-up blanket and sheet. He starts unloading his clothes into the sliding drawer below the bunk.

I put my book down and lean over.

He's got spiky, dark hair and a baby face. He's way too young to be homeless.

"How's it going, dude?" I ask.

"Pretty good." He shrugs his shoulders. "Well, for being at a shelter, anyway."

"Yeah, I hear you." I laugh. "I'm Don."

"Eric," he replies. "You been here long?"

"A month. You just get here?"

"Yeah, like fifteen minutes ago." He puts a pair of shorts in the drawer and stands. "Know if there's any meetings around here?"

"Yeah. I'm going to one in a half-hour," I say. "It's a twenty-minute walk. Wanna go?"

"Hell yeah." He looks down and shakes his head. "Man, I really need to stop getting high."

"I get it," I tell him. "You can do it, dude. If I can, you definitely can."

We talk for a few minutes, then it trails off. I lay my head on my pillow and open my book again, but I can't focus. That really sucks for Eric. He's in his early twenties, but he's just like me. Jail. Drug binges. Always winding up in places like this. I hope he turns a corner. I hope he doesn't go another twenty years before he has his own *aha* moment.

I'M GETTING READY TO GO TO A MEETING. I STEP OUT of the shower and towel my hair, and I start to get dressed.

I've been going to meetings every night. James and Michael

pick me up a couple times. Sometimes Don Dortch gets me. And the other nights I walk to the Serenity Club with Eric, which is what I'm doing tonight.

When Eric and I go, we make our way downtown, zigzagging through side streets and alleys as we talk about what we're going to do when we leave the shelter. We talk about our dream jobs and the cars we're going to get. We talk about which women at the meetings we like.

Eric can never make up his mind. He likes four or five.

But me, there's only one I like.

I finish getting dressed and I step outside. Eric is in the courtyard already, smoking a cigarette. The rain has just stopped, and the streets are wet. We make our way there and when we're a block away, a bus pulls to the curb in front of us. A young lady gets off, and she jumps over a puddle and onto the sidewalk. She's got a hoodie pulled low, and she glances back at us, then looks forward and quickens her pace.

I start talking loudly. "Hey, Eric, that's the cute homeless girl I've been telling you about."

She stops and looks back at us.

"Don?"

"How's it going, Bri?"

We all start laughing.

"Oh my God," she exclaims. "I was like, 'Who are these guys following me?'"

The three of us walk the rest of the way together. She's doing okay, but some days are difficult. It's not always easy doing the right thing when you're used to doing the easy thing. But it's coming together, she says. She's making progress.

When we get there, she finds a seat with a couple of women. Eric and I take a seat by Michael. I'm thinking about what she said earlier, and she's right. It really *is* difficult doing what's right, especially when you're used to doing what's easy. She's struggling, I see. But she's doing it.

And so am I.

I think that when someone follows this path, on some level they've got to believe in their potential to change, and be brave enough to fight for it. Regardless of how beat down they are or how badly they've suffered, they stand upon hope and believe they have what it takes to transcend who they've always been.

They must believe they have greatness within them.

I know I have it. And I believe Bri does, too.

As I think about this something clicks. It sounds crazy, I know, but I don't care. I understand now that Bri is absolutely, positively, the one for me. That we are going to be great together.

Eric already knows I like her. I've told him at least twenty times. But on the walk back, I give him the update.

"Dude, I just know it. I can't tell you how, but I do." I stop walking. "She's the one. She's going to be my wife. The mother of my children. I just know it."

He looks me in the eye.

"You serious?"

"Yeah man, I am. As sure as I'm standing here."

We start walking again, and he waits a whole block to respond.

"Well, maybe you're right. Maybe that will come to pass," he says. "But right now, you know what you sound like?"

"What?"

"Like a crazy motherfucker."

I don't argue because I know he's right. But that's okay, because so am I.

When I climb into my bunk later, I pull out a book and read for a few moments. Then I put the book down. I pull out my phone from underneath my pillow. I'm going to message her. Whenever we've chatted at meetings, I've always kept it light. But tonight, I want to tell her something deep. Something meaningful.

Something *real*.

I tell her I believe in her. That when I see her trying so hard to change her life, I'm amazed. That when I see her sit through discomfort and push through it and get to the other side, I'm in awe. I know she is going to become the person she wants to be.

I tell her that I see greatness in her.

I look over what I've written, and I hold my breath. Do I really believe it? With my entire being?

I do.

I hit send. Then I put my phone on silent and roll over and yawn. 5:30 a.m. comes fast.

Moments later, I'm asleep.

24

DEEP WORK

The bus stop is only twenty feet from my bunk, and I keep my window open. Someone outside yells that the bus is coming, and I climb down, grab my backpack, and get out there just in time. The driver gives me a nod as I make my way to the back and find a seat.

I make this trip to James' house every week. When I get there we usually talk a bit and catch up. Then it's all business. We go over my homework from the previous week – reading and writing assignments. I write about things like what recovery means to me, and why. I answer questions about principles like honesty or integrity. I list ways I've been both honest and dishonest, along with concrete ways I can be more honest going forward.

I know it's good for me to think about all this stuff. And I know I need to put in the work to get to the next level. But sometimes it's a real pain in the ass.

This week my task was to make a list of all the people who have pissed me off. When James gave me the assignment, I didn't get it because I *always* let things roll off my back. I even tried to think of at least one person I was mad at, but I drew a blank. I told James that not being angry with anyone seemed to indicate I was healthy and well-adjusted. Obviously, recovery really *does* work miracles.

He said not so fast.

"You might not think of anyone right now," he said, "but trust me, you've got plenty to write about. Do this – picture the timeline of your life and all the people you know. Then do a quick mental scan of your history with each person. If you feel even the slightest twinge of anger, don't second-guess it. Jot their name down along with a quick one-liner about why you think you're angry."

The next day I began writing. It was slow at first, but soon it started trickling in. Then the floodgates opened. I scribbled like a madman. My face was contorted, and my teeth were grinding. And each time I thought I was finished, I'd remember someone else that had pissed me off. When I was finally done, I had thirty pages full of people.

There was the guy in prison and his buddy who tried to rape me. And my parents, who put me in Straight when I was thirteen. And especially my mom for being the one who left me there. Then there were others who had beaten me up. People who cut me off when I was driving. I wrote about an older kid at the Okeechobee Boys School who snatched my fried chicken in the chow hall over thirty years ago. I had turned my head for a second and then *poof* – my chicken was gone. My face burned with humiliation as he and his friends laughed in my face, daring me to do something about it.

I even wrote down the names of people who had done absolutely nothing to me. I just resented them because they seemed so damn perfect.

I never knew I had so many issues. I thought I was laid-back, like a hippie. But after I wrote the list, I was raw inside. Like hamburger. I was left with a dull, heavy ache that sat in my chest, and the whole rest of the week I had to drag that around with me everywhere I went.

But today it will be over. I'm going to turn that list over to James and forget about it.

When I get off the bus, though, I'm starting to feel a bit iffy about it. It wasn't easy writing it, and now he'll probably want to have a conversation about it.

I walk the two blocks to his house and ring the doorbell.

James swings the door open. He's got a big smile on his face.

"C'mon in, bro!" he almost yells. "How's it going?"

I step in the doorway and we hug.

"Life is good, bro. I'm living the dream."

"That's great, Don," he says. "You just wait – it gets even better."

His wife Sadie stands behind him in the hallway. She's grabbing her keys off a rack on the wall. She goes to meetings, too and she and James are like a team. He works with guys like me, and she works with women and helps them, too.

"How's it going, Sadie?"

"Going well, Don," she smiles and looks at both of us. "Hope you guys have a great session. I'm heading out for a while."

She turns to James and gives him a peck on the cheek.

"See you later, honey."

She walks out the door, and we're alone. Time to get to work.

I take a seat on the couch and dig out my notebook and my list. James brings out a couple sodas and hands me one. He sits in a chair opposite me and sets his own notebook on his lap. He looks up at me.

"You ready?"

"Sure," I said. "Let's do it."

I hand him the list, but he doesn't take it.

"I don't need it," he tells me. "You keep it. I just want you to read it to me."

"Just read it, as is?"

"Yep. Read each name and your note. No commentary – just what you wrote."

No commentary? I grin. This is going to be easy.

I begin reading the list out loud. I don't want it to be over *too* fast, so I read slowly and deliberately. Intentionally. After each item, I take a deep breath and try to visualize the resentment and anger leaving my body. As I exhale, I even imagine a dark, shadowy ghost that scurries away from me, then dissipates into the air.

Anger, be gone!

When I finish the last line, I lay the list face down on the couch next to me.

"That was awesome, Don," he says.

"Thanks," I sigh. "That wasn't too bad."

He opens his notebook and clicks his pen.

"No it wasn't. So now let's get started. We'll begin with your mom."

My heart sinks.

"But I thought that was it," I protest.

"Oh, no," he grins. "Reading it is just the warm-up."

First writing it, then reading it, and now we have to dissect it? He's going to want me to talk about feelings. I'll bet money on it.

"All right, then let's start," he says. "You wrote that your mom left you at that drug program when you were thirteen. At Straight, right?"

"Yeah. But really, my parents didn't have much of a choice. I was a pretty bad kid. Way out of control."

"Okay, but that's not what we're talking about," he interjects. "We're going to focus on what you *felt* about it. Not whether you think your mom was justified or not."

Crap. This *is* going to be all about my feelings. But I don't see how they're relevant. I mean, of course I felt some things about being left at Straight. Who wouldn't? But what matters is the truth. And the larger truth goes way beyond how I *feel* about something. The truth is that I was out of control. And as a result, they really *didn't* have much of a choice.

"Yeah, I get that you want me to focus on feelings. But with old stuff like that, I don't see how it matters."

"Tell you what, if you let me walk you through it, I think you might see it."

I groan under my breath.

"Okay, let's do it then."

"Good. Now, what I want you to do is go back and think about the moment she walked out that door. Try to remember what you felt, then tell me about it."

He leans back in his chair and waits.

I search as best as I can, but nothing comes to me. It was so long ago that even if I do remember how it really was, it won't change anything. I press my lips together.

"This is stupid, James," I snap. "I mean, it was frigging decades ago."

"But Don, you're the one who wrote it down. And I have to say, you *do* seem a bit troubled."

He's right – I am. It feels like there are termites in my guts right now, gnawing at my insides.

"It *does* still bother you, right?" he prods.

I nod my head yes.

"Okay, so maybe it's time you face it and embrace it. Agree?"

"Yeah," I admit. "This really sucks, man."

He nods.

"I get it, Don. I've been through this process and I under-stand. But this is how you get better. It takes work and lots of courage, but you can do this."

I take another deep breath.

"Okay. I'm angry because she lied to me about where I was going. And then she just left me there."

He just listens and doesn't say a word. I continue.

"She didn't even say bye. She just snuck out the door and fucking left me."

My chest is burning.

"You're doing great, Don."

"It doesn't feel great."

I want to run out the front door. The hell with James and all of this crap.

"I know. But stay in touch with that feeling," he says. "What does it feel like? Hurt?"

"Yes," I whisper. "It does."

I feel the tears as they begin to well up in my eyes.

"And why do you feel hurt?" he asks.

My jaw tightens. Who *wouldn't* feel hurt if that happened to them?

"What kind of question is that?"

"Stay with me, Don – what I mean is this: What exactly is making you feel hurt right now? Can you describe it?"

I close my eyes. Christ, it's like he's twisting the knife.

"I told you already," I snap. "She lied to me and left me there."

"Okay – we know that was the *situation*, but what I mean is this – why does it *matter* to you if she lied to you and left you there?"

"You've got to be kidding me!" I'm almost yelling. "How could it *not* matter?"

"Don, I'm not kidding. Now please, stay with me. Why does it matter to you? Why does it matter if your mom lied to you and left you there?"

I'm starting to tremble. This is getting heavy. I take a couple quick breaths, and I get it under control. At least long enough for me to finally say it. And though what I finally say is technically not a *feeling*, I think I'd know what someone else felt if I heard them say it.

"It means she's throwing me away," I blurt out. "It means I'm, I'm no fucking good."

And then I lose it. I bury my face in my hands and burst into tears, sobbing loudly.

Like a thirteen-year-old.

We make our way through more of the list. It's grueling. He even hands me a box of tissues. But I begin to notice that the same thing keeps coming up. Whatever it is I'm angry or hurt by, when I get down to the root of it, I find fear. Fear that I'm not enough.

That I'm no good.

Which is strange because I don't truly believe that. Especially since the workshop.

"Hats off, brother. That really took a lot."

"Yeah, it did." I laugh as I blow my nose. "What's weird is I don't really feel like I'm not enough. I thought I dealt with that already, but on some level it's still with me."

"Yep, those feelings are still there. But they're beginning to resolve, and they will continue to do so as long as we focus on the truth – which is that you really *are* okay. Agree?"

"Yeah, I do."

"Say it then."

"What? That I'm good enough?"

"Say the truth, however you word it."

"Okay, I'm good enough."

"Can you put it another way? Whatever comes to mind."

"I'm perfect. I'm perfect just as I am."

My voice is getting stronger.

"Great! Say it another way."

"There is no one on the face of this earth who is greater than me!" I shout.

"Okay, once more."

"I am worth fighting for!" I yell.

And right now, I know it's true. I *am* worth fighting for.

"Amazing!" he laughs. "So, now you've got a new tool to add to your toolbox. And you'll need it because those old attitudes and feelings will still come up from time to time and try to take the steering wheel. But today you've felt them. You've named them. Which puts you in a much better position to recognize them. And that, Don, is what gives you the ability to take the wheel back."

When he explains it like that, I get it. This exercise wasn't about being left at the drug program. It wasn't about my mom. It wasn't about discovering precisely what caused all my issues or resolving them.

No, that's a lifetime of work. And right now, the priority is to make sure I *have* a lifetime. It's to develop tools that will help me save my life. And damn, he's *right*. It takes gut-wrenching work.

This shit is hard – but not nearly as hard as the alternative.

When I get back on the bus, I pull out the index card James gave me before I left. On it, he's written my assignment for the next week. The first thing I need to do, it says, is find a sheet of paper and write: "I am a good person who has been through hell, and I deserve to recover and have the life I dream of." The next thing I need to do is hang that paper up somewhere I will notice at least a few times a day.

As soon as I get back to the shelter, I do it. I write the words in black Sharpie on a piece of paper, then I tape it to the wall above my pillow. I stare at it a moment. Those words are true. I *am* a good person. I *do* deserve to recover and have a great life.

I know that believing those words and getting them to stick with me deep down inside is the key to having the life I know I deserve.

This is what recovery looks like, I think. It's not just about abstinence. It's all about *living* clean. Which means seeing new truths and becoming and growing. Constantly taking my life to a new level.

This recovery thing, it's no joke.

25

TUX

My time at HEP is up in a week and I have no idea what I'll do. I meet with Yolanda, and we go over some options.

"There's four or five places we can get you into," she tells me. "Or you can give it a go on your own if you want. Up to you, Don."

Since I have a monthly check and food stamps, programs will get in line to take me. But that's not what I want.

I want freedom. If I get my own place, I know I can make it work. I'll squeak by somehow with that little bit of money. I'll keep going to meetings, hanging out with James and Michael, and I'll keep jogging in the morning. And when I'm ready to add work and school to the mix, I will.

I tell Yolanda I'll need a couple days to think about it.

There's a dude I know from meetings who's been around a long time. He always knows the latest, like who's hiring or has a place for rent. I give him a call, and he answers on the first ring.

"Stevie here."

"Hey, what's up? It's Don – remember me?"

"Yeah, man! How's it going, Don?"

"I'm doing good, but my time's up at the shelter. I need to find a place."

"You still clean?"

"Hell yeah. Over two months now, and I'm doing better than I ever have."

"All right, well funny you called because I just got off the phone with this guy. You know Llama Jim?"

I'm not the greatest with names, but I'm positive about this one.

"Nope."

"Okay, well check it out. Jim's got a llama farm, maybe twenty minutes from you. He needs someone to help out around the place. Feed the animals, do some yard work. He's willing to trade for room and board."

"You kidding?" I laugh. "A *llama farm?*"

"Don't knock it," he says. "It might be a good fit for you."

A few days later, I step off the bus at a busy intersection. The traffic is thick for miles ahead and behind. All four corners of the intersection are packed with strip malls, fast food joints, and parking lots crammed with cars.

It doesn't look like farm country.

I have directions on a piece of paper, and I follow them. I walk down one of the side streets and I head east a few blocks. The noise from the main road begins to quiet as restaurants and stores give way to houses. As I continue, the houses get larger and they begin to have bigger, greener yards. And then, I'm on a quiet back road lined with ranches and farms on both sides. Some have acres of thick woods behind them, and I see a guy behind a barn, riding a tractor in an open field.

A rooster crows, and a horse neighs. I laugh aloud. I never would've guessed it – a pocket of farmland tucked away in the middle of this city.

I find the ranch and let myself through the front gate. I walk to the house and onto the front porch, and I knock on the door.

It opens slightly, and a head pops out. He's got short brown hair with sunglasses pushed up on top of his head.

"You Don?"

"That's me. You Jim?"

The door opens the rest of the way. He smiles and extends a heavily calloused hand.

"Yeah. C'mon in, I'll show you around."

He welcomes me in and shows me the bedroom and the kitchen. Then he takes me out back and shows me the farm and the llamas. Everything is like Stevie described. Maybe two or three hours of work a day, spread out with long breaks in between. My job would be to feed the six llamas and also a horse twice a day and do other odd jobs once in a while. In exchange, I'd get a key to the house, a furnished bedroom, my own bathroom, and use of the kitchen.

And lots of fresh air.

"There's something I need to let you know." Jim looks away for a moment, then continues. "I was doing really good for a few years, but a month ago I slipped pretty bad. I'm doing okay now though."

"Slipped? As in what?"

"I got high again."

"Oh, gotcha. But you're steady now, right?"

"Yeah, I'm back on the wagon." He nods quickly. "It's good you'll be here because, well, it'll give me a little motivation."

"Yeah, well glad you're doing okay again," I tell him. "If you ever need to talk, let me know."

I decide to move in, and in a few weeks I find my groove. Each morning as the sun rises, I'm scooping feed from a five-gallon bucket into the llamas' bins. I yawn as I reach over their gates and pet each of them while telling them good morning by name. They look up for a moment as I do, then they go back to their breakfast.

At mid-morning, I let them out of their pens to graze in an

open meadow where they eat wild berries that hang down from tall, dense bushes. I rake and trim trees and brush, making sure the grounds stay clear for them. Late in the afternoon, I lead them to their pens and feed them dinner.

I talk to them while I do chores. Especially Tux. He's tall with white hair, and he follows me everywhere I go. When I turn around and look at him, he stops and stares back. I think that on some level Tux knows I'm more than just a bringer of food. I tell him my story, and how I wound up here on the ranch. Sometimes, he nods.

Life on the farm isn't bad. When I'm not working I'm reading or I'm journaling and doing the assignments James gives me. Lately they all focus on one basic thing: how each day I get to create who I am by the choices I make. And when I choose to do new things and build new habits, I gradually become a different person.

As I practice this, my life begins to take shape. In some ways, just like I imagined it. But in other ways, like I never would've dreamed.

I'M LEADING THE LLAMAS BACK TO THEIR PENS WHEN my dad calls. It's mid-afternoon, and he's in the area. He wants to stop by and check out the farm. I wash up and change my clothes, and I'm waiting on the porch when he pulls into the driveway. I walk to his truck as he climbs down. He grins when he sees me walking up.

"How's it going, D?" he asks.

I give him a big hug.

"Great, Dad." I nod at the farm behind me and grin. "Want to take a look around?"

I show him the llamas and the meadow. I show him where I start my day each dawn. I tell him about the chores I do. When my dad was sixteen, he worked on a dairy farm. It was a lot different from this, I know, but maybe this is close enough. Close enough for him to be proud of me.

"I have to say, I never imagined you'd wind up on a farm," he chuckles as he looks around. Then he looks back at me and nods his head. "But it looks like it suits you, son."

When it's time for him to leave, we walk back to his truck. He opens the passenger door and turns to me.

"I have something for you."

From behind the seat, he pulls out a guitar case and lays it on the seat. He lifts the latches and opens it.

It's my acoustic – the Taylor he got me when I was still in prison.

I look at the guitar, then back at him.

"How did you get it? I thought it was gone."

"It was," he says. "But one night when you were out of it, you gave me the pawn ticket. You don't remember?"

I don't.

He pulls it out of the case and holds it out to me.

"I hoped I'd get the chance to give this back to you."

I take it from his hands, and I hold it in front of me for a moment and look it over. It's beautiful, and it's comfortable in my hands. It's truly mine, I know; it's finally found its way home to me. I'm grateful to have it again. I look at my dad and I'm grateful to have him again, too. To have another chance. With him. My family. With my friends.

With everything.

"Thanks, Dad."

We hug, and he climbs up in his truck. He gives me a long look, then he drives away.

I LOVE RYE TOAST. I USUALLY GET IT WITH EGGS OVER

medium. I'm finishing my last bite in a booth at Perkins, sitting across from Don Dortch. He's eating a pancake, and he stops and wipes his mouth and clears his throat.

"I don't know why, but I can't seem to get back to where I was." He takes a sip of his coffee. "But I'm glad for you. You seem like you're on the right track. I wish I was, but this time around, I'm just not feeling it."

He shakes his head and looks around the diner.

"I don't know if I'll ever get there," he says.

It's back to this again. I try, but I just don't get it. Okay, he slipped up. But when he did, it's not like he really lost anything. He didn't get arrested and he didn't damage any relationships; he was *already* divorced.

To me, what happened was simple: he got high again for a month or two after being clean for over a decade. It's not that slipping up *isn't* a big deal, because it is. It can be lethal. But he's back on the wagon now, and *that's* what's important. Plus, he's got it going on in so many other ways. He's a millionaire a few times over. He owns properties all over the place and he's got friends all over the world.

It's not like he got stuck on skid row.

I know money can't make you happy and I'm not confused about that. But right now he's been clean longer than me, and he can do whatever he wants and go wherever he wants.

I don't understand why he just can't be happy.

Something's haunting him, it seems. His voice is wistful, and he's wishing he could go back to something that's long gone. I'm not sure what that is.

I've tried to cheer him up and tell him things to snap him out of it. When we meet I try to point out that I'm fresh out of the homeless shelter, but that *I'm* happy – and that he can be, too. He just needs to give it some time, I say. And I always let him know that he can call me anytime.

He always thanks me when I tell him, and I know he really means it.

We have that same talk tonight. He assures me he'll be okay. He just needs to get over the hump, he says.

I like Don a lot. But he sure is one sad dude.

It's late when he drops me off at the ranch. I climb down from his truck and I thank him for the ride. It's been a long day and I'm ready to crash. Today was a longer one than usual; I spent all morning and afternoon clearing brush from the meadow's edges, bundling it and loading it into the back of a truck. Then I took the bus to see James and go over an assignment. Then, another bus to a meeting and the diner with Don.

I'm worn out.

I walk to the porch, fumble with my keys, and then I'm through the front door. When I step inside, I stop in my tracks. Something's not right. The lights are all off, and the house is still.

Too still.

I tip-toe through the living room and as my eyes adjust, I see him. Llama Jim is sitting up straight on the couch. His eyes are wide and he's grinding his jaw, like he's agitated. And that's when I smell it. It's faint, but I know what it is.

He's been smoking crack.

"What's up, Jim?"

"I fucked up," he whispers. "But I'm done. After tonight, I swear I'm finished, man."

I want to help him somehow. I also want to run out of the place as fast as I can. On the other hand, I want to fucking strangle him.

Instead, I decide to just go to bed.

"Call someone, Jim," I tell him, "before it gets too far out of hand."

I go to my room and lock the door and wedge a chair in front of it for good measure. I climb into my bed and think about the past few months. I like it here. In my gut, I know I didn't make a mistake. This is where I was supposed to be.

But it's probably about to get crazy out at the ranch, and I can't be here when it does.

When I wake up, Llama Jim is gone and so is his car. I make a few calls, and James is on his way to get me. I'll couch-surf until I figure it out.

I get my guitar and put my belongings together in a few bags and set it all on the steps out front. Then I walk out back to the llama pens. I feed them one last time, while telling them I'm leaving. I pet Tux, and I say goodbye.

Tux looks at me for a long moment, then nods.

I walk back to the front of the house to wait, and I tell myself that everything is going to be okay.

26

YOUNG AVE

I'm in the library at St. Pete College, rereading a paragraph in my textbook *Introduction to Computers and Programming*. I'm shifting around in my seat. I still don't get it. The lesson is about how the internet works. The web and the internet are kind of the same, it says, but different. Both are made up of layers and protocols, and there's ports and hubs and things called *nameservers*.

It's confusing.

It's been three months since I left the llama farm. I'm renting a room for a hundred bucks a week in the city, not far from HEP and the Serenity Club. My routine is the same – bus rides and meetings and hanging out with James and Michael and Eric. When I left the farm, James suggested I add school to the mix. Take a class or two, he said, and see how it goes. So I did.

I want to get a degree in software development. In a way, computers are boring. But I want to create stuff, and there's no doubt that computers are going to be a huge way to do that in the future. So to me, it's a no-brainer.

Some days I focus well, and other days not so much. Today,

it's not so much. I get up and throw my books in my backpack and walk out the library. As I do, I almost bump into someone. As I pull back, I recognize who it is.

"Hey, what's up Kim!" I exclaim.

"Hey! Good to see you!" She grins, and we hug. "I'm up here helping some of the women from the home get signed up for classes. How about you?"

"Homework. On my way to catch a bus to the Serenity Club."

"Now that's what I'm talking about!" she says. "So, you're going to make it to the wedding, right?"

She and Kevin are getting married in a month. It's an open wedding in a park, and they've invited anyone and everyone.

"Yeah, for sure! I'm so happy for you guys!"

"Good, and you're going to sing a song, right?"

"At the wedding?" I blink. "You're kidding, right?"

"Nope." She grins and folds her arms. "You willing? I need to know, Don."

I've mentioned casually to more than a few people that I play and sing. Now, I wish I'd kept my mouth shut.

"Um, I'd be honored."

"Okay, that's great! You'll need to see Bri about the details. She's helping us organize it." She narrows her eyes. "You'll be really sad about that part, I'm sure."

I get to the bus stop and sit on the bench. I can't believe I just said yes to all of that. I'll get to talk to Bri more, and the thought of that makes my entire body tingle. But I'm getting butterflies in my stomach about something else, too.

I'm not so sure I can really pull it off. It's true that I've played in several bands, both as a lead guitarist and vocalist. And I've played in front of some pretty big crowds, too. So, I've never lied about any of that. But it's complicated.

I've never done any of that in the free world.

IT WAS 2004, AND THE SUN WAS SCALDING. EVEN though the prison was just fifteen minutes inland from Daytona Beach, there was no breeze. Not the slightest waft. The heat was dense and suffocating. I was on the rec yard and my knees were knocking and my legs were wobbly. Beads of sweat rolled down my brow.

I stood behind the mic with an old Fender Strat strapped across my shoulder. I reached out my hand and gave the mic a couple taps. It worked. I stepped back and waited.

I thought I might throw up.

I'd been playing in prison bands a few years. It was always me on lead guitar, and I'd do some background vocals here and there. When I was at Raiford in the nineties, I'd even played at different prisons. They'd make us load the equipment on a truck, then they'd shackle and handcuff us and off we'd go – a traveling prison road show. Playing guitar in front of people wasn't that big of a deal.

But now, I could no longer hide behind a band. It would be my voice and my band. I was the front man. Stripped down raw before a bunch of prisoners.

Figuratively speaking.

This gig would be my proving ground. If I could rock *these* guys, I thought, I'd know for sure whether I had something to work with. But as I stood there all wobbly at the mic, I wasn't so sure I wanted to find out. I thought about running off the rec yard and hiding in my cell.

I was afraid I didn't have what it takes. But I was also scared that I did.

Before I could chicken out, Tank stepped up and introduced us.

"All right everybody, this is the moment you've been waiting for!" he shouted into the microphone. "Live, at Tomoka Correctional Institution, it's the one and only, Groove Dogs!!"

I stepped up and stared at the crowd.

About thirty-five convicts sat on the grass in front of us. Not a single hand clapped. Not a single cheer or welcome. Their eyes were glazed over, and they looked straight through us.

Like zombies.

I looked beyond them across the field. There were three hundred other prisoners inside the double razor-wire fences, scattered across the rec yard. Some played basketball or lifted weights. Others shuffled around the track or sat on bleachers, talking or smoking weed or gambling.

Then someone in front of me yelled.

"What's up, motherfucker? You gonna play or what?"

I looked back at Stix. He nodded and counted us in, and we dove into the Allman Brothers' version of Statesboro Blues. A few measures later, it was time to start belting it out. There was no turning back, and I opened my mouth and I let it go. I was singing to a woman, begging her to come take off with me to the country. I didn't care whether I looked tough or not, or how I even looked at all. I just sang from my guts, like the prison yard didn't even exist.

Halfway through the song I remembered where I was. I looked up. The crowd of thirty-five had become a hundred. And after the next song, it became two hundred. Heads were bobbing up and down. Those hardcore, face-tattooed, perpetual frown-wearing dudes were cheering and smiling. They liked it.

No, they *loved* it.

When I got back to my cell, I dug around my locker and pulled out my notebook and began writing a song. Two days later, "Ball and Chain" was done. A week after that I finished "I Will Rise." With almost three more years left, I figured if I wrote a song a week I'd have almost a hundred and fifty by the time I got out.

That would give me at least a few hits.

As I wait for the bus, I mull it over. Playing at Kevin and Kim's wedding will be nothing like performing that first time with the Groove Dogs. This won't be about whether I do good or not, and it's definitely won't be some proving ground for me. It's simply going to be a gift. For *them*. I'll write a song for them that will be *to* them, on behalf all of us who know them. When I think about it this way, it takes the weight off. I don't feel so nervous.

The bus pulls up and I get on and find a seat in the back. I start humming a tune and tapping my feet. And forty minutes later I step off the bus with the song completed.

I get to the Serenity Club, and I see a red Corolla in the parking lot. Lately I notice them everywhere. I see red Corollas at intersections. In parking lots. Whizzing by on US-19. I didn't know they made so many of them.

It all started last month when Bri got one.

The car door opens, and she steps out and walks toward the entrance. I half run to catch up to her.

"I didn't know you organize weddings."

"I didn't know you play guitar and sing."

"I'm a better player than I am a singer."

We stop outside the door and she turns to me.

"What song are you going to do?"

"An original I wrote. It's called 'Friends.'"

"A wedding song called 'Friends'?"

"Yeah. I wrote it on behalf of all of us, to them."

She stares.

"I know it sounds corny," I continue, "but by the end of it everyone will be singing along."

She puts her hands on her hips and smirks.

"Oh, really?"

"Um, yeah." I look at her. "You don't think so?"

"I'm sorry, it's just that, well, like how will you pull that off?"

"By singing it," I explain. "It's a catchy tune."

She grins and shakes her head.

"Okay, Don. I'll let you know when to do your thing."

A few weeks later, right before Kevin and Kim say their vows, I step out in front of everyone. It's just me and my acoustic and a couple mics. There's at least a hundred people at the wedding, and they're all gathered around close. There's a slight breeze and it's sunny and unlike the prison crowd, everyone actually *wants* to be here.

I take a deep breath and pray everyone sings along.

I sing the first verse, and then the chorus. And after the second verse, it's time for the chorus again. I motion for everyone to join in and sing.

And somehow, they just do.

We are friends of Kevin and Kim
and we thank you for letting us into your life
We are friends of Kevin and Kim
and we thank you, husband and wife

It's simple, I know. No super genius moment when I wrote it. But it's really nice hearing everyone singing it together to them.

I glance over at Kevin and Kim. They're beaming while everyone's looking over at them and singing it to them. And as I watch, I think that sometimes things unfold for a reason. And maybe sometimes, for several. I just know that right now, I'm glad I was in prison. I'm grateful I played with the Groove Dogs. That I wound up at a llama farm and my dad got my guitar out of hock and gave it to me for the second time. Because without all of that, I probably wouldn't have said yes to all of this. And maybe Kevin and Kim are just a tiny bit happier today because of it. And maybe the other people here are too, because they had a chance to sing to them.

What a cool gift I've been given, so I would be able to give it back.

But that's not all. Because as the applause dies down, I scan the faces and I see Bri. Our eyes lock. It seems like forever, and finally, I know.

She sees me.

When I get to my room later that night, I fall backward on the bed. Life is beginning to smile upon me. I feel it, deep in my bones. James is right – I'm a good guy and I deserve to recover and have a good life. And because I finally agree with that truth, my life is taking off like a rocket. It's not easy – my days are long, filled with college classes and meetings and endless bus rides. But thoughts of getting high have begun to fade, and my dreams are awakening.

In my mind, I see them. My dreams are like colorful pictures on a vision board. In one image, I'm smiling and surrounded by good friends who love and care for me. In another, a future version of me is designing and creating software with a group of guys that like me and look up to me. And in another, I'm in front of a house. *My* house. One arm is wrapped around Bri, and she holds a small child in her arms. I'm healthy and vibrant.

I'm *alive*.

I have no idea how all this will come to pass, yet I believe it will. There's a ton of work ahead, I know. But the work is just a fraction of what's involved. The results, those are the mystery. They seem to come from somewhere else altogether. Something far greater than me and my efforts. On some days, I think of it as the laws of the universe. Others, it's just pure energy. And although it doesn't make sense to my brain, some days it's a person. Like a God who is kind and loving and cares deeply for me – despite the wreck that I've been.

I know these are only my ideas. They're just my projections.

I know that in truth, it's entirely beyond me and the words or thoughts I have about it all. Yet I know that's okay, because ultimate reality, well, it's flexible like that.

Whatever it is, I know one thing for sure – it's connected to my heart. It always has been and always will be, and there's nowhere I can escape from it. And if my heart remains open, I know the results will be amazing, whatever they are.

THE TWO WEEKS SINCE THE WEDDING HAVE WHIZZED by. I've gotten A's on two exams. And even though my license was revoked after they figured out it was me who wrecked Rick's car, I've started the process to get it back. I've met James a few times and I'm making great progress.

And, I had my first official date with Bri.

Tonight, it's date number two. We're lying on our backs on a blanket at Clearwater's North Beach. Our eyes are on the stars and moon, and my acoustic is lying in the sand next to us.

I'm biting my lip and holding my breath. I know she's carefully thinking about how to reply. I just told her my story. Including prison. The bank robberies. The insanity.

I told her everything.

"Wow, Don, that's an amazing journey." She sits up and looks me in the eye. "Actually, it's quite intense."

I sit up, too.

"Yeah. It is," I admit. "Um, you think you still want to hang out with me?"

She takes a deep breath and sighs.

"Well, I'm glad you didn't spring that on me months from now."

She's about to drop me, I think. Maybe I didn't get that vision board quite right.

I hold my breath.

"But the past is the past, right?" She smiles and nods. "I feel like I get you. I want to move forward."

I exhale.

"Cool," I manage.

Funny, but I don't feel like she's bat-shit crazy for wanting to be with me. She just gets me, that's all.

"Anything else you need to tell me about?" she asks.

"Just one thing." I clear my throat. "I have a wife and three kids."

Her smile vanishes.

"Just kidding," I laugh. "But I really do want three kids."

"I think two are plenty."

"Okay. Now how about you? Anything I need to know before we plan on having those two or three kids?"

"I said two."

"Whatever. Tell me."

"Okay. You told me yours. I'll tell you mine."

I lean back on my elbows.

"I partied a lot in high school," she began. "I started drinking and smoking. I was always able to hold it together, but by the time I got to college it was out of hand and I couldn't stop. I tried switching colleges. I moved in with my sister in South Carolina. I tried changing my location and my situation, but I wound up hooked on heroin.

"At the end, I was living out of motels and had nowhere to go. I found myself in some really dangerous situations. Ones I should *not* have been in." She looks out over the waves. "I hit bottom, and I was scared. I had burned a lot of bridges and I didn't know what to do."

"How'd you wind up down here?"

"Well, I had finally started going to outpatient treatment, but then I relapsed bad. I was strung out and at my wits' end, then someone helped me find a detox in Florida." She looks at me. "The day after I got out, I met you."

I can hardly believe it. Well, I should because, after all, we met at a meeting. Yet on another level it doesn't make sense. She's such a beautiful person to me, and I just don't get how someone like her could've treated herself so badly.

"I can't picture you like that at all, Bri. I'm so glad you're okay today."

"I can't picture you like that either." She reaches for my hand. "I'm so glad we're clean."

27

AMENDS

It's better to give than to receive, they say. Maybe that's because the one who gives has it to give, while the one who receives probably doesn't. I don't know. But I've discovered that now that I can, I like to give.

Sometimes I realize that in some ways I'm still a taker. I'm not perfect. But I'm becoming more of a giver and it's a good feeling. Most of the time, it's little things. Like today – this morning I get to help my mom do some work in the garage. Some things need to go into the attic, and others need to come down. A bit of sweeping. Some rearranging. For a lot of people, doing stuff like this is no big deal, but for me it is.

I'm finally available.

I come over to help my dad sometimes too, but this morning he's out on his boat. Sometimes he goes by himself, navigating through the intercoastal or through the waters of Old Tampa Bay. He's out there today because it's the day after chemo, and that's when he has the most energy. Tomorrow, that's another story. Because for the next week or so, he'll be groaning under his breath. Of course, he'll try to hide it. But we know. It's been rough on him.

It's been hard for my mom, too.

I finish sweeping the garage, and she throws a dustpan on the floor in front of me. I fill it and dump it in the trash. When I return, I take a seat next to her by the workbench. She's gotten a couple bottles of water, and she hands me one. I take a sip.

"How's Uncle John?" I ask.

My mom has been taking care of her brother lately, too. She can tell by John's voice when he's not doing good. And when he isn't, she cleans his trailer and helps him to the VA and manages his meds. She tries to get him to come stay for a few weeks. John would do the same for her because, after all, family is everything. His first tour in Vietnam was because he was drafted, but the second one was so his brother didn't have to go. It was that final tour that left John broken and haunted. I think that sometimes he drinks like I smoked crack. Now, he's fighting cancer, too.

"He's not doing so great, Don." She screws the cap back on her bottle. "He's going to need more tests. He's been short of breath, and he's having a hard time getting around."

"Oh, that sucks." I look at her. "You holding up alright?"

"I'm a bit tired, but I'm okay. It's a lot taking care of people." She smiles and pats my knee. "But family is everything, right?"

It really is. Yet it's my family who I've hurt the most.

James and I have talked about that. It's important that I own my side of the street. To try to make it right with the people I've wronged, to the best of my ability. It's called amends, and not only is it the right thing to do, but it can give some closure and maybe healing – for them and for me. Some things can never be fixed, though, and sometimes contacting someone I've hurt might cause even more pain. Like the bank tellers. I've sorted some of that out with James.

Some of the people I hurt, I'll probably never see them again. So for some, my amends are to give to a cause they would've believed in. For others, like my grandfather, it's to write them a letter even though I'll never send it. For those I owe money, I must make a plan of payment. Others, it's a simple apology. Some amends will last the rest of my life.

For my parents and Bob and Liz, James and I agreed that a talk and a formal apology is best. It won't change the past, but it could clear the air.

Right now seems like the perfect time to have that talk with my mom.

"I have something I want to tell you," I tell her.

"Is everything okay?"

"Yes, everything's okay," I assure her. "I just wanted to share something with you."

"Okay."

She leans forward a bit, and I take a breath.

"I just wanted to say that I'm so sorry for hurting you and doing all the things that I did over the years. I wasn't a good son, and I know I caused you a lot of suffering."

She doesn't speak. She just listens, and I continue.

"There's no way I can ever make that right. But I want you to know that I love you and that I'm sorry. Going forward I'm committed to not hurting you," I tell her. "I'm going to be the best person I possibly can."

I break eye contact and look down. My amends are puny and weak, I think. They don't make up for the decades of madness. Of causing her to worry. Of losing sleep, of wondering what she and my dad could've done different. And really, my amends *are* weak. But they're all I have.

"And if there's anything I can do to somehow make it better," I add, "I will."

When I say that, I know this is the heart of it. I'm willing, and I've expressed it clearly.

She reaches for my hand.

"Donny, your dad and I made a lot of mistakes, too. We're all learning and doing the best we can, and it's okay. Just keep doing what you're doing. It's the best thing you can do for yourself and everyone else." She smiles. "I love you, and I'm so proud of you."

What a relief. I haven't had the talk with my dad or my brother or my sister yet. But I'm pretty sure those will go okay, too. Finding the right time is hard. I'm lucky to be able to talk with my family about it, though. No, luck has nothing to do with it, I remind myself.

I'm *blessed*.

"Well, since you're such a good son now," she grins, "there's just one more thing I need from the attic."

I stand to my feet and laugh.

"I'm ready."

My phone rings. It's Michael. It's probably important because he usually just texts. I tell my mom I need to take it.

"Hey, what's up?" I ask.

"I got some bad news for you, brother."

"All right. Go ahead."

"Don's gone."

"What do you mean? He's dead?"

"Yeah, bro. I just found out. He committed suicide last week."

It didn't take long for the police to figure it out. The month before, Don had taken his handgun apart, put the pieces in a box, and stored it in a cabinet. He'd been depressed and afraid he might hurt himself. Last week, he went on a three-day bender, holed up alone in his house, drinking hard. And in the midst of his stupor, he somehow managed to find the box and put the gun back together. When he did, he put it in his mouth and pulled the trigger.

It was five days before anyone found him.

It was only a couple weeks ago that Don and I sat together after a meeting. He wasn't in the greatest of spirits that night. But then again, he always seemed sad. Yet I knew something wasn't right. Last week, Bri and I had been driving, and out of the blue I thought about him.

"I'm worried about Don," I had told her.

"Really?" she asked. "Why?"

And I had no idea. It was just a feeling that had come over me. I just brushed it aside.

When I hang up with Michael, I look at my mom. She knows who Don was. And who James and Michael are, too. She's heard all about them.

"I'm so sorry about your friend, Donny."

I don't feel much. I'm numb, but usually that's how I am immediately after something tough happens. The feelings come later. When I'm alone, I know I'll think about him, and I'll need to call James.

My mom is tearing up, and then, I see it on her face. The call I just took was the one she'd always feared getting.

About me.

The amends I made seemed weak and puny a moment ago. But not anymore.

"Me too, Mom."

I reach out and give her a long hug.

I'm so grateful to be alive.

28

NEW YORK AVE

Six months of renting a room and I'm ready to take it to another level. I want to rent a house. I start searching and I run across one for cheap – a two bedroom for only eight hundred bucks a month. I can't swing first and last, but I make an appointment to check it out anyway.

The outside is cute, just like the picture. It's a small cottage with brown siding and light-beige trim. Nice shrubs and flowers surround a small oak porch. When the owner shows up, she unlocks the front door and we walk inside. The floor creaks beneath my feet, and I feel the house shift slightly as a light gust of wind blows against it. The tile on the kitchen floor crunches with each step as we pass through it, and the hallway walls are not completely vertical.

The outside is nice, but judging from the inside I think this house might have been dropped here by a tornado.

When we step out, I ask her about it.

"How old is this place?"

"Oh, a hundred years or so. Originally it sat somewhere else, and then it was moved here." She points to a crawl space under the house. "That's why it sits on bricks."

A couple cats run out from under the house, screeching and chasing each other. They're unkempt, probably feral.

When I get back on the bus, I mull it over. The place feels dangerous, like it could collapse at any moment. But after a hundred years, I think it will probably make it at least one more. And it has a lot going for it, too. First, there's the price. Before I left, she came down to seven hundred. If I rent the second room out, I'd wind up paying less than I do for the room right now. And the location is perfect. There's a bus stop two blocks away, and it's close to a grocery store, the mall, and my meetings.

And it's only three blocks from the women's home where Bri lives.

When I move in a couple weeks later, Bri helps me get unpacked. We put the kitchen together and get my bedroom setup. Later in the afternoon Bri has to go wait tables. I sit in the empty living room and try to figure out how to make it look more like a home. There's no furniture yet except for the bed we picked out together, but I find a couple folding chairs in a shed out back. I put those in the living room and I try to picture them like they're a couch and an ottoman.

I give up for the time being and I take a bus to a meeting. When I walk in the door, Bri texts me.

"Mind if I spend the night?"

"Please do."

"Be over in a few."

Two weeks pass, and she still hasn't left. Her hair dryer and makeup and clothes are piling up in the bathroom and the bedroom and the closet. Her socks are getting mixed up with mine. It doesn't make sense for her to keep paying rent at the halfway house. We drive over there and get the rest of her stuff, and I cancel the ad for the spare room. We'll make it an office instead.

THREE MONTHS OF LIVING TOGETHER, AND I'M reeling. I'm sitting at a coffee shop, biting my lip and running my fingers through my hair when James slides into the seat facing mine.

"Thanks for meeting me here," I blurt out. "Man, I really screwed up."

"What's up?"

"It's Bri. We should've never moved in together. She goes through my phone all the time. She thinks I've been seeing other women."

"Oh, really?" He raises his eyebrows. "You know why?"

"No idea. At first I thought it was cute, but not anymore. Last night when you dropped me off, she asked me where I'd been. She didn't even believe me when I said I was with you. She thought I was lying – told me I was full of shit."

"Yeah? How'd you handle that?"

"Not great. We got into a big argument and I wound up yelling and swearing at her. Then I punched a hole in the wall."

I hold up my right hand. My knuckles are swollen and red.

"For a minute, I actually thought about getting high." I sigh and shake my head. "I just can't live like this. Me and her, we're over. I just need to figure out the best way to exit."

"Okay, let's walk through this again," James says.

"Alright."

"Have you given her any reason to be suspicious? You doing anything shady?"

"Nope. Nothing."

"All right, do you feel like you trust *her*?"

"Yeah, of course."

"Have you ever gone through *her* phone?"

I have, but only like once or twice. Well, maybe three or four. Five?

"Yeah," I admit. "But not too much."

"Why? Tell me exactly why you went through her phone."

"I don't know. I had a few weak moments, I guess," I say. "But I don't obsess about it like she does. She's got issues, man."

He stares at me for a moment and shakes his head slightly.

I'm about to get a speech.

"Don, I love you like a brother – which is why I'm going to be straight with you."

I nod.

"Right now, you need to focus on *you*. It's not about her at all. It might seem like it is, but it's not."

"You serious?" I sit up. "But she's the one who freaked out on *me*."

"Don, look – instead of practicing empathy in her weak moment, you got so upset that you yelled and swore at the woman you say you love. You punched a hole in your own wall and you got so worked up that you thought about getting high. And to top it off, you obviously have some trust issues yourself.

"At least she told you her fears," he continues, "but you kept yours to yourself, then judged her for doing the same damn thing."

I've got to hand it to him. James knows how to flip the script.

"Okay, point taken. But still, this relationship is doomed."

"You might be right, Don. It might not work out – who knows? But I can tell you this: running away can't be your focus right now. Whether this relationship works out or not is beside the point. This is all about your recovery. It's an opportunity for you to grow and learn about relationships – and not just about your relationship with Bri. This is about all of your relationships."

"I think my relationships are pretty good," I counter. "Except for this one."

"Don, your primary relationship is with yourself, and all of your other relationships are just a reflection of that one. Your priority is to take care of *you*, and you do that by acting in alignment with principles – the ones you've committed to live by."

I slump in my chair a bit. He continues.

"Which means that under no circumstances do you repeat what you did last night. If the feelings are too much, that's okay. Call me, and I'll come get you. You can yell and scream and say whatever the hell you need without any filters. But you can't do that with her. You need to practice empathy and patience. If you lose control again, it's only going to make it worse. Maybe *way* worse. Understand?"

"Yeah, I do."

"Can you commit to doing that?" he asks. "You'll call me so we can talk about it instead?"

"Yes. I will," I say. "I'm committed."

"Good. Okay, so about this other thing. Why are you looking in her phone?"

"Just curious, I guess. I wanted to see who she's talking to, who she's texting."

"Why not just ask her?"

"Well, if she *is* messing around, she wouldn't tell me, right?"

"I don't know – would she?" he asks. "And besides, if you don't trust her to not screw around on you, why are you with her in the first place?"

"Because I love her. And the truth is, I really don't think she would."

"Okay, but let's explore that. If she *did* screw around on you, what would it mean?"

Crap. I know where this is going. He's going to ask me questions that get to the root of why I looked through her phone. Which is that on some level I'm afraid. Or insecure. Or both. And then he'll direct me to the solution, which is to affirm what I know and believe *is* the truth. So I just cut to the chase.

"Well, one thing it *wouldn't* mean is that I'm inadequate," I answer. "She's responsible for her behavior, not me."

"Okay, and what would it mean for you?"

"It would mean I'd need to reevaluate our relationship, because I want to be with someone who is honest with me. But right now, I don't need to worry about any of that or go snooping through her stuff because it's not real. It's not actual."

"Good," he nods. "Now, you're angry because she doesn't trust you. Let me ask you – are you trustworthy?"

"Yeah, I am."

"You sure?"

"Definitely."

"And if she doesn't trust you, whose issue is that?"

"Hers."

"Okay, and what about her? Is she trustworthy?"

"Yeah, I believe so."

"Yet, despite what you believe, it's hard to trust her completely?"

I nod my head yes.

"Don, one thing I've had to learn and re-learn, is that trust isn't a feeling. Trust is a choice, and it always involves risk. We have to be willing to choose to trust, and to also accept the risk that we might get hurt. When we snoop around and investigate and try to verify whether someone is who we want them to be, what we're really trying to do is find certainty – and the need for that is grounded in fear. There may be situations where investigating is appropriate, but I don't think you're at that point."

"You ever have trust issues with Sadie?"

"Of course. I think everyone does on some level. But the key is, we choose to trust. Or, we choose to *not* trust. It's up to us and it's okay, whatever we choose. We make those choices and we live with them until we decide to do something different. But in the middle of it all, we don't compromise our principles because of fear."

I want to choose to trust. For both of us to choose to trust.

"What do you think about couples counseling?" he asks.

"Really? We've only lived together for a couple months!"

"And what about it?"

"Well, if we were together for five years and had a couple kids, I could see it. But we're just getting started." I shake my head and laugh. "We're doomed, James."

"I'm not suggesting it so you can save your relationship. It's for you to grow and get more clarity about what you truly want – instead of running away like you always have. And if you both *do* choose to make it work, just know that couples get through a lot more than punched walls and arguments. This stuff is common, and especially with histories like yours. It's not good or bad, it just is. And it's just going to take some extra work." He smiles. "That is, if you're willing."

BRI AND I HAVE BEEN SEEING A COUNSELOR FOR FOUR months now. Pam is kind of like a referee. And a coach, too. When we meet, I tell her my version of things, and Bri tells her hers. Pam asks us a lot of questions about how we communicate, and she always wants all the details. And afterward, when she gives us input, it's like she untangles mysteries. Such as how, when Bri and I try to communicate, our words sometimes leave our mouths and magically transform in mid-air, becoming entirely different words when they land in each other's ears. Pam gives us exercises to do right in front of her, too. She tells us to look each other in the eye and say things like, "When you [do that/say this], I feel [hurt/angry/pissed]."

For us, couples counseling is Relationships 101 and on-the-job training rolled into one. The trick is to actually practice what we learn, and we're doing our best. Bri asked Sadie to sponsor her since she's navigated relationship issues with James. And

I'm always bouncing what I learn off James. Bri and I set aside a half-hour each week to talk about our relationship. We talk about what we're happy with and what we want to work on. We set goals and discuss our progress, and it's working.

I've learned that when I slow down and express my feelings in real time, things turn out better. This is true in all my relationships. It doesn't matter whether I'm telling someone I'm not comfortable with loaning them fifty bucks, or whether I'm telling Bri that I feel disregarded when she uses "that tone" with me. Whoever it is, people seem to respect it when I'm clear, and they appreciate that they don't have to guess where I'm coming from.

I also practice remaining present and staying mindful of my truth. Especially the truth that I am good. That I'm trustworthy and that I matter. And regardless of what happens, I must stand on that truth, and act like I believe it. And if someone disagrees with me, well, that doesn't matter one damn bit.

I can't *afford* to let it matter. Because even though I'm building new memories and habits, the old ones are still there. They're under the surface and dormant, but they're just waiting to have the dust knocked off them so they can get busy again. It gets better with time and practice, but I absolutely *must* stay present. I've got to stay on top of my emotions. Because if I don't, I can lose big. I had a terrifying lesson that reminded me of this.

I came close to losing it all.

"HEY, HONEY," BRI ANNOUNCED, "MEG INVITED ME TO catch dinner and a movie with the ladies. You mind?"

I had been planning to ask her to do something with me that night. I just hadn't gotten around to it yet.

"Sure. That's cool," I told her.

Later when she kissed me on the cheek and walked out the door, I felt hurt. There I was, left all alone in a creaky, old house. But she was going out to have fun.

I don't know why I felt so upset. I just did. And as the evening passed, I kept picturing her laughing and enjoying herself while I was stuck home with my nose against the window, like a dog waiting for its human.

When she finally got home and tried to snuggle up to me, I pushed her away.

"What's your problem?" she asked.

"Nothing, what's yours?" I turned over and faced the wall.

"You're upset because I went out with my friends?"

I remained silent.

"Don't be such a baby," she snapped, then she rolled over and went to sleep.

A *baby*? Fury arose in my chest. That bitch, I thought. If she had even an inkling of the kind of man she shared this bed with, the word *baby* would never have fallen from her lips.

I stewed late into the night. And she just slept peacefully – which pissed me off even more. She didn't even care enough to stare at the wall for hours like me.

This relationship is lopsided, I thought. She doesn't give a shit.

When I woke up the next morning, I was still in a funk. And by the time she left for work, I had a combustible mix of anger and self-pity brewing inside me. It was like gunpowder. And that's when the thought of getting high crossed my mind.

It lit the fuse.

My body picked up right where it left off. It flipped over to autopilot and twenty minutes later, I watched as I took the first hit of crack. The moment I did, I regretted it. Paranoia and fear plagued me instantly. I peeked out the curtains, looking for imaginary enemies, for the police and the FBI.

I was sick to my stomach. There would be no happy end to

this, I knew. Just like that, I'd thrown my entire life away. By deciding to use, I'd made sure that everything I'd worked for would go straight down the drain.

I knew there was no use in trying to stop, so when I ran out of drugs I went out and scored more. But as I was walking up to our front door, Bri pulled in the driveway. She got out of her car and rushed up to me. Her eyes searched my face and eyes.

"Have you been getting high?"

I nodded, my right fist clenching the handful of crack.

"Oh my God!" she shouted. "I knew it! I had this feeling, so I left and came home!"

"I don't care anymore," I said. "It's too late. I'm going to keep getting high."

"No! It's not too late, Don!" She stepped between me and the front door, then she started sobbing. "Is this what you really want? You're going to choose drugs over us? Over me? Over everything we've worked for?"

I stood there, feeling nothing. Like granite.

Her eyes darted toward my hand.

"Give me the dope!"

"No fucking way. I told you, I'm getting high."

She lunged toward my hand, but I raised my fist high above my head. She leaped and jumped, but I held my hand even higher.

"Just give up," I shouted. "Leave me the hell alone!"

She stopped. She backed up a couple of feet and glared at me, her fists at her sides.

And then she kicked me hard.

Right in the nuts.

I keeled over and dropped the crack. And as I gagged and almost threw up in our driveway, Bri scooped up the crack, then ran inside and flushed it down the toilet.

Fifteen minutes later, James and Sadie pulled up. I left with

James, and Sadie stayed behind with Bri. He took me to a meeting, then stayed with me till late in the night.

As my mind returned, I was shell-shocked. Baffled. I didn't understand how things had gone downhill so quickly.

"Bro, I don't get it," I said to James. "After all I've been through, I went out and did the absolute worst thing I could've done. Can you believe that? I thought I'd grown – but I was wrong."

"Don, you've come a long way. You've done some fantastic work and you've had some profound awakenings," he said, "but right now you need to know that you're not bulletproof. Those deep emotions we've been working with are still there, and if you don't stay on top of it, they can be intoxicating – like a drug. They can take on a life of their own, and then take you out. Apparently, you needed a reminder."

I thought I'd already learned this stuff a year ago – it's called the basics. Obviously, I hadn't learned them well enough.

"You cannot afford to sit on negative self-talk and self-pity," he added. "Especially when it involves something so close to your heart."

My face was red with shame. I looked at the floor.

"Yeah, you're right."

"You heard about Llama Jim?"

I raised my head.

"No, what's up?"

"He relapsed again. I just found out today. He was out driving at 4 a.m., and he lost control of his car. He drove it into a ditch, and it burst into flames."

"No way! He died?"

"Yep," he nodded. "Burned alive."

"Holy shit!" I shouted. "For real?"

"Yeah, it's true."

I hadn't seen Llama Jim since that night at the ranch, but I'd heard he'd had a rough time staying clean since then.

"Don, this is a great time for you to find out about Jim. You've got to respect where you are at with this."

I could barely believe the news. That could've been me, and on some level, I'd forgotten that.

"You're right. I haven't been practicing the basics like I did in the beginning. My daily routine hasn't been top priority."

"Don, when life gets good and it gets really busy, a lot of people forget about it. They quit meditating because finding that quiet time to get centered can be tricky. But you can't afford to stop your practice. You've got to stay present."

I nod my head.

"You've got to commit to yourself that you will let nothing, absolutely nothing, fuck with your recovery. Not Bri, not your parents, your job, whatever." He smiled. "You ready to get back on the wagon?"

"I am. I don't ever want to go through that again."

"Good, because you don't have to. The first thing you need to do is put down the baseball bat. Don't beat yourself up. Stay in the solution, and in thirty days I promise you'll be in the groove even stronger. Sound good?"

"Yeah," I said. "Thanks, James."

"No problem, bro. Call me tomorrow when you wake up," he said. "I'll swing by and get you."

THAT SLIP WAS TWO MONTHS AGO. I TOOK JAMES'S suggestions, and he was right – I'm stronger than before, and in some ways it's like it never even happened. I've lost nothing. I still have my house, my friends, and Bri.

But there's one thing that's different. That vision board I keep in my mind has an addition. On the very top, above the images of the successful job and wife and all the happy smiles, there's a new one.

It's me. I'm sitting on a mat in a bamboo garden. My eyes are closed. I'm meditating. I'm always practicing.

I'm staying present.

I don't have a bamboo garden and I've never meditated in one. But that's not the point. This image is just figurative. It's on top because it's my first priority. It's my number one commitment for life.

I don't try to stay focused and grounded because it feels good or it's spiritual or because it looks good in a selfie. I do it to stay on my path.

I do it to survive.

Lesson learned.

29

TILL THE WHEELS FALL OFF

I hold it up to the light as I sit in the back of the bus. It's a round, well-cut diamond. It's just under a carat, and it's set in a modest, white-gold band, and it sparkles like a little disco ball. It cost me almost everything I have, and I had to take out a small loan, too.

I put it back in its box and close the lid, and put it back in my pocket.

I know it seems crazy. We've only been living together six months, and it's definitely been a bit...turbulent. But I'm going to do it anyway.

I'm going to ask Bri to marry me.

Being in this relationship has its challenges, but there's a lot of good times, too. We go on road trips. We go skydiving. We eat out whenever we can and try new food. We go see the Dave Matthews Band. Once in a blue moon, we go dancing at clubs, though when we do, we stay together tight and we just drink Red Bull. We go to the beach a lot, and sometimes we swim out as far as we can until we're scared, then swim back to shore as fast as we can.

I just know this relationship is good for me. That Bri is good for me. I was even inspired to finally write, record, produce, and publish a song. It's called "Little Tree." Since the day I got out of prison I wanted to do that, but I always dragged my ass. Now I finally did it – and for my bedroom studio debut, it's not too bad.

We still have relationship work to do – but who doesn't? The other day I read something that I've been thinking a lot about. It said that when people fall in love, they see only the positives. They're oblivious to each other's faults. Then after some time passes, reality sets in. They discover each other's weaknesses, and those shortcomings become glaring. Eventually it takes effort to find the good anymore, and loving each other becomes hard; each begins to wonder if what they once had together was real.

I think maybe it's actually the other way around. It starts out real, then becomes *un*-real. I think that when people initially see only the good, what they're seeing is actually the truth – they're seeing who the other person truly is. And the flaws, well maybe those *aren't* real. After all, if you get to the bottom of it, most flaws are based on something that's not true, like some kind of fear or self-doubt. And those kinds of flaws can't possibly align with who we truly are.

That's what it seems like to me, anyway. I choose to believe the real Bri has no faults. She has no suspicion, no lack of trust.

She lacks *nothing*, for that matter.

And neither do I.

I'm trying to keep my focus on the real Bri, and she's keeping her's on the real Don. And if we do that, the real and the good and the true will grow. With everything that's happened over the past couple years, I'm convinced this doesn't just apply to falling in love.

It's how all things work.

We're going to the Florida Keys in a couple weeks, and I have a plan. I have this tiny metal treasure chest I bought at a gift shop, and I'm going to put the ring in it. When we get to Key Largo, I'm going to dive in the ocean and pretend I find it at the bottom. I'll show it to her on the shore, and her eyes will be wide with curiosity as we open it together.

When I pull out the ring and propose to her right there on the beach, she's going to absolutely freak out.

It's going to be epic.

The bus stops and lets me off. I walk to our house quickly because I want to find a hiding place for the ring before Bri gets home. But she's already there, and she's waiting on me so we can go to the grocery store.

Putting the ring away can wait, I think. I get in the passenger seat and buckle up. But as she puts the keys in the ignition, all I can think about is that ring in my pocket. My stomach gets jittery. It's one thing having it, but it's another having it on me while I'm sitting right next to her.

"What?" she asks.

"What do you mean?"

"You're over there snickering to yourself."

"No, I'm not."

"Whatever."

I've never been great at keeping secrets about gifts. When I was a kid, I couldn't help but blab to my family what I got them for Christmas before it ever even arrived. I can't let that happen tonight. I wipe the grin from my face, and I get it under control. But a mile down the road I catch myself laughing again.

It's going to be a long two weeks.

The sun has barely set when we park at the grocery store. We walk through the parking lot in silence. When we near the entrance, she turns to me and stops and plants her feet. Her hands are on her hips, and she has a scowl on her face.

"What's going on?"

"What do you mean?"

I start laughing aloud.

"I want to know what's up!" she demands. "Now tell me!"

I regain my composure and sigh. There's no way I'll make it two weeks. I reach in my pocket and pull out the little box. I open the lid, and the diamond blings under the parking lot lights. She gasps, and I propose to her as shoppers pour around us on their way into the store.

"Will you marry me?" I ask. "Please?"

"Oh my God! I can't believe you!! Oh my God!"

"Um, is that a yes?"

"Yes! Yes!!"

So much for Key Largo – I just settled for a Publix parking lot. But its own way, it's still epic.

A MONTH LATER WE SET OUT ON A JOG IN OUR neighborhood in the morning. We cut through Hammock Park, breaking into a sprint and then we start racing. We get winded and slow to a walk and catch our breath and laugh, making our way through a winding trail surrounded by tall oaks and pines, a canopy of mossy branches spread out above us.

Abruptly, the trail ends and spills out onto a sidewalk in an adjoining neighborhood. Before us, on the corner, is a small chapel.

A white picket fence lines the property, and inside there's flower gardens and tall oaks. The grass is lush and green. We look at each other, then lift the latch on the gate and walk inside. There's a wooden post with a short blurb about the place. It's an old Scottish church from the late 1800s, preserved as a landmark.

The chapel is whitewashed, with arched stained-glass windows. A walkway leads up to the entrance, and we make our way up and peek inside a window. The floors are hardwood, stained dark, and the pews are aged. Amber-hued sunlight beams in through a round stained-glass window perched just above the altar.

We look at each other and grin. It's amazing. And as we face the front doors, we notice a sign that has a number to call for scheduling events.

Like weddings.

It's December 7, 2013, almost two years ago to the day since I walked through the doors of HEP. There have been a lot of important days since then. Like the day I went back to school. Or when I finally got my own place. There was the day I went skydiving, and there was Kevin and Kim's wedding. The day I finally got my driver's license back, and all the days I met new friends.

Important days are coming, too. I'll be off disability soon because now I've got a telemarketing gig selling solar panels. It's only eight bucks an hour plus tiny commissions, but it's a start. I'll have my software development degree toward the end of the year.

But none of those days are, or ever will be, quite like today. Because today is a day for reflection. And it's a day for looking forward, too. It's a milestone for me if there ever was one.

Today is our wedding day.

I'm with my dad and Bob at my place. My brother is my best man. He's helping me with my tie, and there's a photographer snapping shots of our every move. Michael's on the way, along with Bri's brother and nephew.

I'm excited, but my stomach is in knots.

"How you feeling, D?" my dad smiles. "Nervous?"

I tug at the tie in the mirror one last time and I turn to him.

"Hell no."

Bob is standing next to me with a big grin on his face. He puts his hand on my shoulder.

"You do seem a bit tense," he laughs, "but you're looking pretty damn good."

We all laugh, my dad and my brother and me.

"Y'know, I'm glad you're here with me." I look them in the eyes for a moment. "It's a big deal to me. Without you guys I, well, I don't think any of this would be happening."

I cut it short because I'm starting to choke up. They nod, and I know they get it. They've seen me at my absolute worst, and now today, my absolute best. It *is* a big deal, and I'm so glad we're here together. I've had my amends talk with both of them, just as I did with my mom and Liz. And like them, my dad and Bob aren't focused on the past one bit. They just want me to keep doing what I'm doing because it's working.

There's a knock at the front door. It's Michael.

"Wow, looking good, man!" He stands there and nods his head. "It's a great day, brother."

"Yeah, it sure is," I say. "You're looking good too."

"Thanks bro," he laughs. "It's good to be alive."

Bri's brother and her nephew follow moments later. We all pose for some pics, and then it's time to go.

Though it's winter, it's in the low seventies and it's sunny and crisp. A thick crowd of people are standing outside the chapel when we pull up. My mom and Liz are out front, and I give them a hug and a kiss, and we talk for a moment. I give Bri's mom, Pat, a hug. I shake hands with Mark, Bri's dad. I greet James and Sadie, and Kevin and Kim are here, too.

There are so many others here, too. It's a mixed bunch; our friends are all in recovery, and then there's our families, who have come from all over the country. Seeing them all at the same place seems odd, but it feels so right.

Even our grandparents are here. They smile upon us from within picture frames that sit on a table surrounded by bouquets of flowers. Both the living and the dead are witnesses as Bri walks down the aisle and we read our vows before them all. We swear to always be there for each other. We commit to always take care of ourselves so we can bring our best to each other. Through sickness and health, we vow to love and cherish each other. We've written our vows separately and we didn't share them with each other. But it sounds like we sneaked a look at each other's vows and copied the ideas. Especially our promise to travel on this journey together until the very end – *till the wheels fall off*.

Our friends and family, they're generous with gifts. A week later, we leave on a seven-day cruise through the Caribbean. We explore the Mayan ruins near Cozumel. We zipline through tall trees in the rainforests of Belize. We swim with huge swarms of stingrays in the clear blue ocean that surrounds the Cayman Islands. We eat and dance and watch shows on the ship.

We have a blast.

At the end of night three, we're back in our cabin.

"I can barely believe this is really happening," I tell her.

"Me neither." She steps close. "It's just...amazing."

"Yeah, it really is." I pull her closer. "God has been so good to us."

"Agreed." She puts her hands on my shoulders and kisses my lips. "Let's trust God with everything going forward."

"Yeah?" I grin. "Including when we start a family?"

"Yes." Her lips curl into a smile. "Starting now."

A few weeks after we return, I come through the front door and Bri is standing in the middle of the living room. She's got a huge, silly grin on her face and she's nodding her head *yes*, like I'm supposed to somehow just get it. But I don't, and for a moment it's like charades.

"Um, you got some Ben and Jerry's in the freezer?"

That's a no.

"We saved a bunch of money on our car insurance?"

Another no.

Then the lightbulb turns on, and I almost reach for the counter to steady myself. I'm going to be a dad? We're going to be a family?

"You're pregnant?" I stammer.

Bingo.

We hug. We yell. We jump up and down and we shout.

We're going to have a honeymoon baby, and my heart is about to burst.

When we climb into bed, there's no sleep. Instead we're seated upright, our pillows at the small of our backs against the headboard. There's a glow illuminating our dark room. We're gripping our phones, searching online for anything and everything that has to do with having babies. Feeding them. Raising them. Being good parents.

There's so much information. So much to learn.

The sun is about to rise when we finally fall asleep.

30

JUNIOR PROGRAMMER

I'm seated at my cubicle, staring at the green phone I just hung up. I don't want to ever pick it up again. I'm not enthused about cold-calling people and reciting words from a script – especially when it's about something I don't believe in. When I came aboard, I thought it was to sell solar energy. Then I came to understand that what they really want me to do is hard-sell fixed-income retirees on solar financing that will cost them more in the long run. Plus, a lot of the people here use drugs, and I bet half of them have been to jail more than once.

I hate my job. No, *strongly dislike* is better. I want to quit but now that Bri is pregnant, it's complicated. I need to stick with a plan, and I think I have a good one.

First, for now I'll keep this job. With a baby on the way, I can't quit until I have something better to go to.

That's rule number one.

Next, I'll keep working toward my degree. We'll squeeze by with the solar gig somehow until I graduate, and when I do, doors will swing wide open for me. I'll find an entry-level programming job and start making decent money.

Then, and only then, is when I'll quit the solar gig.

Getting the degree is non-negotiable; without one I'll have no future. If I weren't an ex–bank robber, maybe it wouldn't be such a big deal. But for me, a degree will be the only thing that can show an employer that I even *might* be worth a shot.

The boss walks out on the floor, right by my cubicle. He's on the short side, a bit heavy, and he's chewing a fat cigar. He stops and looks around, then he removes the stogie from his lips.

"Wrap up the calls!" he shouts. "Two minutes and we're having a meeting!"

Time for one of his pep talks, which aren't too peppy. Which is another reason I strongly dislike this place.

"Now listen up," he says. "You all know how lucky you are to find a job like this."

He pauses, and looks around the room

"You don't have to be here till 9 a.m. You only work five lousy hours. You can dress how you want, smoke when you want, and you can even eat at your desk. You miss a day or come in late? I don't give a shit. We're here for you. Every Friday, like clockwork, we hand you a check, and the bank's right over there."

He points across the street.

"You can't get any better than this – what more could you want?"

He eyes one person, then another.

Then me.

"And you know as well as me," he continues, "that most of you couldn't find a job anywhere else."

What a cheap shot, I think. We might be a motley crew, but that's still a shitty thing to say.

"Now listen." He wags his finger at us. "Some of you are screwing off. You're not staying on script. Not making enough calls."

He paces the floor and continues.

"I'm going to tell you something. Don't let me catch you

without that phone in your hand. You need to stay on it and stay on script because I didn't hire you because I needed friends. I hired you to make me some goddamn money. You'd better get with the program, or I will take whatever commissions you think you've earned and send you on your fucking way. Understood?"

Heads nod yes.

"Good. Now get your asses back to work."

He sticks the cigar back in his mouth and walks back to his office.

His words sink in, and I'm not okay with it. I don't like being spoken to like that. It's not that I'm taking it personally. Actually, it's the opposite; I know what he said doesn't fit me at all. And at once, I know that this entire place is no longer a fit for me. Maybe a couple years ago it would've been. But not today.

The truth is, that guy should thank me for being here. *He's* the lucky one – not me.

I glance at the phone in front of me and I know in my heart I'll never pick it up again.

I sigh. So much for rule number one.

I rise to my feet and tell the manager I'm finished, right in front of everyone. I walk out the door and unchain my bike from a post outside, and I push off. The breeze hits my face and I smile, then I laugh as I race home down the Dunedin trail. I did the right thing; I have no doubt about it. I deserve better, and I'm starting to understand my worth. Going forward, *that* will be rule number one. I will stick to that rule, and trust that God is always with me.

No matter what.

IT'S 6 A.M., AND I'M SEARCHING FOR JOBS ONLINE. IT'S

been three weeks since I left the solar gig. I've submitted a lot of resumes and filled out several applications.

I'm shooting for an entry-level software development job. But I'll accept website developer or tech support, even. And if this runs on another few weeks, I'll take bus boy. I'm thinking I just might have to do that, too, because the feedback I'm getting is that I don't have enough experience. Or, I don't have a degree.

Or, they don't hire felons.

I'm starting to freak out, and I've even had a few thoughts about going back to the solar gig with my tail between my legs.

But this morning, I run across something that makes me sit up straight. It's an ad for a junior software developer. It's local, just a couple miles from our place. I reply to the ad and I attach my resume. It's mid-afternoon when I get a response from the owner of the company, inviting me for an interview the next day.

I can barely contain myself. I tell Bri. I call James. I call my mom and dad. If I can just get my foot in the door and land that position, it's over. I'll be a *junior software developer*. And after a year I might be able to replace that junior with *senior*. Then with experience *and* a degree, I'll land an even better gig in one of those higher income brackets.

Like, maybe even over 40k.

I do some research on the company. They help merchants who get dinged by online credit card fraud. It sounds complex. I don't know squat about how that stuff works, but I try to work with what I do know. I memorize the bullet points. I practice breathing and letting go. I tell myself it will unfold just as it's meant to.

When I arrive for the interview, the receptionist leads me through a hallway to a tiny office. The door is ajar, and a guy in jeans and a T-shirt is sitting back on a big chair with his foot on the desk. He's talking on the phone and looks at me over his glasses.

"Your three o'clock is here," she whispers.

He waves me in and motions for me to sit, then wraps up his call. He stands up and sticks his hand out.

"How's it going?" he asks. "I'm Gary, CEO of Charge-backs911."

I shake his hand. He covers the company history briefly, and then gets right down to it. He tells me they need a good programmer to get on board and learn the business. He and his wife, Monica, own the company and in the next few years they'll go international. They're going *big*, he says, and soon, Fortune 500 companies will be lining up to do business with them. If I come aboard, I'll be getting in at the perfect time.

"How many people work here?" I ask.

"About twenty-five. But that number will be going up," he smiles. "*Way* the hell up."

He walks me back to the lobby, then turns to me.

"You ready to work your ass off, Don?"

"I'm ready," I tell him. "I'm all in."

"Good. That's exactly what we need." He nods his head and grins. "My better half will be out to see you in a few. Just wait here."

He walks back to his office, and I stand in the lobby and read an article about the company. It's framed on the wall and has a picture of a businesswoman smiling widely.

"Don?"

I turn. It's the woman in the picture. There's a guy with her, too.

"Monica?"

"That's me." She extends her hand, then introduces the guy with curly hair and glasses standing next to her. "This is Jay, our Director of IT."

We all shake hands and go to a room. They tell me about the position, Jay quizzes me on my skills, and I explain why I want to work at Chargebacks911.

I tell them that I want to learn and grow with a company. That creating awesome products with cutting-edge technology is my passion.

I think I nailed it, but I'm not sure she agrees. She abruptly stands and politely shakes my hand.

"You'll hear something by morning," she says. "Thank you for your time."

I don't hear anything by the next morning. So I email Jay. Then I email Monica. Then, for good measure, I email Gary, too. I want the job and know I'm the one for it – and I let them know it. All day, I monitor my inbox like a hawk.

Nothing.

Later in the day I call and leave a message. And then a while later, I leave another.

They probably think I'm psycho, I think, but at least they'll remember me. Plus, I'm not going to take no for an answer until they keep their word and tell me what's up.

I finally get an email from Monica. She tells me to come in the following Monday – and to be ready to work.

My title is going to be *Junior Programmer*.

I run into the living room.

"I got the job! I got the job!" I yell at Bri.

We're nearly jumping up and down, and we're hugging. Finally, I'm going back to work full-time – with a real career that can take us places. I'm a *professional software developer!* It's only twelve bucks an hour, but that's four more than I was making a few weeks ago. And after ninety days they'll give me a substantial bump. If I deliver, Monica said, I'll be amazed at where things go.

I don't have to wait ninety days to be amazed. I already am.

31

LEVI

"Okay, now hold your partner's hips, take a deep breath, and squeeze gently."

The squeeze is supposed to relieve the pent-up pressure from six months of pregnancy. I squeeze Bri's hips and she groans.

It's prenatal yoga night, and we go twice a week. It's a six-week series and one more night and we'll be finished. Practicing yoga will help Bri be stronger, the instructor says. She'll be more flexible and prepared for birth.

I don't know much about yoga but Bri does. She thinks it's the solution for everything. It helps you get connected to God, she says. It cures back pain. It even helps with weight management. She's even been taking classes to become a yoga instructor, and she plans on mixing her recovery knowledge with yoga and developing a yoga style for recovery.

Me, I'm just happy to be here. I want to learn because I need to do this parenting thing right. And also because this whole thing of becoming a dad freaks me out. I want it more than anything, but it's bringing up some deep feelings. Yes, I know I'll make mistakes and that I'm not perfect, and I accept that. So it's not that. And I also know without a doubt that I'll be a good dad, so it's not that, either.

It's this: I've actually passed on my genes to my child – which is a terrifying thought. And not only that, we found out we were having a boy a few months ago, which is even more scary.

The last thing I want is a mini-me.

If anything, I want him to be a mini-*he*. The less like me, I think, the safer he will probably be. The safer we *all* will be.

So I've got my work cut out for me. If I'm going to parent the best I can, I need to learn all I can.

My dad and mom say you learn how to be a parent by doing it. That you love your child before they're even born, and that love just grows and grows. And as it does, it shows you the way. You can't plan it all out or anticipate everything that happens.

That sounds good, and I agree in principle. But still, I'm going to prepare in every way I can.

I do my research. I read all the links Bri sends me, too. There's *attachment* parenting style. There's the *helicopter* approach. Private versus public school. Schools of thought about how youngsters learn best. There are discipline theories. My dad spanked me occasionally when I was a kid, but not nearly as often as the dean in junior high swatted me.

Obviously, it never worked for me.

Maybe my parents are right. I need to keep it simple. Besides, I'm getting way ahead of myself, anyway. Our boy isn't even born yet, and right now I need to focus on learning how to help Bri bring him into the world – not on whether or not he will go to Montessori.

We've decided on a name. His first name will be Levi. His middle name is going to be Herman, after my grandfather. My *dad's* father. When I told my dad his full name, his eyes welled up with tears and for a moment, he couldn't speak. I'm glad it made my dad happy. But the truth is, I'm not naming my son after my grandfather for my dad's sake. No, it's for my grandfather. It's a tribute to him. And I believe that somewhere, somehow, my grandfather will be proud.

IT WAS 1989 WHEN I CALLED COLLECT FROM A FEDERAL prison in Arizona. My grandmother answered, and she knew why I was calling. She handed the phone straight to him.

"Hi, Grandpa," I said. "How are you?"

"Donny?" he whispered. His voice trembled. He'd been released from the hospital just the day before, after having half a lung removed.

"Yes, it's me, Grandpa. How are you doing? Are you okay?"

He was silent for a moment. I pressed the phone closer to my ear. And then, I heard him begin to cry. It was faint at first, but then quickly it gave way to loud sobs.

"Grandpa? What's the matter?" I'd never heard my grandfather cry before. I began to panic, and I didn't know what to do. And then, he quieted down. After he blew his nose, he managed to speak a few words.

"Donny, when are you going to stop conning and lying to us?" he asked, his voice cracking. "All of us, Donny, we love you so much."

He broke out crying again, and then suddenly, my grandmother was on the phone.

"We love you, honey," she said. "I need to take care of him now. Call back soon."

I hung up the phone, stunned and heartbroken.

I was twenty-two years old, and I was serving my first sentence for bank robbery.

My grandfather saw the world in black and white. If you said you were going to do something, you just did it. If you didn't, then you were lying and bullshitting everyone.

Technically, he was right. I'd sworn again and again to my family that I'd stop using drugs and start doing the right thing. I truly wanted to make good on those promises, but I didn't know how. The truth was that I was just damaged, and I had some hard lessons ahead of me, and I don't think he ever really understood that part of it.

And really, that made two of us.

My grandfather was a hell of a guy. He was a World War II veteran, a fireman and a police officer. And later on, he became of those rare, honest salesmen with a big booming voice who people naturally trust and like.

God, how I wanted to make him proud of me. That would have really meant something.

But those few words he managed to speak to me that day, they were the last I ever heard from him. Because just a couple days later, he was gone.

SO LEVI HERMAN, YES, THAT'S FOR MY GRANDFATHER. And to the best of my ability, I'm going to make sure that my son, his namesake, is well-adjusted and healthy. Both Bri and I are going to make that happen. We've done our homework and planned well.

We've decided on a birth center. We're going all natural – we'll avoid epidurals or inducing, and it will be a water birth. We've attended special classes on natural birth, and we've gotten to know the midwives who will be there to help us. We've selected some soothing music to play as he comes into the world. We've been through drills for the day Bri goes into labor.

We know what do.

When Bri goes into labor at 11 a.m. on a weekday, we report to the birthing center with our duffle bags full of water, towels, meditation music, and baby clothes. They show us to our room, which is more like a suite. It's spacious and luxurious. Soothing scents fill the room, and a large whirlpool bath sits in the center.

It's going to be a spiritual experience.

But after twenty-four hours of labor, Bri has to transfer to a hospital. She's worn out, and Levi is nowhere near arriving. Once we are admitted to the hospital, right away they start pushing us to induce and get an epidural. A few hours later, Bri relents.

More hours pass, and inducing isn't working. Nothing is going as planned, and we're dismayed and exhausted. Finally, after thirty-eight hours of labor, they wheel Bri into the operation room for a C-section.

It goes by like a blur. I stand behind Bri, holding her hand with one hand and stroking her forehead with the other, whispering that everything's going to be okay. A curtain hides her midsection from both of us. Then suddenly, I hear my son cry. The surgeon holds up his tiny, wrinkled body, and a doctor swaddles him and hands him to me. I gaze at my son in astonishment, then hold him close as he screams. And at that moment, the surgeon tells me I need to take Levi to another room. Bri is hemorrhaging, I hear him say, and I can't stay in the room. They need to focus on her.

I kiss Bri's forehead and tell her Levi and I love her. I'm still telling her it will be okay as the nurse rushes me out the door and down the hall to a private room. The nurse says she'll be back with an update as soon as she can. Then she leaves me there alone with my son.

I lay him gently in a small bassinet next to the bed and I take off my shirt. I pick him back up and hold him close to my bare chest. He needs to feel skin.

He needs to feel connection.

I'm almost trembling. I don't know if we're going to lose Bri. I take a few breaths and get centered, and I focus on Levi.

It's just me and my boy.

I whisper in his little ear how much I love him. How much his mother loves him. I tell him that his grandparents love him and that he's going to be great. I tell him he will be a leader. That he will help others. I speak these words directly into his soul, to let his spirit know how incredibly valuable he is.

How perfect he is.

I want him to be certain of the very things I always doubted about myself.

An hour later, the nurse comes through the door, wheeling Bri into the room.

She's awake and she's okay, and all is well. I gently place Levi in her arms, and she cries as she holds him close to her chest.

The past forty hours have been one hell of a journey. Nothing played out like we planned, but as we look at Levi, none of that matters anymore.

Everything is perfect.

32

FINLEY DONALD

My mom sets an iced tea on the living room table in front of me, and she takes a seat next to my dad on the couch. She puts her hand on my dad's shoulder and rubs his neck. His face is narrow, and his neck is thin. It's been ten years of on and off treatment, and he's tired.

I stop by after work some days, or sometimes when I'm just out and about.

"How's Bri doing?" my mom asks

"She's doing okay," I say. "Real achy, and sleep is hard. She's definitely ready."

I take a sip of the tea and set it back down.

"He's constantly kicking and waking her up all the time," I chuckle. "He definitely wants out."

I can barely believe it. When Levi came almost two years ago, I didn't think I could ever love another human being as much as I loved that little boy. But then, almost nine months ago, I came home from work and there was Bri, giving me that crazy smile again.

Boy number two.

Since then, whenever I place my hand on Bri's belly and feel him kick, or when I look at his ultrasound pics, I know I have more than enough love. Plus, this time around I have no expectations. There's no telling how it will go, but I know that however it goes it's going to be a rollercoaster ride – and I'm ready for it.

"That's really something, D," my dad smiles. "I can see it in your face. You're starting to understand. The love you have for your children, it's like a miracle. It just keeps growing."

"You guys finally decide on a name?" my mom asks.

"We have." I sit up straight and look at her, and then my dad.

"His first name is Finley."

"Now that's a wonderful name!" She grins and pats my dad's knee. "The Irish side!"

"And for a middle name," I announce, "we chose Donald."

My dad leans forward on his seat.

"Donald?"

"Yeah. But we're not naming him after me. It's after you, Dad."

He nods, but says nothing.

We talk a bit more, and then I have to get back home. I give my mom and dad a hug and kiss, and I walk out to the driveway.

"Y'know something, D?"

I look up. My dad's standing by the front door.

"What's that, Dad?" I take a step toward him.

He takes a long look at me. Then he smiles, shaking his head.

"You amaze me, son."

"What do you mean?" I walk up to him. "Is everything all right?"

"Oh, yes." He puts his hand on my shoulder. "It's just that, well, you're really something. I mean, you're clean. You're a husband and dad who loves your family. You're a hard-worker.

You're a manager at a big company. It's like your entire past never really happened."

He's starting to tear up.

"It shows who you really are." He squeezes my shoulder tight. "You're a real class-A guy. You always have been, and I've always known. But now, you can see it. Everyone can. It's nothing short of a miracle."

I've heard old-timers say that before. *Class-A guy.*

That's someone you respect and trust. It's a guy who's solid. Someone other guys look up to. A model of what a good guy really is.

"I'm so damn proud of you, son."

I wipe the corner of my eye.

"Thanks, Dad. I love you."

When I drive away, I look in my rearview mirror. He's still standing in front of the house, watching me as I turn the corner.

He's right. It *is* miraculous. It was like I was down for the count, the referee standing over me, shouting. *Seven... Eight!... Nine!*

And on nine, it happened.

Somehow, I got up. And when I did, everything began to change. And now, it's as though all things are new. The former things, they've passed away. Even the bank robbery charge – they finally dropped that months ago.

It's amazing what has happened in my life.

Then there's my career. Now *that's* a real mind-blower. As Gary promised, our startup company went international. We grew exponentially in the financial technology sector. Or *FinTech*, for short. I'm the software development manager now, and within the next year or so, I'm probably going to become the Director of Software Development.

WHEN I FIRST STARTED, MY JOB WAS INSANE.

I'd be at my desk, gripping a burrito with my left hand and typing an email with my right. That's how I did lunch. Sometimes that's how I did breakfast and dinner, too. I got there early, and I left late. Then I'd work from home a bit before I crashed.

My job requirements were steep, and they continually changed. For three weeks, the focus would be a project doing technical stuff I'd never even heard of. After a little research, I'd be convinced that no one else had, either. I'd wake up in the middle of the night, my heart racing and my brain clueless as to how I'd figure it out. When the solution came to me, it was usually as I slept. I'd wake up with my answer and I'd bounce into work, practically skipping and giddy that I'd solved it – only to find out everything had changed. The project had been put on hold, and I'd been assigned a different task, usually one twice as hard.

I got jerked around so much I was getting whiplash.

I thought about doing something different. Something easier and less demanding. Something carefree, like getting an ice cream truck and making a living cruising the beaches, bringing the joy of fudge popsicles to my fellow humans. I even considered doing gigs at local clubs, playing acoustic covers of classic rock and R&B.

Now *that* would be living the dream.

But I couldn't justify quitting. Not after I began to understand what it was like to leave for work every morning and kiss my wife goodbye. To tell my little boy that his daddy loves him. To walk out that door knowing it wasn't about just me anymore. My dad, he understood this. So did my grandfather.

And now I did, too.

Quitting wasn't an option for me. But I still thought about it a lot. And when I wasn't thinking about quitting, I worried about getting fired.

I envisioned exactly how it would play out. Jay was going to stick his head in the door and call me into the office down the hall. And there, he'd have the talk with me.

"Hey Don, we need to have the talk with you."

"Oh. What's up?"

"Well, you're a great worker, but unfortunately everyone here now knows that you've been arrested. Like, way more than just one or two times. Or even ten or twenty."

"Oh, crap. What are we going to do?"

"Um, I'm really sorry to tell you this, but we have to let you go."

"But I'm a good worker, Jay. I always deliver."

"You are. And yes, you do. But the fact is, well, some people are afraid that you're actually here among them. Like, in the flesh."

It wasn't as bad as thinking the FBI or CIA was after me. But it was still nerve-wracking. For the first year, I went through the whole *I'm getting fired* stuff at least every other day. Then it slowed to a weekly thing. Then it was monthly.

When it got really bad, I'd call James and he'd talk me off the ledge.

"Okay, what would it mean if your co-workers found out about your past?"

"That they're some real nosy bastards."

"Seriously. What would it mean, Don?"

"Okay. It would mean they wouldn't look at me the same anymore."

"And how do they look at you now?"

"They think I'm polite. Funny. Maybe a bit of an airhead. But I think they really like me."

"Okay, and if they found out about your past, how would that change?"

"They would think I'm a horrible person."

"Okay, and why would that bother you? Are you really a horrible person?"

"No, I know I'm not. I guess that would be their problem. I'd still be okay with me."

"Okay, then why do you care if they find out about your past?"

"I could lose my job."

"And what would it mean if you lost your job?"

"I don't know. That my life would be ruined."

"Wait a second. Time out."

"What?"

"You, Don Cummins, the former homeless, insane ex-convict who has practically come back from the dead, are saying that all it would take to ruin your life is losing a damn job?"

"Okay, point taken. But it still would suck."

James and I would talk a lot about success, too. What it means, and what it doesn't. He pulled no punches with me. He'd tell me that if I wanted to succeed at anything, I had to find a way to make recovery the basis of everything I do. This journey of recovery, he'd tell me, is *my* journey – not anyone else's. I couldn't compare mine with anyone else's because it would always be changing. What worked for me yesterday might not work for me today, and it was my responsibility to pay attention to it so I could keep up.

And that required *work*.

If I practiced this, he'd tell me, I'd get in touch with my greatness. And when challenges came, I'd be ready even if I felt like I wasn't. I'd be able to give more. To help more.

To love more.

James was right. There would be no *easy*. There would be no lying down. No selling ice cream on the beach for me. And the more I began to accept that, even though I was still working my ass off, something within me began to find rest.

My life was hard in many ways. But the truth was, I loved the challenge.

And, I loved the results.

In the two years since I'd been there, our company had expanded our office space twice. First, we had a small office in a tiny strip mall. Then we annexed the office to our left, and then the one to the right. Then we moved the whole operation to a big, two-story building that we leased all for ourselves. And before long, we were making plans to do it all over again. We opened up offices in other countries and began to partner up with big names. Our employees tripled and quadrupled. We wound up with fifteen software developers, and we projected that with all the business headed our way, that would double over the next year or so.

When a new guy would start, I'd shake their hand. I'd smile and show them the ropes. I'd tell them about our company and what we did, and where we were headed.

Which was to the top.

The new guys, they were razor sharp. They were younger than me and they were degreed. They wanted to prove they knew their shit – and they did. Sometimes when they opened their mouths, I'd have no idea what they were talking about. I'd nod my head, and later I'd go look it up online.

A lot of them would confide in me. They'd complain about each other. Other times they'd look to me for advice. About love or balance or finding out how to be happy. Maybe it was because I was older, I don't know. But they seemed to trust me.

As my role evolved, so did my focus. It wasn't just about programming anymore. It was about helping all of us succeed. I didn't want to be a manager because keeping track of people and nagging them about stuff, well, to me that was disgusting. But I could encourage people. I could be positive and lead as well as I knew how.

So that's what I did. I focused on leading the team and being the best person I could. And it was that, more than some technique or three-point process, that helped me to bring value, reach our goals, and help develop solutions that meet the needs and challenges in our industry.

And as a result, I wound up helping create and grow a solution that has improved the entire globe's online payments industry.

Sometimes I'd have a moment, and I'd be proud that I did all of that. But then I'd remember the truth, which was that I really didn't do that. Not by myself, anyway.

No, *recovery* did that.

I PULL INTO OUR DRIVEWAY AND I SIT A MOMENT, thinking about what my dad had just told me.

I'm a Class-A guy, he'd said.

I chuckle. Now *that* is rich, I think.

I look across the front yard. There's a blue swing that hangs from a small oak. Levi loves that swing. I've pushed him in it, and so has my dad. We rent our house, but we're thinking about buying it. Then again, maybe not. Either way, we have options today. We've worked hard, and we can come up with the down payment. Over the past few years, our credit has gone from poor to excellent, and we qualify for all the first-time homeowner deals.

My Dad's right. For a guy like me, this really *is* a miracle.

I go inside. Bri's in the kitchen cooking dinner. I come up behind her and give her a light hug and kiss her neck.

"How can I help, honey?"

"Tell Finley to come out right now."

We laugh. Dinner's in ten minutes, and I go to the living room to read a Dr. Seuss book with Levi. That lasts about five minutes.

"Oh my god! Honey, come here!"

I run to the kitchen.

"What's the matter? Are you okay?"

"My water just broke." She breathes heavy. "Call my mom."

I call her mom *and* mine. They race each other to our place, and I grab a duffle bag and the backpack of belongings we have on standby. Fifteen minutes later, Bri and I jump in the car and head across the causeway to Tampa General Hospital. When we get there, the staff is waiting for us, and moments later I'm in scrubs, holding Bri's hand in our room.

We're trying for a natural birth again. Our hospital supports it because Bri's in shape and she's passed all the tests. Which is no surprise – she's a yoga teacher now. I'm a bit nervous, though. I hope it's easier this time around, and I say a quick prayer under my breath that it will be.

Finley Donald Cummins takes three hours to arrive. The doctor helps guide him right from the birth canal straight into my hands. He is so tiny. So vulnerable. I gasp as I hold him, but I manage to cut the cord and hand him to my wife gently. She holds him close to her chest, and she's crying with joy and exhaustion. Finley's eyes are wide, and he's looking around the room while he nurses.

When he stops, I take him into my arms and hold him close. I pace the floor while whispering into his ear. I tell him how loved he is. How glad we are that he's finally here. How he is going to be great and be a blessing to people and bring happiness into the world.

A couple days later, we bring Finley to my parents' house. My dad holds him for the first time, cradling him and planting kisses on his tiny head. My dad seems even thinner than a week ago, and his eyes are slightly sunken. But he's smiling. I think he wants to say something, so I lean closer.

"I love little Finn so much," he says. "And I love his dad so much, too."

Maybe I should see it coming, but I don't. Maybe I can't. Because no matter how thin or tired or sick my dad may be, he's still my dad. And my dad, he's going to be with us for at least a few more decades. Maybe even forever. But it's just a few days later when my mom and dad break the news.

He's begun hospice home care.

I SEE MY DAD MOST DAYS AFTER WORK. WHEN I GET there, he's always propped up on the couch. His face lights up when I come in, and I sit and talk with him and my mom. He's not eating much, and he's weak. My mom has to help him hobble around – to the bathroom, the bedroom, then back to the couch. He's having a hard time, but he doesn't let on.

He's still telling lots of jokes.

I think he's going to make a comeback. Something is going to happen that will have him back on his boat. Driving his truck. Puttering around the garage and doing all the other things he likes to do. He's nowhere near there yet, but at least during the past week he's remained stable. And that can take a turn for the good any minute. I believe it can, because I believe in miracles.

I'm in the parking lot at the grocery store after work, and I'm putting a couple bags in the backseat of my car when I feel my phone buzz. It's my mom, texting me. She's had a talk with hospice, and she has some news for me.

I call my mom.

"He may have only a couple days or so left," she tells me.

"Okay. I'll be right over."

When I get to my parents' house, my dad's in bed, propped up with pillows. My brother and sister are in there with him. I take off my shoes and lie on my back next to him.

He's feeling okay, he says. His voice is soft, but even and

steady. He's telling us that we always need to see the glass as being half-full.

"Remember when I had my balls removed?" he asks.

We tell him we do. It was a hard decision for him to make. He did it because at the time he thought it could improve his chances of beating prostate cancer, and of being with all of us longer.

"Well, I can focus on the fact that I have no balls," he says. "But y'know, I don't do that half-empty shit."

We look at each other, wondering where this is headed.

"Instead, I look at it like this." He grins. "Down there, I'm all dick."

I burst out laughing and I can't stop. Bob is too, and he's wiping a tear from his eye. Liz has to get up and go to the bathroom.

That's my dad. Irreverent and funny. Always taking the high road and keeping it light, putting everyone at ease.

Even when the wheels are completely falling off.

My brother and sister leave the room, and for a while it's just me and him. We're both staring at the ceiling as we talk. His left hand reaches out and grips mine. His voice is low, but steady.

"You see that breaker box up there?"

He lifts his other hand and points at the middle of the ceiling.

There's nothing up there but the ceiling. But I play along.

"Um, what about it, Dad?"

"That's what powers all the circuits in the house," he explains. "And those circuits, Donny, they power everything else in this house. They keep it all working perfectly. Just like it's meant to be."

My dad contracted this house to be built, and he oversaw it from the ground up. He'd stand there with a blueprint in his hands while workers scurried around and put it all together. If there was a breaker box in that ceiling, he would know.

But still, I'm pretty sure there isn't. It's just not where they go.

"Donny," he says, "that breaker box, it generates love."

He grips my hand even tighter.

"It generates it and sends it all out, and it keeps everything working," he whispers. "And that's how it all works."

My dad's not a religious guy. We've never talked about this kind of stuff before. But I think during these final days, he's seen something. He's come to some kind of understanding. And I know he's right. When you get down to it, it's love that sustains everything. It's what makes everything function.

It always has, and it always will.

"Yes, it does," I say. "I believe that, Dad."

I squeeze his hand back.

His birthday is the following day, and we gather to celebrate it quietly. Jackie and Chris are down from New York to be with him, and to be with us. It's difficult, and everything's happening so quickly. He's not talking anymore, and he's uncomfortable. He is propped up in a chair while we sing Happy Birthday to him, and Levi doesn't understand what's wrong with Pop-Pop.

The next day, it's just past 2 a.m. when they come to get him. My brother and I gently lift his frail body and place it on the gurney, and the undertaker wheels him out in front of the house. I stand in the driveway with my mother and Bob and Liz. The undertaker zips the bag that surrounds his body, but only up to the neck. He gives us a chance to say our goodbyes. My mother kisses his forehead and whispers something to him. My sister does the same, and then my brother does, too.

I don't. I just look on and say nothing. I don't feel, I just think. And what I'm thinking is that he's not in that body anymore. I think that whether that body is a few feet or several million miles away from me, I will never be any closer or further to him than I ever have been, or ever will be.

The undertaker zips it up the rest of the way, covering my

father's face forever. When he does, I realize I really do want to kiss his forehead. I'd just rationalized it all away. I was afraid to let myself feel. I still do that sometimes, and it's only afterward that I see it.

Sometimes, like now, I regret it.

As the van pulls away from the driveway, my mom and brother and sister and I hold each other and watch it drive away till we can see it no more.

It's almost sunrise when I walk through my front door. My brother and sister are staying behind with my mom, and I need to be with my family and young Finley Donald. I make my way to my bedroom. Bri is bed with little Finn, holding him as he cries.

I am too. I really wish I'd kissed my dad goodbye.

I lean over and kiss Finn gently on the forehead, and I hope that somehow, somewhere, my dad can feel that kiss on his grandson's face.

And then, I lie down next to them in the dark.

33

GIVING BACK

"**D**on, would you be willing to speak at a graduation ceremony?"

I'm sitting at my desk when Monica asks me.

"A graduation ceremony?" I ask. "Are you sure?"

"Of course!" she says. "It's for the Paid for Grades program at Boca Ciega High in a few weeks. The graduates might be inspired by your story - think about it at least!"

Our company sponsors a program that pairs students with tutors to help them improve their grades. If the students stick it out over the school year, we make a cash donation to the student and the tutor.

I've already been thinking about doing some volunteer work and telling my story. I haven't taken any concrete steps yet, but I know I want to help. The further I get from the insanity that once was my life, the more I see how incredible all of this has been. I believe I have something to offer – that my story might help someone.

I have a plan how I'll do it, but it's loose. I've decided that sometime soon I'll get a speaking coach and try to learn how to tell my story. I'll start small and build a little confidence. I'll find my voice, and slowly learn where I fit in. Then when I'm ready, I'll try to actually speak in front of people.

But *this*? Speaking in a school auditorium for my first speech ever? With no training?

In three weeks?

The thought of it terrifies me. I have absolutely no experience. I'm not even sure what my "message" is yet.

I'm simply not ready.

But I know what James would tell me. He'd say that this one event will probably teach me more than months of coaching. That I should do it. To go ahead and make the mistakes, because those are the most effective teachers. If I'm willing to pay attention, that is.

"Count me in," I hear myself tell her.

"Great! You'll be the keynote speaker, then." She walks out the door. "See you there!"

I'M SEATED IN THE FRONT ROW OF THE AUDITORIUM as the students and their families begin to fill the seats. It's the last week of school, but the summer weather has already begun. The air conditioning is broken. Sweat is trickling under my collar and down the small of my back. My heart is racing. Bri looks at me and smiles, and she puts her hand on my knee.

"You're going to do great, honey."

The ceremony begins, and a few people take turns talking about the program. Then Derek Craun, the school principal, steps up to the podium.

"And now, it's time for our keynote speaker. Let's give a warm welcome to Don Cummins, Chargebacks911's Director of Software Development!"

I make my way to the podium and I shake Derek's hand. I turn to the students and their families. I don't have an exact count of many people are here, but it feels like a thousand – and they're all staring at me. I grab the podium and hold it tight. Chills are running down my spine. I take a breath and remind myself why I'm here.

I need an icebreaker to loosen things up. I ask how many students here have completed the Paid for Grades program. A few hands go up. Then I ask them how many of them are ready to get paid.

Hands fly up, and they begin to holler and laugh.

I feel a bit better. Then I begin telling them about myself and a little bit of my background. I tell them I dropped out of school. That I became a drug addict and homeless, but that I turned my life around and found love, created my own family, and wound up with an awesome career.

I tell them that if they practice self-honesty, ask for help, and work hard, then absolutely anything is possible. That if it worked for someone like me, it definitely will work for them.

The speech goes okay. Some of the students smile and thank me on their way out. But I'm disappointed. I had hoped people would be inspired. I wanted them to be impacted in a life-changing way. But there were no earthquakes. No clouds opened up with beams of light shining down upon all of us. And none of the students broke out into tears or spontaneously rose to their feet, shouting out commitments to pursue greatness.

It seemed like they were just there to, well, get paid.

On the drive home, I replay the speech in my mind.

"You think it went okay?" I ask Bri.

"Oh my God, yes. It went great," she exclaims. "You came across as likable and sincere and honest, and you stuck to your message. You were right on point."

"How about some constructive criticism?"

"I can't think of much, really. I could tell you were nervous. You said *um* a bit. But it was your first time. You'll get better the more you do it."

She looks at me directly and smiles warmly.

"You really did great, honey. I am so proud of you."

Maybe she's right. It wasn't a bad speech at all for my first one. With experience, I know I'll improve my delivery. But really, that's not what's bothering me. There's something beyond the nervousness and my *ums* that's not sitting well with me.

I didn't *connect* with the students.

That's what it is. I feel it. I *know* it. And I also know that connection is necessary if I want to inspire people and motivate them to become their best selves.

I look out the window and watch the streetlights as they pass. Bri wants to do the same thing in her own way, and she's already started. She mentors other women in recovery and she's a yoga instructor. She's even teaching *Yoga for Recovery*.

I want to find my groove, too. I want to help people full-time. It's not that I don't like developing software, because I do.

It's just that I want to help people develop *themselves*.

I'm not sure how to start, so I do the only thing I know. I go back to the basics. I make a decision that I'm going to start speaking and working with people. And I decide that when I do, I'll connect with them and have a meaningful impact. I don't need to know how it all will unfold – I just need to decide that it will. And having made that decision, I trust that something within will take me there.

Just like Johnny taught me.

A FEW DAYS LATER MY PHONE RINGS.

"Don, how's it going brother?"

It's James. His voice is strained and weak. It's almost 11 p.m.

"Hey, I'm okay. What about you? You all right?"

"I'm hurting, Don. I wanted you to know what's going on with me."

I sit up.

"What's up?"

"It's Sadie," he whispers. "She got high again."

I groan. The past year has been rough for them. They're deeply in love, but they have an understanding that's equally deep. If one of them returns to using drugs, they'll try to work with each other. But it could also mean the end of their relationship. It's an understanding borne of necessity, for each other's survival. And she's fallen hard a few times now.

There's no judgement. Not from me. Not Bri. And not from James or anyone else I know. We all love Sadie. And we hate this, this – what can I call it? Some call it a disease. Some think of it as a mindset. Others call it a choice. But whatever they call it, the result is the same. It causes people to sabotage their own lives. And no matter how hard others may try to help, each of us has our own path. And at some point, we know that letting go is the right thing to do. For everyone.

I don't know when that time is for anyone else. But James came to that understanding for himself. The last time she got high, he told us he would try one more time. But after that, he'd said, he would need to protect himself – even though the pain would feel unbearable.

And for James, now is that time.

The next day, four or five of us gather around him. He bawls. He cries. He shares what's been going on and lets it all out. And finally, he laughs.

"Damn it." He pauses and blows his nose in a huge hanky, then sighs. "This isn't going to be easy. But I know what I need to do, and I will. I've already talked with my sponsor, and I'll keep doing that. I'll be available for all of you as usual, like nothing's changed. I just wanted to let you know what's up with me so you don't have to guess."

In another life, I would not have understood this. I probably would've laughed at him. What a push-over, I would've thought. How *unmanly* it is to mourn over a relationship!

But not today. Today, I only see him doing exactly what he has told me to do – to reach out and ask for help. James does this because he doesn't just talk the talk. He lives it.

We all tell him we'll be there for him, just as he's been for us.

"Thanks for showing up for me," he says. "We all take turns helping each other save our lives. It's what we do."

A month later, I meet with James for coffee. It's still rough on him, I know. But so far, he's gotten through it like a champ. I've had a front row seat, watching him deal with ending a marriage while staying true to what is right for him on multiple levels. When we sit down and catch up, he tells me something I'll never forget.

"One thing I learned early on is to commit to being vulnerable," he says. "I do that because it accomplishes two things that are so important. First, it helps *me* in so many ways. It keeps my ego in check and helps me stay humble. When I put myself out there like that, others know where I'm at and they offer to help. And bro, I still need plenty of it!"

He laughs, then continues.

"The second thing is, it helps *others*. If I'm not real about my experiences and I'm not willing to be open about what's really going on with me, I'm just projecting a bunch of bullshit. But when I'm vulnerable, others can relate to my true experience on the level of emotions – and they find connection. And that helps them get honest with *themselves*. It can motivate them to take action that will change their lives forever. Our stories, our individual, raw stories, are mighty, and telling them is the most powerful way we can truly help others."

His words speak directly to my heart.

"Don, we can never let fear stop us from showing our

authentic selves. The good, the bad, and also the ugly. Whenever we get the opportunity, we must tell our story." He smiles. "Because when we do, miracles happen."

AFTER TALKING WITH JAMES, I KNOW WHAT I NEED TO do. I'm going to take the leap. I'm going to lay the groundwork for my vision. And once I do, there's no turning back.

The story I told at the high school, it was weak. I see that now. And it doesn't have to do with how I delivered it.

It's *what* I delivered.

I delivered the vanilla version. Yes, I used drugs. I dropped out of school. And yes, I finally turned my life around. That's all true. But what makes it vanilla is that it leaves out the *real* stuff. Like my deep feelings of abandonment and extreme isolation. My fear and low self-worth. It leaves out prison and mental wards, and the incredible awakening I finally experienced.

If I'm going to connect with others and impact their lives, there can be no vanilla in my story. I've got to tell it all – the good, the bad, and, as James said, the downright ugly.

I realize that I've been hiding. I've been living a double life. Somewhere along the line, I got so damn clean that I started to pretend the past didn't happen, and that it wasn't as extreme as it truly was.

My past had become my secret.

Because at work, in my neighborhood, and to all the other parents at our kids' birthday parties, I'm squeaky clean. I'm successful. I'm the guy down the street with the nice family, the house and two cars, and a good career.

What it is, I realize, is I'm still afraid. What will the neighbors say if they find out? What about my wife's yoga community and all the moms she works with and has become close with? And what will happen if my company's business partners find out that a bank robber helped direct and manage the creation of the software they depend upon?

I could lose my job. And what kind of person takes that kind of risk and puts the security of their family on the line?

A horrible person, that's who!

That's what I still hear in my head sometimes. But I recognize that lying voice. And if I obey it, it certainly will lead me to a place I don't ever want to go again.

I must always remember the lessons that Johnny and James have given me, and what the trust I've placed in God has taught me. I must hold the lessons I've learned close and dear, because they weren't easily won. No, they cost me something; they came to me slowly while I clawed and scraped for my dear life.

I've witnessed it again and again as this power unfolded in my life, at times defying all common sense. And when it comes down to it, it's all that I really have. It's the only thing I know beyond any doubt that has brought me again and again to the place I need to be.

I'm going to take action and do what I know is right, and trust that God has the steering wheel. Not me.

I'm going to tell my story.

I TAKE A FIRST STEP AND I MAKE IT OFFICIAL ON social media. I say I'm coming out of the closet. That's an attention-grabber. I go on to summarize my childhood, the insanity and bank robberies, and how I had an awakening that allowed me to start forgiving myself and ask for help. And how awesome my life has turned out after realizing I am worth fighting for.

At work the next day, no one treats me any different. Some people thank me for sharing. One says they're amazed and have a new respect for me. Another says that what I wrote touched them. And as I walk to lunch, one person stops me in the hallway.

"Don," he says, "I never knew you've overcome so much. I am honored to know someone like you."

There are a few people who avert their eyes, looking at the floor as we pass in the hallway. But it's got nothing to do with me, I know. I don't regret coming out. I'm *liberated*. And now that I've come out, it's *on*.

I start taking action in other ways, too. I visit a homeless shelter and share my story with the residents. I find a non-profit that helps people find recovery resources, and they let me speak at an event. I even decide to put on my own free event at the public library.

For that, I advertise and hand out fliers. I walk the streets and talk to homeless people and try to get them to come. But only my friends and my family show up for support – ten people total. I wind up getting nervous and forget everything I was planning to say.

It's a total train-wreck.

But I learn a little with each experience. And what it boils down to is this: What makes the message powerful isn't whether I say *um* a lot, or whether I have two or two hundred people show up. Instead, it's about being real. Because when I am, I connect with them. I can *feel* it – they get what I'm saying on a deep level. And afterward they thank me.

My story, they tell me, gives them hope.

My nightmare has become my gift, I think. It has the power to change lives – if only I am willing to share it. And every time I do, I know it's the greatest thing I can possibly do while this heart still beats.

THE NEXT YEAR I'M INVITED TO SPEAK AT THE PAID

for Grades graduation again. As I stand before the students and staff spread out across the auditorium, I hear that voice.

You aren't like them. If you tell them your story, they'll think you're weird. They'll wonder what your crazy story has to do with them. Stick to the vanilla version – the truth is inappropriate for high school students!

I swallow and blink, and doubt seeps into my limbs. I feel frozen. But then, I hear another voice.

The truth is that you are just like them – more than you will ever know. There will be at least one person here tonight whose life will be changed if you will just speak your truth. You must do it – for them.

I take a breath and then I begin. I share how badly I wanted my grandfather to be proud of me, and what he said to me the last time we spoke. I share how he died days later as I sat in prison. I use that story as a lead in to talk about how I had spent my entire life stealing, doing drugs, and even robbing banks. I share how alone and isolated I felt, how badly I wanted to be normal, but how I was trapped and felt like I was unable to change.

As I share, the room is silent. They're right with me, and I can feel the connection. I move on to explain how my mindset prevented me from seeing who I truly am. And how, after I awakened to that truth, my life began to do a complete one-eighty.

And then, I share what I believe and know is the truth – for *them*.

There might be a Nobel prize winner among them, I say. One of them could be the person who discovers a way to travel at the speed of light. One among them may be a world leader who reminds all of us of our need to be connected and show compassion and love toward one another.

I tell them they have greatness in them, and that I believe in them – that if I went from the absolute gutter to the person I am today, then absolutely anything is possible for them. That they can become whoever they want to be if they just accept the truth of their own greatness.

As the students make their way out, many of them stop and thank me.

One seventeen-year-old stops in front of me, then extends his hand. I take it. I look at him and smile. His eyes are moist with tears, and he glances down at the floor.

"How's it going, man?" I ask him. "You all right?"

He nods his head slightly. His mother is standing at his side, and she speaks up for him. She says my message hit home.

"I have another son," she explains. "He's in prison right now. There are so many similarities with your story. It gives us hope that he might turn around. We really needed to hear this tonight. Thank you so much."

When I lie down later, I realize that what my grandmother said to me so many years ago is coming to pass. I'm telling my story about what God has done in my life, and it's starting to help others.

It's been seven years since the workshop I attended with James and Michael. It took me over four decades to get there. What a long time coming that was.

I know I've got to keep telling my story. Because if I do, someone, at least one person, will see the same thing I saw that day. And if they see it – if they can just get a glimpse – I know they will never be the same again.

34

HOME

"I'm ready to do this," I announce.

The sun is beginning to rise, and the house is quiet. Bri's in the kitchen in her robe, leaning against the counter and holding a cup of coffee.

"You sure you feel good about it?" she asks.

"Yeah, I'm ready."

"Okay, honey. Call if you need help – we'll come get you."

"I'll be fine." I smile and give her a kiss. "Love you."

"Love you, too."

I wheel my bike out of the garage and out to the driveway. I swing my right leg over and plant my foot on the pedal. I'm about to push off. But then, I freeze.

I want to jump off the bike and walk it right back to the garage.

I shake my head and laugh at myself. I'm afraid to ride my own bike!

I begin to push off a second time, but my body resists. My limbs protest and my heart accelerates; I can hear it pounding in my ears.

Don't do it!!

I'm in full-blown panic.

We remember what happened! my body says.

I'm taken back for a moment. After all, *I* sure don't remember what happened. I recall most of it, but not the moment it happened.

It's maddening because I want to. I really do. Maybe it's *certainty* I'm after. Maybe I think that knowing exactly what happened will somehow help me feel more in control of the whole thing.

I close my eyes and try to remember, just one more time.

But I can't. It's just a blank.

IT WAS OVER FOUR MONTHS AGO, THE DAY BEFORE New Year's 2019. We stood in our driveway as Bri strapped a Little Tikes helmet on Finley and fastened him in the child's seat on her bike. I helped Levi put his helmet on and get seated on his new blue bicycle. He'd gotten it the week before, on Christmas.

I jumped on my bike and we took off, heading for the trail just a block from our home. After we pulled onto the path, I sped up ahead of my wife and boys and looked back at them all.

"Levi and Finn!" I shouted.

Their eyes snapped toward me, and I popped a wheelie. It was only six inches off the ground, unworthy of being called a wheelie. But to my boys, it was amazing.

"Daddy, do it again!" Levi squealed.

"Yes, Daddy, do it again!" Finn echoed.

I decided to take it up a notch.

The second wheelie was an honest foot off the sidewalk. Still small, but no doubt about it – a legitimate wheelie. Plus, I rode it for a full three feet.

"Wow!" they squealed. "Again!! Do it again!!"

"Okay, but this is the last one!"

I decided to give them something to really cheer about. I'd pop a big wheelie and ride it, maybe twenty or thirty yards if I could. It had been decades since I'd done it, but so what, I thought. What's the worst that could happen?

A skinned knee? Scraped elbow?

When I pulled the front wheel up, I pulled too hard. The bike flew out from under me and rose in the air above me. The next thing I knew, I was lying on my back, the wind knocked out of me. My right foot was heavy and dull, and it felt strange. I raised my head to take a look. It was dangling from my ankle, like it was dislocated. And my ankle bone, it glistened white as it protruded through a tear in my skin.

Levi ran to me as I lay there, then Bri and Finn followed. My boys were wide-eyed, staring at me with their mouths wide open.

I couldn't tell if they'd noticed my ankle. I propped myself up on an elbow and motioned for them to come closer to me. They did.

"Hey, you guys," I said. "Daddy fell off his bike and got hurt, but it's going to be okay."

Levi reached out and put his hand on my shoulder, and I reached out and held Finn's hand.

"Daddy's going to be okay, all right?" I smiled at them.

They nodded their heads in unison and smiled back at me.

I turned to Bri.

"Honey," I said in a low voice, "call 911. My ankle's broke."

When I got to the ER, they took x-rays and wheeled me to a private room. Bri and my mom arrived and sat with me as I lay back, my foot elevated with a pad of gauze lightly strapped to my ankle. Then Bob walked in. I told him to lift the gauze and take a peek. He stared a moment.

"Whoa."

"Gnarly, huh?" I said.

"Yeah, bro." He shook his head. "So how did it happen?"

"I popped a wheelie and landed wrong."

"Yeah, I heard. But I mean, like, how did it happen? Did you land like this, with your foot pointed out?"

He planted his right foot on the floor in front of him, his toes pointed outward.

That was option one.

"Or was it like this?"

He pointed his toes inward.

Option number two.

I remembered being in the air, and then I was flat on my back. I couldn't recall anything in between.

"I don't know, Bob. I can't remember."

"Really?" He scrunched up his face. "You don't remember?"

"No, it's all a blank."

As I lay there trying to make sense of it, the doctor came into room. They had to do surgery right away, he said. There would be a second surgery in a few weeks, and possibly a third. He explained that the x-rays showed I'd broken my fibula in two places. Not only that, but one of my ligaments had ripped off my ankle bone, and another had snapped altogether. That explained why my foot had been dangling. To top it off, there was the exposed bone, which complicated everything.

"I'm the one who will do your surgeries," Dr. Taylor continued. "You're in good hands, Don. I've handled quite a few of these just like yours."

"Will I be able to jog again?"

He hesitated.

"We'll have to see about that. It depends on how you heal – and everyone heals different."

Later that day, I awoke from the surgery. My eyes focused slowly on the room around me. And then, I noticed my leg. It was propped up a couple feet, and two steel rods were screwed into my shin bone. Another long rod protruded right through my heel. Thick metal rods were bolted to all of *those* rods, holding my foot and shin together.

My right leg was enclosed in a steel cage.

As I stared at it, I tried to remember again. I wanted to recall the moment I hit the ground and my ankle snapped. But I couldn't.

I laid my head back down on the pillow.

Maybe it wasn't that important.

TODAY I STILL DON'T REMEMBER. BUT MY BODY SURE does, and it's not too thrilled that I'm perched on this bike in my driveway, and that I'm ready to take off and ride. Apprehension surges through me, and my nervous system is freaking out. It's trying its damnedest to make me get off this bike and return it to the garage.

The crazy thing is, I know I'm ready to ride.

It was just a couple days ago that I saw Dr. Taylor again. He looked me over and gave me the green light.

"Wow, Don," he chuckled, "some people heal fast, and others, well, it takes some time. You? You're definitely a healer."

But right now, it's clear something within me *hasn't* healed. It's still afraid.

I laugh to myself because I see it for what it is, and it's taken a mountain of pain for me to learn this truth.

I know that the split second my fibula snapped and my ligaments ripped clean from the bone, my brain seized the memory of that event and filed it away in some undisclosed location in my gray matter.

It did that on purpose. It made an executive decision to seal off that memory. To make it off limits. But it knows it's there. It *remembers*. Which is why it's throwing a fit right now as I'm about to ride this bike again.

It's trying to do me a favor, really. It's trying to protect me from pain. From injury.

From more trauma.

My brain just wants to help this body survive. And I've got to say, it does a hell of a job. But sometimes it goes too far. It bends over backward to avoid danger and anything remotely associated with it. It flees from aches and pains, and even the tiniest emotional discomfort.

Being human is a delicate thing. And my brain, smart as it is, doesn't always get those finer, human points. Because the truth is, I want – no, I *need* – more than just for my body to survive and be protected and "safe."

I need to be happy. I need to be fulfilled. I desperately need to live with purpose, and to live my truth.

For so many years it was my brain that practically begged me to self-medicate. To avoid pain. To run like hell from every perceived threat. And I obeyed, which spread sickness, dysfunction, and insanity to every area of my life.

Today I know the truth. I can't trust my brain. Not completely, anyway. I must remember that I am *not* this brain and I am *not* this body. I am something more than these. I must remember that without me, they are nothing.

If I want to truly live, I don't need to be pain-free or danger-free.

I just need to ride.

I push off and leave the driveway behind me. I pass the stop sign at the end of our street, then I speed up on the sidewalk and burst onto the trail, under the canopy of oak branches at the entrance. I pedal hard and race by the spot where it all happened. I slow down and stop for a moment and look back on it. I see it all over again. My boys and my wife, I see them gathered around me as I lie sprawled out by that tall oak.

I still don't remember that break, and I probably never will.

And that's okay. I don't need to remember it. It's not my responsibility, anyway. I know what my responsibility is.

It's to keep riding.

I push off once again and tell my body to pedal as fast as it can. It obeys, and as it does, my heart begins to lift. And then, it soars.

I PARK MY BIKE IN FRONT OF THE MARINA AND FASTEN it to a pole. It took ten minutes to get here, and the sun has just risen. I walk past the row of sailboats that are harbored in the docks, and then over to the pier. A few photographers are packing up their cameras and tripods. They come here at dawn to take shots of that old wooden pier and the waters of Old Tampa Bay that lie beyond it. At its farthest northern shore, thick mangroves line the water's edge, and I see something large break the water, making a light splash before it disappears.

It's a manatee. I'm sure of it.

It was thirteen years ago that my dad and I launched here on my first day out of prison. We were right by the spot where that manatee just emerged. It was there that we cast our nets for baitfish and spent the morning fishing. The water had been like glass that day, and the wind was nowhere to be found.

It was a day just like today.

And today, I'm alive. I have a heart and I know where it is. I also know where it is not. It's not out there somewhere at the bottom of the sea. It's not encrusted with barnacles or sick or on the verge of death. No, it's beating and it's alive, and it connects me to all of this. I know because I can feel it. I know when it hurts and when it laughs. When it's strong, and when it's afraid.

I know when it nudges me to push forward despite the risks. It reminds me that this body and this brain, and even this very existence, are so weak and temporary. I know my hope is not in those things, because everything that my eyes see and my mind thinks, one day all of this will surely vanish.

Yet I know that somehow, I will remain.

I breathe deeply, and I stretch. I think about taking a light, slow jog on the sidewalk that hugs Bayshore Drive. Yet something within says *no*. It says I'm not ready yet. But I miss jogging. So I make a deal with myself. I'll do it for five minutes and keep the weight off my foot. I'll jog-limp, I tell myself, and I'll see how it goes.

I take off. I run past the Safety Harbor Resort and Spa. A group of women are beginning their morning power-walk and they barrel toward me. They smile and wish me a good morning. I do the same as I trot by with a slight limp. As I continue north on Bayshore Drive, I start going over my list of things to do for the next few weeks.

This afternoon I have a speaking engagement. It's a graduation ceremony for addicts and ex-convicts who've completed a life-skills course. I have a couple events that might be lined up at at-risk and alternative high schools in the next month as well. I'm planning a presentation called "The Hero Within: Bringing out Your Inner Greatness," and things are starting to take off. I'm starting to give back in the way I know I'm meant to. Another chapter in my life is beginning, and I'm thrilled.

But regardless of what chapter it is, some things aren't going to change anytime soon. Like my recovery. Next weekend I meet with James and Michael and the rest of the guys like we have once a month for the past seven years. We eat and talk and get current. It's good to see those guys. James is doing well – he's actually dating again. Michael's expanded his tile business and has employees and his own place, and he's doing great. The last time we all got together, we talked about Eric for a few. He's still around and he's clean – he's married and even has a little boy now.

There's twice as many, though, who didn't make it. People

we all know personally. Some overdosed. Some committed suicide. We see it happen at least a few times a year. We think about them, and we remember them.

Yet today, we live. It's amazing to watch as our lives become something almost unrecognizable compared to what they once were.

We're grateful.

Rick called me last night, but I missed him. I'll call him back later this morning. He moved to Tennessee a few years ago and became a pastor of a small church. I think he's finally found his calling, and I'm happy for him. I might head up that way and visit sometime. Bri and the boys love the area – we've done a couple family vacations at a cabin around the Blue Ridge Mountains, and it's amazing.

After I jog a hundred yards, I slow down to a walk. I stop and put my hands on my hips and take a few deep breaths. My right ankle is stiff and there's a stabbing pain in the shin just above it. It's the same pain I had the other day when I chased two-year-old Finn across the yard after he ran out the front door, trying to make his escape.

It's hurting pretty bad. Reluctantly, I accept it: I'm not ready to run. And really, I knew better when I negotiated with myself a few minutes ago.

I chuckle to myself. Yeah, I've gotten a lot better at listening to my heart. But my foot, not so much.

I stretch again, then walk back to my bike. I'll ride it the rest of the way this morning. But I really do miss jogging.

As I reach my bike, I look out over the water again and it occurs to me. And as it does, I'm grateful beyond words. Running was great, and maybe I'll do it again someday. But today, I'm blessed.

I get to ride.

AFTERWORD

Thank you for reading *The Prison Within*. I hope you loved it. If so, please take a moment to leave a review wherever you got it. It might help someone.

MAKE A DIFFERENCE

Today, I want to be part of the solution and I hope that you do, too.

There are so many among us who, in some form or another, suffer from their own *prison within*. And, as I found, there is a *hero within* as well.

It exists in all of us.

I'm offering a free course to inspire others to take up the challenge of self-discovery and pursuing greatness. It's called *The Hero Within: Bringing Out Your Inner Greatness*.

The course is aimed primarily at High School students and young adults. But really, the message applies to anyone. I believe we all have a unique, special gift, as well as an inner longing to become the best version of ourselves we possibly can. I believe that we are called to greatness, whatever that means for each of us. And as we make progress, we extend our hand, offering to take others along for the ride.

If you or someone you know might benefit from this challenge, please send them!

Find out more at https://theherowithin.org

ABOUT THE AUTHOR

Don lives in Safety Harbor, Florida with his wife Brianna and his two boys Levi and Finley. When he's not hanging out with his family or working on a project, he's probably riding his bike or playing guitar.

    facebook.com/DonCumminsLive
    twitter.com/_doncummins
    instagram.com/don_cummins
    youtube.com/doncummins1

CPSIA information can be obtained
at www.ICGtesting.com
Printed in the USA
BVHW031349211120
593887BV00010BA/32/J

9 781734 892611